Registered by FRANK CARREL, in the office of the Minister of Agriculture, in conformity with the Law passed by the Parliament of Canada, in the year 1908.

The Quebec
Tercentenary Commemorative
History

Compiled and Edited by
Frank Carrel and Louis Feiczewicz, B.A.

Revised by
E. T. D. Chambers,

With Introduction by
Dr. A. G. Doughty, C.M.G., F.R.S.C.

Dominion Archivist and Author of "The Battle of the Plains
of Abraham," "Quebec Under Two Flags,"
"The Cradle of New France," etc.

Quebec
Published and Printed by
The Daily Telegraph Printing House
A. D. Nineteen Hundred and Eight

mariners of his time, but a hero in the full sense of the word; the second is that the handful of men led by him in Canada has grown up strong and valiant.

JACK TARS
Parading in the street.

Champlain, when 20 years of age, had one ideal: to promote the glory of God and the honor of the King, and his sole ambition was to devote his life to the discovery of far distant countries where could float side by side the standard of Christ and the flag of France. All deeds born from such thoughts, now that they are developed, cast a brilliant glory upon the name of the man whom we honour to-day and with him the birth of New France; also it was due to the French-Canadian young men to first acclaim the founder of their country. Why this enthusiasm on the part of the young and especially of the young members of our A. C. J. C.?

ONE OF THE ENGLISH FLEET

It is that four years ago, they also have enlisted into the service of a noble cause when they took the vow to be in the future as they are to-day, men of

principle, men of action, apostles inspired with the spirit of love for God and country.

The main deed accomplished by Champlain, we may say the deed of a lifetime, was the founding of this courteous and valiant city of Quebec and his main idea is still here found, the glory and the honor of his King, and until his death he remains always the indomitable soldier of Christ and of France. Never has his patriotism weakened, never has faith diminished, never ideal varied. And we should be thankful to Providence for having chosen such a worthy founder for our nation. Not only should we be thankful and adorn our progress to God for this favor, but we should also make it our duty to take up the work where it has been left and contribute our share for completion. Our patriotism must be awakened.

I am not prepared to say that our nationality is being betrayed. But we have heard too many times

THE LEON GAMBETTA
One of the French War Vessels present at the Tercentenary.

the theory that peace in this country must repose on mutual concession, only to find that concession being made by one race only, by our's. We know also that unsavory and dangerous doctrines are being spread amongst our people in view of destroying the strong ties that have always allied the French-Canadians to their clergy. We know also that the day we shall listen to these theories will mark the death of our race.

Let us vow, we young men of the A. C. J. C., and also you who are not yet our comrades but are our compatriots, let us vow to put before and above all party consideration the good of the country.

Mr. Ernest Legare after reading a letter from Sir J. G. Garneau, regretting his unavoidable absence, proceeded to discuss the present situation of the Church in France, saying in part:—

DUFFERIN TERRACE

On the first day of the celebrations showing some of the British Warships in the Harbour.

mon love and admiration. Let us profit by the lessons of history and let us remember what has been our strength in the past and let the future borrow its experience from it.

We have not yet seen the end of our route as a people. We are profoundly convinced that we have yet hardly made our first step. Up to this day, our efforts have met with signal success. With a strong will and the help of God, we will follow the glorious pathways so evidently marked for our nation by a fatherly Providence. Do we want to become a strong people, equally powerful in war and in peace? Let us then follow the examples set by Champlain as a true and faithful son of the Church, let us be Christians before the forum as well as in our churches and our homes. Let us never separate our national from our religious interests, because the destruction of the former will entail the ruin of the latter. Let us remain true to the traditions of our race; and before this monument let us make the solemn vow to put into practice the sublime lessons of our great ancestors

never to desert the splendid examples immortalized in marble and bronze. We must write our page of the national history and in a language that our children will be proud of as we, to-day, are proud of that history of the past.

✱ ✱ ✱

Mr. George Baril's Address

Amid the acclamations that followed the speaker, Mr. George Baril was introduced, who delivered an eloquent discourse in which a psychological and accurate description of Champlain's motives was outlined. He said in part :—

There are two reasons why the attention of the world is drawn upon the man to whose memory has been erected the monument in front of which we are assembled to-day; the first is that this man from Saintonge was not a mere adventurer like so many

"Croissez! Multipliez!" Au mot sacré fidèles,
Nous avons su grandir avec l'épi des champs:
Autour du premier nid battent des milliers d'ailes
Dans l'érable plus dru qu'emplissent d'anciens chants!
Sois tranquille! Où tu bus tout un peuple s'abreuve!
Nous veillons sur ton cœur, inlassables gardiens;
Et d'un cours plus puissant, en dépit de l'épreuve,
S'étend et s'élargit, parallèle au grand fleuve,
     Le beau sang de tes Canadiens!

Samuel de Champlain, ô patriarche! apôtre!
Si ton divin appui, nos soins l'ont mérité,
Si tu sens rejeunir ta vaillance en la nôtre.
Elu de Dieu, du haut de ton éternité,
Bénis de nos sillons cette moisson féconde
Que d'un immense vœu déjà tu caressais!
Bénis nos fils! bénis nos filles! et seconde
Le rêve que par toi nous vivons dans ce monde!
     Bénis ton Canada français!

GUSTAVE ZIDLER.

Following Mr. Rivard, Mr. Maurice Dupre delivered an address in which he paid a glowing tribute to the work of Bishop Laval who conjointly with Champlain did much to build up Canada. In part, he said:--

Mr. Maurice Dupres' Address

This demonstration is the glowing tribute paid by a remembering youth to one of their ancestors who has won the title of "Father of his country." It was nothing but just that the young French Canadians should also take an active part in the festivities organized in honor of Champlain. A few weeks ago we were celebrating the memory of a great bishop, a man who shared with Champlain the honor of founding and upbuilding New France, in taking a jealous care of his newly born flock. Now is the turn of the hero, who, equally religious in public and private life, had the special care of the material interests of the country to which he was to be devoted with all his intelligence and heart. With these two monuments Canada has rendered a well-deserved tribute to both and by placing their monuments on neigboring sites it has intended to teach the coming generations that the French race, so strongly settled in this land of liberty by their endeavor, entertains for both a com-

LORD ROBERTS
Leaving the English
Cathedral.

CELEBRATION OF LA JEUNESSE CATHOLIQUE

Around Champlain Monument. (Drawn by N. Savard, special artist for "La Patrie.)"

people had already gathered, the monument was at once bedecked with a shower of flowers delicately interwoven and neatly superimposed. These were presented by the Catholic Association of French-Canadian youth, the Loyola Circle, the Chevalier de Levis circle, the Champlain guard, and by the youth of St. Sauveur.

The monument now overlaid with pacific garlands was then encircled with Zouaves and other military guards. Several thousand voices sang Canada's national anthem; the bands played; ensigns fluttered; military commands were given, and the Quebec Tercentenary was on!

Mr. Rivard's Address

Mr. Maurice Dupre, president of the Association presented Mr. Adjutor Rivard, who, renowned for his oratory and elocution recited *La Prière du Canadien-Français au Père de la Nouvelle France;* written for the occasion by Mr. Gustave Zidler, a well-known French poet who was recently honoured by the Royal Society of Canada for his poetic works on Champlain. The poem reads:

La Prière du Canadien-Français

Depuis ce jour, Champlain, bon Français de Saintonge
Où ta barque accosta l'ancien Stadaconé,
Depuis qu'à coups de hache a pris forme ton songe,
A l'horloge du Temps trois cents ans ont sonné!
Et nous, fils des héros qu'un triple siècle embrasse,
Sur ta tombe, devant ton image, à genoux,
Par tout le cher pays où nous baisons ta trace,
Nous t'allons demandant, nous ton sang, nous ta race

O père! es-tu content de nous?

Es-tu content de nous, Père, qui nous contemples,
Toujours présent, d'un ciel de gloire et de vertu?
Avons-nous profité de tes virils exemples?
Pour tes nobles desseins avons-nous combattu?
De la croix, que ta main planta sur cette grève,
Qu'avons-nous renié, couvert d'un sombre oubli?
Au-delà de ta vie impuissante et trop brève
Par nos cœurs et nos bras ton vaste et puissant rêve
S'est-il tout entier accompli?

Père! ce que tu fus, nous aussi nous le sommes;
Pour tes fils, défricheurs et soldats tour à tour,
Tout fut dur, les hivers, la forêt et les hommes...
Et pourtant cette terre est notre unique amour!
De sueurs et de sang plus notre terre est faite,
Plus elle nous aspire et plus elle nous prend;
Et tu nous vois encore à son nom seul en fête,
Tous tels que tu revins, conquis par ta conquête,
Mourir aux bords du Saint-Laurent!

Nous portions trop au cœur ces graves paysages
Pour n'en pas refouler nos ennemis,—les tiens!
Avec les Cinq Tribus et de Pâles Visages
Nous avons prolongé les sanglants entretiens.
Montcalm succomba—— Mais l'âme toute meurtrie,
"Plus grand que son malheur", et vainqueur de l'échec,
Comme toi, sans changer de foi ni de patrie,
Le Canadien-Français en français pense et prie,
Libre sur son roc de Québec!

Es-tu, content, semeur? Vois ces plaines, ô Père,
Sur la cendre des bois dérouler leurs grands blés!
Dénombre en cet instant ta famille prospère,
Pour le même banquet tes enfants assemblés!
Ajoute aux premiers fruits de ta persévérance
De trois siècles d'efforts les robustes présents:
Tu pourrais, exalté d'orgueil et d'espérance
Retrouver la saveur de ton pays de France
Dans le pain de nos paysans!

THE TOWER OF WELCOME

Erected in front of the Archbishop's Palace.

LA JEUNESSE CATHOLIQUE

Pays homage to the memory of Champlain at the foot of his Monument.

First Day, Sunday, July Nineteenth

Homage to the Memory of Champlain

WITH the honouring of the memory of Champlain at the foot of his monument on Dufferin Terrace by l'Association Catholique de la jeunesse Canadienne-Francaise, the celebrations which marked Quebec's Tercentenary were commenced.

It was Sunday, the nineteenth of July. The day was an ideal one. Quebec had assumed a festive air, pacific spirit yet pervaded all, making Champlain's old city an enviable spot.

The youth of French Canada formed into a body organized for the purpose of welding the ties which binds the French element of the population and for the strengthening of the Catholic spirit among its members, took the first step in honouring the memory of the revered founder of Quebec. Formed into a procession consisting of about five thousand persons, these youths marched toward the Terrace and after depositing floral tributes on Champlain's monument,

THE CROWDS VIEWING PROCESSION
Of La Jeunesse Catholique on the way to the Champlain Monument.

emphasized by the profuse decorations which covered every part of the city. It had lost the normal and peaceful spectacle that it usually represents, and metamorphosed, as it were, was now the scene of animation and din. On its ever quiet streets now perambulated men dressed in the military garb of Wolfe and Montcalm, courtiers of old France and primitive settlers of New France, her off-spring. A

orations were delivered, eulogistic of Quebec's founder, and at the same time an urgent appeal for the unity of French Canadians in matters of nationality and religion.

In the procession were deputations of the different branches of the Association scattered throughout the province. Arriving at the Terrace towards three o'clock in the afternoon where a large number of

The National Battlefields Commission

B. E. WALKER, D.C.L., C.V.O., LL.D., F.G.S.
President Champlain Society.

Hon. A. TURGEON, C.V.O., C.M.G.

Col. G. T. DENISON

Sir G. DRUMMOND, K.C.M.G.

SIR J. GEO. GARNEAU.
Chairman

Lt.-Col. J. S. HENDRIE, C V O.

Hon. L. A. TASCHEREAU, K.C.

J. M. COURTNEY, C.M.G.,
Hon. Treas.

Joint Secretary
H. J. J. B. CHOUINARD, C.M.G.,

A. G. DOUGHTY, C.M.G., Joint Secretary

The Eve of the Tercentenary

By

Louis Feiczewicz, B. A.

FROM the day when the idea of celebrating the three-hundredth birthday of Quebec was first launched, preparations for the great event were constantly under way Slowly at first and causing but a slight stir in some official circles, the Tercentenary idea gradually spread. At first but the cherished object of a few Canadians, the spirit of the event expanded and permeated the entire Dominion, until in a very short time the idea which had originated in the old city of Quebec was taken up by the Dominion and executed on a scale never originally contemplated.

During the beginning of the summer of 1908 the preparations were hurried and final plans adopted As the time wore on more bustle and energy were thrown into the work and marvellous rapidity marked the final arrangements.

The city was gaily decorated during the whole summer. Street arches erected for the Laval *fêtes* several weeks earlier were left standing. They now needed but a fresh coating of flowers and flags. New ones were also put up. Public buildings were lined with rows of electric lights which illumined their dull greyish forms, bespeckled as they were with mottoes and pictures amid a mass of bunting. Private citizens had caught the spirit. Houses containing occupants of every degree were almost hidden from view by the numerous flags which protruded from every window, all fluttering in unison when disturbed by the breezes of the summer nights.

Visitors were continually flocking to the city from all parts of the world. Every family had its quota of friends and relatives. Hotel accommodation was not sufficient to meet the demands. To house the numerous thousands a tented city was erected. Streets were laid out, tents erected thereon, and furnished with all necessary equipment. Big dining-rooms were set up. In the new and white city of refuge was a post-office, a baggage-office, hotel offices, parlours, and all the other conveniences that make modern hotels what they are. Nothing was lacking.

As the date of the celebrations drew near the pageant performers received their costumes and were every evening practising for the performances. With enthusiasm at its height the historical scenes were being prepared, none shirking their duty, all eager for their success. Quebecers costumed as in the days of yore walked the streets. The uniform of the men who fought on the Plains of Abraham was already a common sight and mingled freely with that of the modern soldier who was daily arriving in the city from every part of Canada.

The British war vessels arrived several days before the commencement of the celebrations and gave to Quebec that Imperial aspect which marked the Tercentenary. Their huge grey forms rested upon the surface of the river before the city and were ever conspicuous save when concealed in the smoke which covered the water when the naval cannons boomed their frequent salutes.

No detail was left unfinished nor any requirement remained undone. All was at last ready. Only the word to start was being awaited and when the many events of the elaborate programme were executed it was seen with what care and efficiency the preparations had all been made.

PRINCE OF WALES

The Tercentenary of Canada

By

Dr. A. G. Doughty, C.M.G., F.R.S.C.

THE more the history of Canada is studied the more will it be seen to present peculiar characteristics. From the little fort constructed by Champlain on the crest of Cape Diamond it is possible to trace the history of New France for nearly two hundred years. But while Champlain was founding his colony on the banks of the Saint Lawrence, British colonization had taken root at Jamestown, to the south. For a long time the course of each community was independent; but it was their subsequent expansion that brought about the contest for supremacy in North America between England and France. The Battle of the Plains of Abraham and the surrender of Montreal preceded the cession of Canada to England; but few could have foreseen that the withdrawal of French influence from this continent would pave the way for colonial independence.

The American colonies, in their impatience to realize national aspirations, threw off the yoke of England long before they had attained the degree of social and political independence which Canada has reached. The predominating idea in the mind of the revolutionary party was that freedom and colonial relations, however attenuated and ameliorated the latter might be, were wholly incompatible. The remarkable example that Canada was to give to the world of two races achieving constitutional liberty in union with the British empire, was beyond their powers of imagination; or possibly, being bent upon a larger and freer life, they did not much care to exercise their imagination in that direction. So they took their way, gained the desire of their heart, and as a people developed on lines of their own with no restraint or guidance from the outside world. This step on the part of the colonies threw into Canada a large loyal element—loyal in the sense of devotion to British connection. The extrusion of this element by the emancipated colonies simplified conditions there; but to some extent complicated them here, by stamping a special character on those parts of the country—Upper Canada particularly—to which the new settlers be took themselves. But what has especially given a unique stamp to Canada is its dual population.

It was a serious responsibility which the mother country assumed when she took over a colony peopled by over six thousand souls to whom the English language, not to speak of English laws and customs, was unknown.

The American revolution was not at the time foreseen by the British Government, and it is doubtful whether the colonists themselves were conscious of the forces which were gradually moulding them into an independent people. And probably the expectation in England was that the French colony would in course of time be modified and in a measure transformed, not only by emigration from the British Isles, but by the close relations which would spring up naturally between it and the old established English colonies to the south.

H. E. THE COUNTESS GREY

H. E. RIGHT HON. EARL GREY, G.C.M.G.
Governor General of Canada.

Not so, however, was it written in the book of fate. The American colonies revolted, drove their loyalists into Canada and alienated the French population in the first place by the anger they showed at the liberal provisions of the Quebec Act, and then by the actual invasion of Canadian soil. Thus was French Canada preserved from those influences that would have made against the continuity of its development: and how striking a social and political phenomenon it presents to the world to-day it is needless to emphasize.

There are those who think that a country, where two languages are spoken and recognized, must necessarily labour under serious disadvantage. This, it may be said, is a common place, surface view of the matter. Another view is that this complication of conditions makes rather for intellectual vigour and political stability. It is on the level prairie that the tornado usually rages with the greatest fury, and popular gusts of passion are perhaps more to be dreaded where all speak and think substantially alike than where there are well established and well defined differences of culture, habit and opinion.

To-day Canada does not find that she is carrying any disabling burden. She has lately, upon the heights where fortune threw her into the British system, been reviewing her history, not without pride and satisfaction—a pride and satisfaction shared by all her provinces alike. The central figure in the celebration which has just closed was Samuel de Champlain, the founder of New France. But the significance of the festivities lies not in the commemoration of the passing of a small boat up the Saint Lawrence or the founding of a little village : not in the commemoration of the beginning of one *régime* with Champlain at its head and the inauguration of another by Wolfe; but in the fact that both races united in celebrating their mutual co-operation in the political development of Canada.

Champlain was not permitted to see the far-reaching effect of his heroic life. After twenty-seven years of hardship and disappointment in the New World he passed away, leaving apparently only a struggling village on the banks of the Saint Lawrence. But this is not the measure of his service to posterity. He had ever before him the vision of a greater New France than that confined by the limits of Quebec. It was his boundless confidence in the future of this country—a country which he felt he had been called upon by God to develop—which gave him courage to overcome every obstacle, which consoled him in the darkest hour and enabled him to accept with resignation the decrees of Providence. This was his great service to France and to Canada. The ships of three powerful nations assembled lately at Quebec to pay homage to his worth; and the heir of an empire vaster than any known to Champlain placed a wreath upon his monument in memory of the greatness of his achievement. Upon the ground sacred to Canadians as the special sphere of Champlain's activities, other scenes were enacted that brought about a change of rule. But with the passing of the old *régime* in Canada the work of Champlain did not cease. Gaining strength by transfusion, the sons of the old *régime* and of the new have wrought out their destiny, fitting themselves nobly for the proud position that awaits Canada amongst the nations of the world. In no other way, therefore, could we render justice to the memory of Champlain than by associating him with that larger Canada which is really the fulfilment of his vision.

The festivities at Quebec have shown to us, as nothing else could have shown, how great a debt we owe to the men sent forth from France. We have all read the voyages of discovery; and are familiar with the work of Champlain, of Laval and the missionaries, of Talon, Frontenac and the other great names in history ; but the best written description seems tame when compared with the animated scenes arranged by Mr. Lascelles upon the heights of Abraham. Comparatively few were able to witness this splendid illustration of our early history, but thousands and tens of thousands have been led to take up the story of Canada as a result of the interest which has been focused on Quebec during the past six months.

Canada has been looming large in the public eye for many years ; but it has been mainly through her material products that she has gained special attention. Few, perhaps, have thought of Canada as a country where deep problems in self-government have been solved, or have realised what interest its history presents to the student of human affairs. Canadians themselves, it is to be feared, have not fully grasped the significance of the events which have taken place in their midst, and have not done all that they might have done to make their history known beyond their own borders. But with the incentive given to the study of

THE DUKE OF NORFOLK
Leaving the Seminary after his visit.

many ecclesiastical institutions which still flourish; the struggle of the brave Dollard des Ormeaux and his companions, whose fatal contest with the Iroquois was but a heroic incident in the lengthy wars with the Indians with whom our forefathers had to contend; the arrival of Marquis de Tracy in whom we see a representative of the government of New France; Frontenac, the brave defender of Quebec, so often the target of strange warriors; and lastly the two armies standing side by side amicably on the ground where the men whom they represent once fought each other.

On the scene nothing has been changed. It is the natural site for a panorama such as is being enacted. To the north is a thicket of trees as of yore; to the west, the forest; while to the south still glides as peacefully the St. Lawrence river, washing on one side an old city revered by all; on the other, green villages scattered with white as in days of old.

The pageant deftly winds on. Scene after scene passes on the undulating plain. The spectators, ordinary men and women of to-day, become absorbed in the glory and tragedy of the past. They forget the cares of the morrow and heed but the irrevocable. The last scene comes on the stage. It is enacted. The actors depart. The witnesses of the pageant rise with a start. They rub their eyes and once more realize that it is but a picture, that the seventeenth century is gone and cannot be recalled, and that they live—here and now. Yet, how real it all was! One would again live in the days of the past. But the scene changes. On the river below passes a modern freight steamer. Her whistle shrieks and her steam puffs. Slowly the spectators wind homeward with an impression not easily effaced. A feeling of solemnity steals over them, but is quickly dispelled by the sense of pleasure at having witnessed so great a spectacle.

which regiment Lord Roberts is an honorary lieutenant-colonel, were in turn inspected. The Canadian
soldiers, who in common with their English brethren
idolize the hero of the South African war, cheered him
enthusiastically as he passed by each regiment.

✱ ✱ ✱

The First Official Pageants

At five o'clock commenced the first official representation of the famous pageants. The clouds in the
sky appeared to be suspended as was the sword of
Damocles. Yet the grand stand was filled with ten
thousand people who came to see the hand of time

rolled backward and to watch the incidents which loom
conspicuously in Canadian history again revealed as
faithfully as history can record.

The stage on which the historical scenes were presented consisted of a portion of the Plains of Abraham. No boards covered the natural sward. The
stage was the stage of the sixteenth, the seventeenth
and the eighteenth centuries, and the events of those
ages were represented there.

The valorous deeds and sufferings of the founders of
Canada were retold. After thirty generations had
gone their way in the ancient capital the settling of the
first was recounted. Again was seen the splendour of
old France, the mother country; the arrival of the
Ursulines in Quebec who were the forerunners of the

BRITISH SAILORS
Hauling up cannons on
Mountain Hill, for Day
of Sports

THE MEN-OF-THE-WATCH,

Familiar figures in Quebec during the celebrations—Sketched for the "Montreal Star" by H. Julien.

ing from broad-rimmed felt hats, the Heralds-at-arms accompanied by martial strains proceeded on their duty.

Halting on the Battery near Flavien street, one of the oldest sections of the city, the heralds made their announcement which was repeated at different important sections of the city. The eager citizens and curious visitors who assembled around the men of another age heard :

———

"Oyez! Oyez! Oyez! inhabitants of Quebec, gentry and burgesses!

"The principal events of the day were :—

"This morning at ten o'clock, the New Hampshire, a man of war of the United states specially sent to Quebec to represent the government of the

a long mantle studded with violet doublet embroidered with fleur-de-lys of gold, green trunks and purple hose with long white and violet coloured plumes float-

neighboring republic at the Tercentenary of Champlain, arrived in the roads.

DIFFERENT TYPES OF CHARACTERS

Seen on the Terrace during the celebration.— Sketched for the Montreal Star by A.C. Racey.

Second Day, Monday, July Twentieth

Heralds-at-Arms March Through City

OYEZ! Oyez! Oyez! Inhabitants of Quebec, gentry and burgesses!

On the second day of the celebrations the heralds and men-of-the watch appeared. This proved to be a matter of great interest to Quebec during the Tercentenary. With retrogressive steps, the city was again pictured in one phase as it was several hundred years before.

Clad in casque and corselet of steel they forced their way through the crowds. Close behind them were armoured men on foot, bearing in their hands huge gilded truncheons, the insignia of their office.

As in the days of Frontenac, the heralds-at-arms once more passed through the streets of the city proclaiming to the citizens the events of the day and the occurrences of the morrow. The curfew was again sung in the simple style of yore, everything being carried back to an age romantic in appearance and evidently attractive.

THE MEN-OF-THE-WATCH AND HERALDS

centenary. With retrogressive steps, the city was again pictured in one phase as it was several hundred years before.

Clad in casque and corselet of steel they forced their way through the crowds.

From their headquarters issued the Men-of-the Watch, an anachronism, but one in keeping with the spirit of the people and the desire for antiquity.

Thus defended and garbed in a picturesque costume,

... Preface ...

N compiling this volume it is the desire of the Editors to produce a complete historical record of all the important events that took place in Quebec during the Tercentenary Celebration. There is no doubt of the fact that the importance of the Tercentenary and of its meaning will be realized in the future to a larger extent than it is to-day by many people. Those who witnessed and took part in the pageant and who now regard it but as a masterly historical performance will in a generation look back upon the event and see in it a greater significance. The youthful soldiers who gathered from every part of Canada to what appeared to some a monster pic-nic will relate to their grand children events which breathed the spirit of Empire unity and strength. If this volume will but aid in commemorating these events and through them demonstrate the real spirit of the Tercentenary, the Editors will have been amply repaid.

History is never better illuminated than by actual representations of the scenes explained. In this connection we must thank the following publications who lent their kind assistance in providing a large portion of the drawings and photographs of their best artists: The Canadian Pictorial, P. F. Collier & Son, The Canadian Courrier, the Toronto Saturday Night, The Toronto Globe, The Toronto World, The Canadian Magazine, The Star, La Presse and La Patrie, of Montreal, The London Graphic, The Montreal Standard, The Canadian Photographic Stores, Captain Guenette, Messrs. J. E. Livernois, M. Montminy, Jos. Beaudry, S. H. Kennedy, of Quebec, and the Intercolonial Railway Advertising Department.

Thanks are also due to the organizers of the pageants and their assistants who kindly lent their list of names of those who took part, to Capt. the Viscount Lascelles, A.D.C. to His Excellency the Governor-General, for furnishing lists of the guests present at Lord Grey's banquets, to Mr. U. Généreux who did the same in connection with the Lieutenant-Governor's functions, to Mr. Lawford Dale, designer of the " Don de Dieu " for information about the *fac-simile* of Champlain's ship, and to many others whose small favours have all been appreciated.

F. C.
L. F.

Quebec, Sept. 1908.

HER MAJESTY QUEEN ALEXANDRA

HIS MAJESTY KING EDWARD VII.

its picturesqueness and the unequalled beauty of the magnificent St. Lawrence. He, as a stranger could appreciate this scene all the more, but he was no stranger to Canada for said the General ''I rejoice to

U. S. S. NEW HAMPSHIRE

Present at Quebec during the Celebrations.

think that the Canadians and myself can never be regarded as strangers to each other. England will never forget and I can never forget the assistance which Canada rendered to us when the appeal went forth for your assistance in 1899 and 1900, nor how freely that assistance was given.'' He could state that Brigadier-General Otter and those who served under him fully proved how much they deserved the confidence he had placed in them and could testify to services rendered by them in the campaign from Rhodesia to the Cape. He was proud to be a member of the Canadian forces in his capacity as Honorary Colonel of the Queen's Own Rifles and looked forward with much interest to the review of the Canadian troops on the Plains.

The official list of guests for this dinner at which Lt.-Col Turnbull presided, were :—

His Excellency the Governor-General, His Excellency's Military Secretary, His Excellency's A.D.C., His Honor the Lieutenant-Governor, His Honor's A.D.C., Vice-Admiral Curzon-Howe, Vice-Admiral's staff, Rear-Admiral Jellicoe, Vice-Admiral Jaureguiberry, Admiral Cowles, Admiral Cowles' A.D.C., Lt.-Col. Denison, A.D.C. to Lord Roberts, Col. G. T. Denison, Sir Fred Borden, Sir Wilfrid Laurier, General Otter, Vice-President Fairbanks, General Otter's A.D.C., His Grace the Duke of Norfolk, General Sir R. Pole Carew.

The list of subscribers was as follows:—Col. Turnbull, Col. B. A. Scott, Lt.-Col. Turner, V.C., D.S.O., Lt.-Col. Gaudet, Lt.-Col. Wurtele, Capt. J. J. Sharples, A. H. Cook, Major Petry, Major Panet, William Seaton, Colonel Benson, G. H. Balfour, Capt. H. E. Price, Major-General J. F. Wilson, Hon. Lt.-Col. Wm. Macpherson, Murray Kennedy, Wm. M. Dobell, Lorenzo Evans, R. M. Beckett, J. C. McLimont, Major A. C. Dobell, Capt. A. E. Doucet, E. Slade, Capt. J. B. Peters, Major, J. D. Brousseau, H. C. Foy, Hon. R. Turner, Major J. A. Scott, Major J. Homliston, C. A. Pent

land, G. G. Stuart, J. S. O'Meara, Capt. J. Burstall, F. J. Cockburn, Col. J. L. H. Neilson, R. C. Smith, C. E. L. Porteous, D. C. L'Esperance, G. C. Renfrew, Capt. A. B. Whitehead, W. G. Hinds, Jas. Muir, jr., J. W. Hamilton, Capt. D. Watson, J. W. Killam, Capt. F. M. Wells, Col. Lessard, E. T. D. Chambers, Captain J. A. Benyon, Major G. K. Addie, H. E. Heustis, Stuart H. Dunn, J. K. Boswell, C. E. A. Boswell, A. W. Boswell, C. L. Hervey, H. S. Thomson, E. T. Nesbitt, A. G. Piddington, A. C. Joseph, Capt. F. Holloway, Lt.-Col. W. J. Ray, Lt.-Col. J. Lyons Biggar, E. E. B. Rattray, F. M. MacNaughton, C. W. Walcot, Lt.-Col. W. Wood, Frank Carrel, Capt. W. P. Lindsay, General W. W. Henry, Col. G. T. Arth. Evanturel, J. W. McCarthy, Major Davidson, C. A. Foy, Major K. Gilmour, P. T. G. Mackenzie, K.C., G. A. Vandry, H. T. Machin, W. H. Delaney, Jules Hone, Sir Thomas Shaughnessy, Major Hethrington, E. J. H. Waagen, D. Johnstone, G. S. F. Robitaille, J. T. Ross, Colonel J. Bell Forsyth, B. H. N. Ross, Lieut.-Col. A. Roy, D.O.C., General Lake, H. Kennedy, General Macdonald, W. A. Weir, J. W. Borden, Col. E. Watkin, Surg.-Major Lebel, E. T. Hale, Senator Edwards, G. Sewell Page, F. G. Wilson, Col. C. C. Sewell, Albert Demers, John H. Holt, Major A. T. Ogilvie, Capt. A. C. Shaw, F. Walsh, A. N. Lyster, G. S. Bacon, L. J. A. Amyot, A. Laurie, Capt. Wm. Price, Major A. J. Price, Sir J. G. Garneau, R. C. Patton, Geo. C. Scott, Senator Jules Tessier, Prof. F. de Sumichrast, General Buchan, Dr. Scott-Ives, Mr. Burns, Judge McCorkill, Hon. L. A. Taschereau, Lt.-Col. Harry Borstall, Lt.-Col. Howard, Major Leslie, Major Jamieson, General Cotton.

✳ ✳ ✳

U. S. S. Battleship Arrives

Monday, the second day of the Tercentenary festivities marked the arrival of the U. S. S. battleship New Hampshire. The war vessels of England and France were already stationed in the Harbour, and with the new addition, the implements of battle of three nations once at war with one another stood amicably side by side contemplating the scene of former activities. The French had founded Quebec, the English had conquered it, the United States citizens would once capture it. This was now but history, and acute struggles were now marked but by pleasant friendship and common rejoicings.

THE ENGLISH ADMIRAL.

Driving through Quebec Streets.

Large crowds had gathered on Dufferin Terrace on all available heights to see the vessel steam into port. At one o'clock in the afternoon, the prow of the New Hampshire swung around the curve of St. Joseph. With a salute of nineteen guns she greeted the Governor-General of Canada, at the same time flying the British ensign. The reply from the citadel over, she, slowly steaming, fired a second salute of sixteen guns to Vice-Admiral Curzon-Howe, H. M. S.

VICE-PRESIDENT AND MRS. FAIRBANKS
And Major Mott driving through Quebec streets.

Exmouth replying. A similar salute was fired as the Amiral Aube was approached, the Tricolor at the same time being made to fly from the mizzen mast of the New Hampshire. A salute from the French flagship, the Leon Gambetta, followed while the Stars and Stripes fluttered over the French ship.

When within a cable length of the Amiral Aube's stern, passing on the right hand side, the New Hampshire's band played "La Marseillaise" while from the French vessels came the tune of "The Star Spangled Banner." The United States vessel then steamed ahead and her band having discoursed "Maple Leaf," "God Save the King," and "Rule Britannia," she dropped anchor between the Albemarle and Leon Gambetta.

Later in the afternoon, Rear-Admiral Cowles whose flag the New Hampshire flies, came aboard to pay his respects to the Governor-General and was greeted with a salute of sixteen guns as he landed on the wharf.

✱ ✱ ✱

French-Speaking Physicians Meet

Quebec during the Tercentenary period revived among other phases the life of ancient Athens. Among the learned bodies which convened here during the celebrations was the Association of French-speaking physicians of North America whose fourth Congress was opened in the evening at Laval University,

with an address of welcome by His Honour the Lieutenant-Governor, Sir Louis Jette. Other speeches were delivered by Mgr. Mathieu, rector of Laval University; Dr. Brochu, president of the association; Mr. J. Delage, official delegate of the French Government; Hon. Mr. Devlin, representing the Province of Quebec; and Mr. Maurice Renaud, delegate of the University of Paris. A garden party in the spacious lawns of the institution ended the first assembly.

✱ ✱ ✱

French Band on Terrace

As on every evening during the eventful fortnight, Dufferin Terrace presented an appearance which once seen by the stranger remains a lasting memory, an impression not soon fading into oblivion.

It was band-night. Moreover, it was French band-night. The musicians of the French vessels charmed the promenaders on the walk with a splendid selection of good music ably interpreted and well received.

The usual crowd of citizens was augmented by numerous strangers. More peoples and more ages, consequently more costumes were visible than on any other occasion. A plainly-clothed citizen of to-day walked with the costumed French nobleman who two hundred years ago was present on the same spot, in the Chateau St. Louis. Soldiers from all parts of Canada walked with the sailors of the United States vessel while British mariners strolled arm in arm with French tars, closely followed by Montcalm's and Wolfe's soldiers forgetting past memories in their fraternization—a living, concrete, entente cordiale.

THE FRENCH ADMIRAL
Driving through Quebec Streets.

The promenade was illuminated all along while overhead hung suspended crowns resplendent with the glowing effects of electricity. The river below was covered with ships in still darkness while once in a while a vessel would pass bearing a light on its course, smooth and stealthy. Levis, across the river, was dotted with illuminations, here an electric sign visible from Quebec, there a sparkling decoration. And all is quiet. The music sends its waves over the flooding mass of humanity. All are silent, contemplating the spectacle with admiration and reverence.

We protest our loyalty to the British Crown, but before the interest of the Empire we place the interest of Canada and before all the rest, the love of our Province.

Cheers were given for the king, Champlain, L'Association Catholique de la Jeunesse Canadienne-Francaise. The national anthems again re-echoed to the sound of music, salutes were given, and the crowd dispersed.

* * *

Official Guests Arrive

In the evening, some of the eminent official guests whose presence added great interest to the Tercentenary arrived. They were Marquis de Levis and Marquis de Levis-Mirepoix, descendants of Montcalm's faithful successor as commander of the French troops in Canada after the eventful battle of the Plains, and Count Bertrand de Montcalm, a member of the family to which belonged the ill-fated French general. These visitors, the official guests of the Tercentenary Commission, were met at the train and welcomed by Sir Francois Langelier, Hon. A. Turgeon, Lt.-Col B. A. Scott, M. Broet, M.P.P., Lt.-Col. Bacon, Major K. Gilmour, Major A. Dobell and Capt. J. S. O'Meara.

* * *

Tercentenary Greetings

The same day Sir J. G. Garneau, Mayor of Quebec, received a number of congratulatory telegrams among them the following :—

"Fontainebleau.—Vive Quebec.—LYONNAIS, Pres. Canadien."

Pekin.—Felicitations.—CRONHOLM."

THE CATHOLIC YOUNG FRENCH CANADIANS
Doing Honour to Champlain.

Mr. Ernest Legare's Address

Champlain has not worked in vain, and we are here, thousands in number, a living proof of this fact. Our race has developed pure from alloy, loyal, chivalrous, and as spotless as the lilies of its flag. Sons of Frenchmen, and all the glories of Old France are justly moving our souls. Indeed so many glories followed on their footsteps, our discoverers, our missionaries and the civilization which they carried broadcast on this continent; nowhere else have they made a more endearing impression than on this rock of Quebec, where fought in such great numbers, the "hauts seigneurs," the valiant captains, the heroic apostles.

France, gentlemen, Christian France is the one beautiful, is the one appealing to our hearts, the one which alone can produce men stronger than defeat, because they have faith in Him who has vanquished the world and who loves the Franks. In vain will the

and aspirations agree with our's, with those young men to whom we send a fraternal salute across the seas will revive the France of the Gospel, the France of St. Louis, Joan of Arc, Champlain, Montcalm and Levis, the France of Laval, Brebeuf, Lalemant, Mazenod and Jean Baptiste de la Salle. And we, it is that France that we love, that we salute when passes the French flag; it is to that France that to-day, in front of this monument, we convey the assurance of an everlasting remembrance.

✳ ✳ ✳

Mr. Leon Paradis' Address

The last speaker, Mr. Leon Paradis, spoke in a similar strain urging the French Canadian especially to assume a position of eminence in the Dominion, to make himself a force commanding respect and deserving admiration. He said:—

THE SIX BRITISH WARSHIPS
Anchored in the Harbour. From the Plains of Abraham.

principles of '89 try to obscure its glorious past. Always are there rising men, who dissipate the clouds. Only a short time ago, we, members of the A. C. J. C. were acclaiming one of these Frenchmen still true to their country's past. He had come here, a delegate from the "Association Catholique de la Jeunesse Francaise," a true representative, in our midst, of the thousands of young French Catholics who, like himself are fighting to save for their country the title of "Eldest Daughter of the Church." On their account France will keep that title and wear it through centuries while giving to Christ the blood of its children and filling the world with the light of faith.

With those valiant young men whose sentiments

Champlain and the Youth, it is the future saluting the past, it is the past throwing its light upon the days yet to come. In the past appears an heroic character, a brilliant figure, hallowed with glory and fame, Champlain, the founder of this nation, and with him all those who helped through ages and have contributed to complete his enterprise.

Our ancestors have opened this land to civilization; they have conquered for us those liberties we are so proud of. And we cherish that hope—a dream for others—of seeing Canada playing in this new world the role played in the old world by France. But our dream goes still further. We desire that French Canada become the force that commands respect, the brain that thinks, the hand that accomplishes.

Rentrez, habitants de Quebec,
Tenez-vous clos en vos logis,
Que tout bruit meure.
Quittez ces lieux, car voici l'heure
L'heure du couvre feu!

A select programme of music was furnished by the orchestra of the State band under Mr. Vezina's accomplished leadership.

The "terror for his size" met with a reception at the Club perhaps unrivalled in the annals of vocifer-

LORD ROBERTS AND MISS ROBERTS
Return from a Drive.

Lord Roberts Dinner

In a more modern manner and with as much interest was held a banquet in the evening at the Garrison Club in honour of Lord Roberts, perhaps the most popular man in Quebec during the Tercentenary.

The dinner was marked by a novelty, being held on the Club's lawn under a large marquee. The tables were set in horseshoe shape, the head of the boards facing the Club building. The sides of the big tent being open, gave vent to the delightful evening air, and the function was as enjoyable as it was picturesque.

ous welcoming at banquets. As he arose to respond to the toast of his health he was cheered to the echo and after some minutes' wait succeeded in making himself heard. He alluded to the cordial welcome that enhanced the pleasure with which he found himself in Canada which he had long wished to visit. He had always been prevented from complying with his desire until His Majesty had prayed him to attend Quebec's three hundredth birthday as the representative of the British army.

Referring to Quebec city, Lord Roberts said that he had never seen anything so perfectly satisfying as

"The Vice-President of the United States, the Hon. Mr. Fairbanks, officially represents his country at our great celebration.

"This afternoon on the Plains of Abraham in the midst of magnificent weather took place the second dress rehearsal of the pageants which represent with gorgeous decorations the principal events of our history and the great deeds of our ancestors.

"The events of to-morrow: to-morrow afternoon will take place on the historic soil of the Plains, the

assisted by a large number of outside singers and musicians.

"Oyez! Oyez! Oyez! Inhabitants of Quebec, gentry and burgesses; the old city which was the cradle of New France celebrates by these remarkable festivities the glory of its founder. Thousands and thousands of strangers have come from all parts of this country, and of the United States, and throng within our walls. Receive them well, and keep up the good reputation for French politeness left you by your forebears."

THE DUKE OF NORFOLK AND LORD LOVAT

In the rear seat, being driven about the city by Sir Charles Fitzpatrick.

first grand representation of the pageants at which the seats will be reserved.

"In the evening at eight o'clock at the Drill Hall, Felicien David's symphonic ode 'Christophe Colomb,' will be given by the Symphonic Society of Quebec,

The citizens apprised of all the news and information so liberally furnished by the heralds now listened to the chanting of the curfew bidding them retire and cover all fire-grates. In poetical language, the order was given—

REMINDERS OF THE PAST

American Horse and Champlain.

cessary legislation for the Tercentenary to be held over till his return. It was also hoped, at the time of the postponement, that by the summer of 1909 the inauguration of the bridge over the St. Lawrence at Cap Rouge would be able to form an interesting feature of the Celebration.

The proposed postponement caused but little interruption in the preparations for the Tercentenary fetes, and the work of preparing a suitable programme and arranging its various details continued to occupy the attention of the different committees.

On the 10th January, 1908, Colonel J. Hanbury-Williams appeared before the Executive Committee on behalf of Earl Grey, to suggest that in consequence of the impossibility of inaugurating the Quebec Bridge in 1909, there seemed to be no longer any good reason for deferring the celebration of the Tercentenary to that year, which would be twelve months beyond the actual three hundredth anniversary of the founding of Quebec. After a careful consideration of the possibility of completing the necessary preparations for the fetes by the summer of 1908, it was unanimously resolved to recommend that the celebration be fixed for that period ; and this recommendation was adopted by the General Committee on the 13th of January.

The various committees continued their work with renewed vigour; and in keeping with his promise to His Worship Mayor Garneau, Sir Wilfrid Laurier lost no time in submitting to Parliament his legislation for the appointment of a National Commission and for a vote of $300,000 to the funds under its control. The bill received the sanction of the Governor-General on the 19th March, 1908, just a fortnight after the official announcement had been received from England that His Royal Highness the Prince of Wales would reach Quebec on the 22nd July and leave again on the 29th; thus finally fixing the dates for the leading events of the fetes.

From the date of their appointment the members of the National Battlefields Commission have laboured assiduously for the success of the Tercentenary celebration. They are at present seven in number, and were appointed under the provisions of the Act of 1908 "Respecting the Canadian Battlefields at Quebec." The act authorized the appointment of five Commissioners by the Governor-General-in-Council, and one by every province which may contribute a sum of not less than $100,000 to the purposes of the Commission. The Governments of the two provinces of Ontario and Quebec voted $100,000 each to the Commission, the first named appointing the Hon. J. S. Hendrie to represent it on the Commission, and Quebec naming the Hon. L. A. Taschereau as its representative. The five Commissioners appointed by the Dominion Government are Mayor Garneau of Quebec, chairman ; Sir George E. Drummond, K.C.M.G., Montreal ; Byron E. Walker, Esq., C. V. O., and Colonel George T. Denison, of Toronto, and Hon. Adelard Turgeon, C.M.G., Minister of Lands and Forests of the Province of Quebec.

Besides being charged with the establishment and maintenance of the National Battlefields Park, the Commissioners were authorized to expend a sum not exceeding $300,000 on the fetes attending the celebration of the Champlain Tercentenary at Quebec. This $300,000 is the entire amount voted by the Dominion Parliament to the National Commission for the current year ; but the Commission's work is likely to last over many years ; and, for several sessions to come, it is expected that additional votes of money will be forthcoming towards the project of the Battlefields Park. To this object, all subscriptions, given either by private individuals or by public bodies other than the Dominion Government, are to be solely and strictly applied, including, of course, the $200,000 already subscribed by the two provinces of Ontario and Quebec, and the large sums flowing in from private subscriptions in different parts of the world. Until after the close of the Quebec fetes the Commissioners devoted almost their entire attention to the Tercentenary celebration in honour of Champlain's founding of the city, which was the actual birth of the Canadian nation. In so doing they earned the gratitude, not only of the citizens of Quebec but of every true Canadian. Thanks are equally due to Sir John Hanbury-Williams, K. C. V. O., who represented the Governor-General at the meetings of the Commission, to Mr. J. M. Courtney, C. M. G., Honorary Treasurer and to Messrs H. J. J. B. Chouinard, C. M. G., and Dr. A. G. Doughty, C. M. G., Interim Secretaries.

In addition to the $300,000 or thereabouts expended by the National Battlefields Commission for the Tercentenary fetes, the greater part of the sum of $50,000 voted by the City Council was used for the same purpose. Some $31,000 of this amount was entrusted to the local Executive Committee of the Tercentenary, and the remaining $19,000 was expended under the direct supervision of the Mayor and Finance Committee of the City Council.

Much credit is due to the members of the local Executive and its sub-committees for the enormous amount of work done by them, and Quebecers will not easily forget how much they owe to His Excellency Earl Grey, Governor-General, for the vast amount of interest he has taken in the fetes, and to Sir J. George Garneau, Mayor, for his untiring exertions in the same good cause for more than two years past.

SIR WILFRID LAURIER
Prime Minister of the Dominion
of Canada.

our own development by the celebration which has just closed, we may look with confidence to the creation of an historical literature worthy of the country's past and the magnitude of the issues that have here been decided. Our own people have been shown, and the world has been shown, that Canada is no longer a dependency : but a political entity for which a large place is reserved in a greater system. The mighty ironclads in our river that thundered forth a salute in honour of the founder of Quebec, were not the ships of a foreign power that might be trained against us at any moment: but our own, under the one flag to which great and greater Britain look for protection.

In the final scene of the Pageant when all the historical characters were massed on the Plains, the soldiers of Montcalm, of Lévis, of Wolfe and of Murray,—English, French, Irish, Scotch—marched together in one grand parade of honour. And this surely is the lesson to take to heart from this great national celebration. There is no longer any room in Canada for a narrow provincial spirit. The ancient fields of strife have been consecrated anew, not to the victor on either field but to the larger and more ample national life that has resulted therefrom. Henceforth it should be our pride and our duty to march forward side by side as Canadians of Canada to a common destiny.

Honour to Champlain ! Eternal honour to his name. Honour also to all those who toiled and bled that we might one day enjoy the blessing of peace.

A. G. D.

Sports for Soldiers and Sailors

The day was essentially one of sports. The evening witnessed the spectacular military tatoo while the afternoon was marked by a series of horse races at the exhibition grounds and a demonstration of sports on the Quebec Athletic Association field.

The sports held on the Q.A.A. grounds varied in character. There were races of all descriptions for the sailors and soldiers, as stilt races, sack races and

magnificent and evoked the admiration of all the spectators.

More exciting was the driving exhibition given by the detachment of the Royal Canadian Horse Artillery. It was thrilling. As the field guns, each drawn by six horses, dashed through their evolutions, all were still. The rapidity with which the movements of the heavy armament were gone through was marvellous and beyond the credence of the frightened witnesses who feared at every moment a catastrophe that appeared

SAVARD MILITARY CAMP,

Where 15,000 men were under Canvas.

wheelbarrow races. The contestants entered all with vim and provided genuine displays of the art of Atalanta. No such prizes as were offered by the fleet maiden were distributed, but this did not detract from the running qualities of our defenders.

The features of the sports were the excellent gymnastic display given by the Royal Military Cadets and the sensational driving of the members of the Royal Canadian Horse Artillery.

The Cadets whose reputation and skill made them very popular during their stay gave a fine exhibition of calisthenic drill. Their marching and movements were executed with the utmost precision and neatness. They presented a striking appearance in the vaulting horse exercise. The acme of their demonstration and the pleasant effect that they produced came when the pyramid work was performed. The tableaux were

to them inevitable. The spectacle was a new one and certainly perilous. In a circumscribed space the guns, horses and men drove. In the intricate passages the carriages glided by each other, and what seemed wonderful, missed each other.

✤ ✤ ✤

Lord Robert Inspects Troops

In the afternoon, Lord Roberts, who made his whole stay in Quebec an active one, visited Savard Park where many of the militia who came to attend the celebrations were encamped. He was accompanied by His Excellency Earl Grey and by Col. Denison, his aide-de-camp. The forty-eighth Highlanders, the Royal Grenadiers and the Queen's Own Rifles of

Third Day, Tuesday, July Twenty-First

Official Guests Arrive

 UESDAY was a day of expectation. All were preparing for H. R. H. the Prince of Wales who was to arrive on the morrow. Bustle and hurry marked everything. To give the royal visitor a fit reception was the predominant motive in all official and private circles. The third day of the celebrations was consequently marked by events which bore more of a preparatory character than aught else. It was dotted with happenings of every description which were but a harbinger of what was to follow.

Tuesday was set aside on the programme as the day for the reception of all official guests. These had, however, been arriving for some time past and were individually met by the members of the special reception committee, organized solely for the purpose of extending a welcome to official visitors.

Among the guests who arrived on Tuesday were Mrs. Cowles, wife of the commander of U.S.S. New Hampshire; Hon. J. Stewart Pitts, C.M.G., who represented Newfoundland at the celebrations; Sir Wilfrid and lady Laurier; Mrs. Aylesworth, wife of Hon. Mr. Aylesworth, Minister of Justice; Hon. Mr. Rodolphe and Mrs. Lemieux. With the exception of Mrs. Cowles, who remained on the New Hampshire and Hon. Mr. Pitts, the new arrivals above mentioned were guests of Sir Louis and Lady Jette at Spencer Wood. His Honor's other guests were Vice-President and Mrs. Fairbanks, Major Mott, Mr. J. de Loynes, wife and daughter, Mr. Louis Herbette, Conseiller d'Etat, representative of France, Mr. and Mrs. F. D. Monk, Mrs. Hurlbut, Mrs. Sturgeon, Miss Quigley and Dr. Eugene Lemieux, who acted as extra A.D.C.

Accommodation was provided for the other official guests at the Governor-General's headquarters in the Citadel and at the famous Chateau Frontenac Hotel.

SOME OF THE BRITISH WAR VESSELS
In Quebec Harbour.

Consuls Visit Warships

The members of the Consular Corps in the city visited the French flagship, the Leon Gambetta and U.S.S. New Hampshire in the afternoon. They were cordially received by Vice-Admiral Jaureguiberry and Commander Cowles respectively. The former stated that the visit testified to the existing harmony between the two races in Quebec which was in the best interests of humanity and of progress.

Little else except of fragmentary importance occurred during the afternoon.

* * *

Soldiers Hold Tattoo

The sporting events of the day ended with the spectacular military tattoo, an event not often seen in Quebec and long to be remembered by all who witnessed it. Arranged and organized by Mr. John Slatter, W. O., Bandmaster of the 48th Highlanders the event proved a complete success and was well attended at both performances, the tattoo having been repeated shortly after. Those who took part in the performance came from all parts of Canada, but everything was executed with precision and skill. Eleven bands drawn from different parts of the Dominion took part. These, with a number of torch-bearers who composed the performers, numbered five hundred.

As darkness was falling, the bands playing their regimental marches came on the field, escorted by the torch-bearers. Having assembled opposite the grand stand the buglers and trumpeters on duly called "First Post" after which the massed bands followed with popular selections. The massed drum and bugle bands followed by the Scottish pipers then marched around the arena playing military airs. Then

came gunfire. The signal call was sounded and the bands played "La Marseillaise" which preceded several selections of a devotional character. The illuminations were in harmony with the music and as the hymns were played the lights were gradually subdued presenting an appearance of tranquility and piety in strange contrast to the somewhat noisy and highly illuminated state of affairs of but a few minutes before.

Fires were then lighted and a typical camp scene portrayed. Songs of glee resounded while the soldiers amid the darkness were seen to "flit on winged fantastic toe." The torches were then extinguished and the camp was at rest.

The spectators next witnessed a sudden night attack on the camp. An outburst of bombs and fireworks giving the semblance of fire-arms awoke the air. The sleeping soldiers were at once astir and for a few moments the confusion of a camp attacked at night was on the tapis. Repulse and victory followed. A splendid display of fireworks of variegated hues amid the strains of martial music ended the pleasant and novel entertainment.

* * *

Five Hundred Perform Symphonic Ode

In the evening over two thousand people gathered at the Drill Hall to hear the symphonic ode "Christo-

THE ROYAL MILITARY CADETS

Giving a Calisthenic display on the Q. A. A. grounds.

phe Colomb" rendered by the Quebec Symphony Society. This was the first of the concerts which the Tercentenary committee on music had arranged for the celebrations.

Four hundred vocalists and one hundred trained musicians told the complete story of the discovery of America in music and verse, as composed by Felicien David. To hear four hundred voices in perfect unison is no ordinary event. No less striking was the completeness of the concord with which the large number of musicians produced harmony.

The ode has different phases all of which were well rendered. The audience was taken from scene to

"A toi, chef Immortel" forms a finale which lends a finishing touch to an excellent musical treat.

The soloists who gave the programme that charm which true musicians only can appreciate were Miss Godbout, Miss Lacroix, Mr. Paul Dufault, Mr. Moise Raymond, Mr. J. A. Gagne and Mr. Jos. Saucier.

Mr. Dufault's rich baritone voice was heard to advantage in the opening solo "La Brise qui se Leve" and in "Amis Fideles". Mr. Gagne's rendering of the orphan sailor boy's pathetic song "La Mer est ma Patrie" evoked from the audience rounds of applause which could only be satisfied with a liberal volume

THE STERN, UPPER DECK, OF H. M. S. EXMOUTH.
Showing the sailors at rest.

scene and as with a vivid histrionic representation the struggles and trials of the great navigator are recounted. Words as it were are put into the mouth of the instruments which tunefully pour forth the tale of David.

The tropical ocean storm which figures in the ode is vividly pictured before the audience by a violent outburst of music. The roll of the waves, the groaning of the labouring ships and the fury of the gale are all heard. The monotonous voyage is told by the strings while a joyous ring of music proclaims the sight of land. The Indian mother's lullaby as she rocks her child is mimicked by the tender strains. A combined chorus of five hundred voices greeting

of song from his luscious baritone voice. A similar reception met Mr. Raymond's "Attendez la Nouvelle Aurore." The "Indian Mother's Lullaby" was sung by Miss Lacroix whose melodious and sparkling voice was a contrast to the high sounding chorus which had preceded it.

The work of the chorus was very good. This was well demonstrated in its rendering of "Dieu de Bonte," a prayer for protection on an hazardous ocean voyage. "The chorus of the Ocean Spirits" and "Les Douces Voix des Genies" were sung with that sublime grandeur which is rendered possible only when several hundred voices are ably combined.

The narrative forms a fit subject for symphonic execution. In the hands of the Quebec Symphony Society and under the extremely able leadership of Mr. Joseph Vezina, the special traits of the ode, which under incapable management might otherwise have been disregarded, were assured their full significance.

✳ ✳ ✳

Lord Roberts Again Banquetted

A dinner was given by the Honorable Sir Louis Jette at Spencer Wood in honour of Lord Roberts. The invited guests were His Excellency the Governor-General, Col. Hanbury-Williams, Capt. Newton, Major Sheppard, Major Panet, Hon. Mr. Gouin, Hon. Mr. Archambeault, Hon. Mr. Taschereau, Col. O. Pelletier, Major-General Wilson, Major-General Lake, Brigadier-General Otter, Col. Buchan, Sir Chas.

LANDING PIER
For the launches of
the Visiting Warships

Fitzpatrick, Sir J. G. Garneau, Mr. Jos. Pope, Vice-Admiral Sir Curzon-Howe, Commander Haggard, Capt. A. J. Henniker Hugham, Rear Admiral Sir John R. Jellicoe, Lt. Buxton, Capt. Goodenough, Capt. Ricardo, Capt. Chapman, Capt. Huddleston, Capt. Ewart, Vice-Admiral Jaureguiberry, Captain Clements, Captain Hebert, Capt. Gres, Mr. Brandelis, Lord Roberts, Marquis de Levis, Marquis de Levis-Mirepoix, Count de Montcalm, Mr. George Wolfe, Capt. H. A. Murray, Count Dudley, Count Ranfurly, Lord Lovat, Duke of Norfolk, Lord Howick, Sir H. de Villiers, Hon. Jas. Pitts, Hon. P. Dandurand, Sir Mortimer Clark, Hon. D. C. Fraser, Hon. Jas. Dunsmuir, Hon. H. O. Bulyea, Hon. A. E. Forget, Col. G. T. Denison, Mr. Byron Walker, Sir Geo. Drummond, Hon. A. Turgeon, Lieut.-Governor McKinnon, Commander Cowles, Capt. T. Winslow, Judge Davidson.

Ball by British Officers

The grand finale of Tuesday's events was the naval ball at the Parliament buildings. The invitations were issued in the name of the Admiral the Hon. Sir Assheton G. Curzon-Howe, Rear Admiral Sir John R. Jellicoe, and the captains and officers of the Atlantic fleet. Almost one thousand persons were present. In the social annals of the Tercentenary, the naval ball was one of the greatest events of the celebrations.

The Parliament buildings were a blaze of light outside which did not however betray the decorations that marked the interior. The Legislative Assembly and the Legislative Council chambers are in their usual state highly ornamented halls. Add to this the bunting and naval paraphernalia which covered the walls and some idea of the splendour may be obtained. The halls were lined with ferns and flags while at equidistant intervals were placed men from the different vessels and guns effectively arranged. Half way up the stairway and facing the hall below was a trophy formed of small arms and various nautical devices, a sailor and marine flanking the central arrangement and retaining their positions without budging, the effect being very novel and picturesque.

The guests were received by Admiral Curzon-Howe and Madame J. G. Garneau in the ball-room which was lavishly decorated. The gallery was hung with great flags between which were placed life belts bearing the names of the various battleships and cruisers belonging to the fleet. The orchestra was stationed on the gallery.

There were twenty dances including a number of extras. Supper was served at midnight in the chamber of the Legislative Council. Dancing was kept up till an early hour when one of the great social events of the celebration ended. The invited guests were:

A

Hon. Jules and Mrs. Allard, Hon. H. and Mrs. Archambeault, Sir Montague and Lady Allan, M. B. Allan, Hon. H. G. and Mrs. Ahern, Miss E. Wright, Mr. and Mrs. Aylwin and Miss Ross, Mr. F. Aymar, Mrs. A. Aylesworth, Rear-Admiral Cowles, U.S.S. New Hampshire, Captain C. McR. Winslow and officers, New Hampshire, Vice-Admiral Jaureguiberry, Leon Gambetta, Captain and officers Leon Gambetta, Captain and officers Admiral Aube.

B

Archbishop Begin, Justice and Mrs. Blanchet, Justice and Miss Bosse, Captain and Mrs. Benyon, Mr. and Mrs. J. F. Burstall, Hon. P. and Mrs. Boucher de la Bruere, Mrs. and the Misses Burstall, Mr. and Mrs. R. Beckett, Mr. John, Mrs. and the Misses Breakey, Mr., Mrs. and the Misses Boswell, Lt.-Col. H. and Mrs. Burstall, Mayor Brandelis, Major T. Bentley Mott, Sir John and Lady Burron, His Honor and Mrs. G. H. Bulyea, Sir Frederick, Lady and Miss Borden, Hon. L. P. and Mrs. Brodeur, Brig.-General and Mrs. Buchan, Col. and Mrs. Benson, Lord Bruce, Mrs. Bell and Miss Johnstone, Mr. St. G. P. Baldwin, Mr., Mrs. and the Misses Bradley, Mr. Belleau, Major Berdaw, the Misses Beauchamp.

C

Mr., Mrs. and Miss Culman, Justice and Mrs. Chauveau, Hon. P. and Mrs. Choquette, Justice and Mrs. Caroll, Mr. and Mrs. P. B. Casgrain, Mr. and Mrs. L. A. Cannon, Justice and the Misses Cannon, Hon. T. and Mrs. Chapais, Mr. and Mrs. L. H. Carrier, Mr. and Mrs. H. J. Chouinard, Mr., Mrs. and the Misses Cook, Rear-Admiral and Mrs. Cowles, Mr. and Mrs. Courtney, Captain the Hon. Dudley Carleton, Mr. Convent, Mr. E. S., Mrs. and Miss Clonston, Rev. W. C. Clarke, Mrs. and Miss Crombie, The Editor of the "Chronicle," Mr. Frank Carrel, Mr., Mrs. and Miss Crosby, Miss Carling, the Misses Cooke and Miss Cassels.

D

Bishop Dunn, Mrs. and Miss Dunn and party, Mr. and Mrs. W. L. and Miss R. Dobell, Hon. C. R. and Mrs. Devlin, Capt. and Mrs. Doucet, Mr. and Mrs. Dumoulin, Col. and Mrs. Geo. and Miss Denison, Lt.-Col. Septimus Denison, Capt. the Hon. Hugh and Lady Susan Dawnay, Sir George and Lady Drummond, Dr. Doughty, His Honor James Dunsmuir, Mrs. Dunsmuir and party, Hon. R. and Mrs. Lemieux, the Hon., Mrs. and Miss Dandurand, Consul-General, Mrs. and Miss des Isles, the Marchioness of Donegal, Mrs. and the Misses Dobie, Mr. and Mrs. Sumichrast and party, Mr. and Miss De Parkyn, Sir John De Villiers, Mr. A. C. Dobell, Brig.-General, Mrs. and the Misses Drury, Mr. and Mrs. Dyer, Mr., Mrs. and Miss Dandurand, Mr. and Miss Dowd, Mr. and Mrs. Davis, Mrs. Dodge, Mr. Delicure.

E

Lt.-Col. English, Lady Violet Elliott, Col. Oscar and Mrs. Evanturel, Mrs. and Miss Fitsrandolph Eaton, Mrs. and Miss Evans, Mrs. W. Edwards and party.

F

Chevalier O. Frechette, Lt.-Col. and Mrs. Bell Forsyth, Major and Mrs. Fages, Mr. and Mrs. Foy and Miss Grant, Vice-President and Mrs. Fairbanks, Viscount and Lady Falmouth and Hon. Hugh Boscowan, His Honor and Mrs. Fraser, Hon. W. S., Mrs. and the Misses Fielding, Rt.-Hon. Sir Chs., Lady, Mr. and the Misses Fitzpatrick, Mr. and Miss Meredith Finneane, Sir Keith Alexander Fraser.

G

Hon. Lomer Gouin, Lt.-Col. and Mrs. Gaudet, Mr. and Mrs. Garneau, Mayor and Mrs. Garneau, Mr. and Mrs. Grenier, Dr. and Mrs. Grondin, His Excellency the Governor-General and Countess Grey, Lady Sybil Grey, Hon. G. and Mrs. Graham, Col. T. H. and Mrs. Grant, Mr. and Mrs. W. Gillman, Mrs. and Miss Gooderham and Miss Nadine Kerr, Mr. W. A. Griffith and the Misses Phinney.

H

Mrs. J. H. and Miss Holt, Mr. and Mrs. John Hill, Mr. M. J. Hale, Mr., Mrs. and Miss Hamilton, Mr. and Mrs. W. Henry, Viscount Howick, Col., Mrs. and Miss Hanbury-Williams, Louis Herbette, Col., Mrs. and Miss Hendrie, Hon. J. D. and Miss Hazen, Mr., Mrs. and the Misses Hays, Mr. and Mrs. Huestis, Mr. G. G., Miss Hill and Mr. Hill jr., Miss Holland, Mr. Angus Hooper, Mr., Mrs. and the Misses Hall, Mr. and Mrs. W. A. Home, Mr. and Mrs. Hill, Mr. and Mrs. E. A. Hoare, Miss Home, Miss W. Hoare, Mrs. and Miss Hurlbut, t'e Misses Hughson.

J

His Honor Lieut.-Governor, Lady Jette and party, Captain Johnston, A.D.C., Colonel C. James, Mr., Mrs. and Miss Joseph, and Miss Ramsay.

K

Mr. and Mrs. Kennedy, Hon. and Mrs. Kaine, Captain Kincaid Smith, M.P., Rear-Admiral and Mrs. Kingsmill, Capt Knowlton, Miss Kerman.

THE GARDEN PARTY AT SPENCERWOOD.

Lord Roberts is seen in the foreground while Hon. Mr. W. S. Fielding is seen at the extreme left.

H. M. S. MINOTAUR.

L

L. J. Lemaire, Sir Frs. and Lady Langelier, Mr. and Mrs. J. de Lotbiniere, Hon. P. Landry, Mr. and Mrs. Langelier, Mr. and Mrs. Lanctot, Mr. and Mrs. Lachance, Sir Henry de Lotbiniere and Mrs. Nanton, Viscount Lascelles, A.D.C., Mr., Mrs. and Misses de Loynes, Mr. G. B. Lockwood, Marquis de Levis, Marquis Mirepoix de Levis, Hon. Mr. and Mrs. Lindley, Sir Wilfrid and Lady Laurier, Major-General and Mrs. Lake, Lord Lovat, C.V.O., C.B., D.S.O., Major N. LeVasseur and ladies, Mr. T. LeVasseur, Revd. Mr. and Mrs. Love, Mrs. Lockwood, Mr. Robert Loyd, Mr. L. A. Loyd, Captain and Mrs. Lafferty, Miss Lamontagne, Dr. Eugene Lemieux.

M

Mgr. Marois, Mgr. Mathieu, Mr. Justice and Mrs. Malouin, Mr. and Mrs. Wm. Macpherson, Mr. Justice and Mrs. McCorkill, Mr., Mrs. and Miss McLimont, Hon. Angus McDonnel, Comte de Montcalm, Hon. Arthur Murray, M.P., Mr. F. D. and Mrs. Monk, Hon. G. H. and Mrs. Murray, Mrs. F. W. Morse, Mr. W., Mrs. and the Misses McKenzie, Mr. B. McLennan, Mr. and Mrs. Meredith and party, Mrs. and Miss McDonough, Captain and Miss Mills, Capt. Mills, R.C.A., Mr. and Mrs. Machin and party, Dr. V. C., Mrs. and Miss McIlwraith.

N

Mrs. Neilson, Capt. Newton, A.D.C., His Grace the Duke of Norfolk, Mrs. Nordheimer and party.

O

Mr., Mrs. and Miss O'Meara, Major and Mrs. Ogilvie, Mr. and Mrs. O'Meara, Mr., Mrs. and the Misses Obalski, Hon. Frank, Mrs. and the Misses Oliver, Brigadier-General and Mrs. Otter, Mrs. D'Arcy Hutton, Rev. Mr. and Mrs. Orchard, Revd. J. M. O'Leary, Miss O'Brien.

P

Mr. and Miss Piddington, Captain and Mrs. Palmer, Miss Parmalee, Mrs. and Miss Pickering, Sir A. and Lady Pelletier, Mr. Justice and Mrs. H. C. Pelletier, Mr., Mrs. and the Misses Porteous and party, Mr. and Mrs. Price, Mr. and Mrs. Paquet,

Mr. and Mrs. Price, Mr. and Mrs. Panet, Major Poole, Mrs. and the Misses Price, Col. and Mrs. Oscar Pelletier, Mr. and Mrs. H. E. Price, Mr. and Mrs. C. A. Pentland, Major and Mrs. J. B. Pym, Major and Mrs. Pacaud, Mr. and Mrs. W. Power, Mr. H. J. and Miss Petry, Lady Mary Parker, Capt. Pickering, A.D.C., Lieut.-General Sir Reg. and Lady Beatrice Pole-Carew, Hon. J. Stewart Pitts, Mr. and Mrs. Pope, C.M.G., I.S.O., Hon. Wm. and Mrs. Pugsley, Captain and Mrs. W. Price and Miss Lola Powell, Miss Chadwick, Miss Oliver and Miss Morna Ball, Miss Pym, Mr. and Mrs. Bertram Patton, Capt. A. H. Powell, Dr. and Miss Parkin, Lieut. Passy.

R

Captain, Mrs. and the Misses Roy, Miss Robertson, Lt.-Col. and Mrs. Ray, Mr. Justice and Mrs. Routhier and party, Mr. and Mrs. Roy, Mrs. F. E. Roy and Miss Taft, Hon. Rodolphe Roy, Mgr. Roy, Mr., Mrs. and Miss Robitaille, Miss Elsie Ritchie, Mr. and Mrs. J. T. Ross, Field Marshal Earl Roberts, V.C., K.G., Mr. Justice Ritchie, Lady Aileen Mary Roberts, the Earl of Ranfurly, Hon. A. and Mrs. Rutherford, Mr. and Mrs. Reeves, Mrs. and Miss Reynolds, Mr. and Mrs. Hayter Reed, Miss Grace Richardson, Mrs. and Miss Renor, Mr. and Mrs. A. Rhodes.

S

Mrs. Stanton, Hon. Mr. and Mrs. Shehyn, Colonel, Mrs. and Miss Sewell, Lt.-Col. and Mrs. Scott and Miss Shehyn, Mr. and Mrs. J. G. Scott and Mrs. G. G. Stuart and Miss Masy, Rev. Mr. and Mrs. Scott, Captain and Mrs. J. Sharples, Major H. C. Sheppard, Mr. and Mrs. Harcourt-Smith, Mr. and Mrs. Arthur Smith, Mr. and Mrs. W. Sharples, Miss E. Stephen, Mr. and Mrs. Sladen, Col. and Mrs. Sherwood, Lt.-Col. Sillers, Mrs. Sladen, Colonel and Mrs. Scott, Hon. R. W. Scott, Miss Scott and Mr. D'Arcy Scott, Hon. R. F., Mrs. and Miss Sutherland, Sir Thomas, Lady and Miss Shaughnessy, Mr. and Mrs. G. Smellie and Miss Jones, Miss Shaughnessy, Miss Stephen, Mr. and Mrs. Scott-Griffin, Captain and Mrs. Sharples, Miss Mott and Miss Combe, Mrs. Sullivan, Mr. and Mrs. Slade, Misses Shaw, Mr. and Mrs. G. C. and W. J. Scott and Miss Bowell, Miss Scarff, Mr. and Mrs. J. J. Sharples.

T

Lieut.-Colonel and Mrs. Turner, Lieut.-Colonel Turnbull, Hon. Jules and Mrs. Tessier, Hon. R., Mrs. and Miss Turner, Hon. A. and Mrs. Turgeon, Hon. L. A. and Mrs. Taschereau, Mr. Justice and Mrs. Tessier, Mr. and Mrs. G. H. Thompson, the Misses Thomson, Sir Henry Taschereau, Chief Justice and the Misses Taschereau, Capt. Emile Trudel, Chief of Police.

V

Mrs. Vanderwerken, Miss Valliere.

W

Hon. W. A., Mrs. and Miss Weir, the Dean of Quebec, Mrs., Miss and Mr. J. Williams, Lieut.-Colonel Wood, Lieut.-Colonel Victor Williams, Lieut.-Colonel Wadmore, Major-General and Mrs. Wilson, Mr. and Mrs. Hallam, and the Misses, Mr. and Mrs. Cook, Mr. George Wolfe, Mr. and Mrs. Byron Walker, Hon.

Y

Capt. Young, Mrs. Agnes Young and party.

Canadian Army

Major A. W. Ward, Lieut.-Colonel A. Roy and officers, Colonel Benson, Major A. O. Fages, Lieut.-Col. Ashmead, Lieut.-Colonel Martineau, Major Laliberte, Lieut.-Colonel Wood, Lieut.-Colonel O. Evanturel, Lieut.-Colonel O. E. Talbot, Lieut.-Colonel L. N. Laurin, Major Brousseau, Major Houliston, Lieut.-Colonel I. P. Landry and staff, Lieut.-Colonel G. E. A. Jones, Lieut.-Colonel Turner, V.C., D.S.O., Lieut.-Colonel B. A. Scott, Lieut.-Colonel

THE KING'S WHARF
Before the Prince's arrival
showing the arch of welcome.

J. P., Mrs. and the Misses Whitney, Mr. E. F. Wurtele, the Rev. and Mrs. Williams, Capt. and Mrs. White, and Mr. and Mrs. G. West Jones, Miss Walker, Miss Hope Wurtele, Mr. and Miss Kate Webb, Mr. Perley White, Mr. Webster, Mrs. Scott, Miss Bowie, Mrs. Webster, Mrs. Scott, Miss Bowie, Mrs. and Miss Powers, Mrs. Wurtele.

L. K. Scott, D.S.O., and officers, Lieut.-Colonel H. Burstall, Colonel Jones, Major E. A. Lodge, Lt.-Colonel Wadmore, Lieut. Col. Polge Williams, A.D.C., Brig.-General W. H. Cotton, A.D. C., and one staff officer, Colonel W. D. Gordon, A.D.C., and one staff officer, Brig.-General L. Buchan, C.M.G., A.D.C., Captain Panet, Captain Young, Brig.-Sergeant Major Lane.

SAMUEL DE CHAMPLAIN

Fourth Day, Wednesday, July Twenty=Second

H. R. H. Prince of Wales arrives.

EDNESDAY was the first grand day of the Tercentenary celebrations. The promised arrival of H. R. H. the Prince of Wales had made the day a long desired one. All had been looking forward to the coming of the Prince who was the central figure of the celebrations. Old Quebec doubled its population on Wednesday. Many came but for the day, all eager to have a glance at the royal representative and future King of the greatest empire in the world.

Long before any sign was visible of H. M. S. Indomitable, which bore the Royal representative, thousands of people had gathered where they might catch a glimpse of the great war-vessel arriving and of its royal charge. The harbour front was decked with launches and boats of every description, filled to their capacity with anxious seekers for the son of His Majesty. On the wharves sat men and women waiting expectantly. The Terrace above the Lower Town was crowded, being marked by no vacant spot. The heights above had been scaled early in the day by climbers who there sojourned till the vessel glided into the harbour. Even the steep cliffs beneath Quebec's famous walk were covered by people who somehow maintained their difficult position. The

H.M.S. INDOMITABLE

H.R.H. THE PRINCE OF WALES INSPECTS THE GUARD
Drawn up on King's Wharf as he lands.

pinnacle of every house high enough to afford a view of the river fringing the city was ornamented with living occupants.

All were waiting patiently. The clouds which traced their course overhead earlier in the day had, as if nature were contending with man in its reception of the visitor, vanished and were replaced by a strong sun casting its warm rays upon the swarming mass of humanity below. It was hot. But who thought of discomfort? Strangers and citizens stood side by side conversing freely. It seemed as if a family reunited was awaiting the arrival of its chief member. A common feeling pervaded the large multitude. One thought was pre-eminent in everybody's mind—the Prince.

The King's wharf, where the Prince was to land, presented a busy scene and a gorgeous one. The dull walls of the marine storehouse were overlaid with flags and crests. At intervals were placed stands of flags and shields bearing Royal and Canadian arms. Venetian masts and pennants floated gaily adding to the rich hues of the suspended flags.

The landing stage upon which the Prince was to disembark was also bright with decorations, its small roof being festooned with all that goes to make a shelter attractive. On the wharf and to the right of the gangway leading from the landing stage stood a green and white striped marquee, where stood His Royal Highness as he listened to the address presented to him by the Canadian people through the mouth of Sir Wilfrid Laurier. Adjoining this was a small uncovered stand decorated with the many coloured frocks of the ladies who sat on it. Nearby stood soldiers, statesmen, jurists and leaders of learned professions, some in the ordinary dress of the civilian, others in military garb resplendent with gold lace and dotted with medals and ribbons, the whole presenting an appearance of unrivalled colour and magnificence.

Where the wharf ends and the street begins, a double arch of massive proportions was erected. The inner one, supported by double Ionic columns, bore the Royal and Dominion arms upon it, while on top,

THE GUARD OF HONOR
Drawn up on the King's Wharf.

on either side of the Union Jack fluttered the flags of France and the United States.

Leading up to the arch was a flight of stairs, while beyond it a short path led to the second great white and gold archway upon which in gold letters shone conspicuously the cheering "Bienvenu." Between the two arches the way was a galaxy of greenery and flowers.

Shortly before three o'clock in the afternoon, the event for which all were eagerly looking occurred. Turning around the curve of St. Joseph de Levis came smartly the armoured cruiser Minotaur closely followed by the larger and more terrific Indomitable. As if with a unanimous instinct, a vibration seemed to pass through the throngs of people gathered on every view point. A sensation of realization filled all. The Prince had come!

From the mast head of the mighty mystery ship

flapped the Royal Standard of England. In front of her lay war vessels of three peoples all watching with respect the coming of a future King. All around were men and women loyal to the crown. The spectacle was one of peace and goodwill coupled with a demonstration of Britain's power and the venerable front of old Quebec.

As the two ships steered rapidly to their berths, the nine grey war instruments devoid of any colour, were suddenly, from masthead to bulwarks, from stem to stern covered with a maze of brilliant lines. The old colours of Britain were everywhere; coupled on U.S.S. New Hampshire with the stars and stripes, and on the French battleships with the tri-colour. The gay colours were uniform on every ship and in strange contrast with the sombre hues of the grey members of powerful fleets. Every deck was lined with the sailors and marines on board.

The brilliant spectacle was emphasized by the booming of the cannon from the citadel and the ships in port. The bow guns of the flagship Exmouth belched forth the first roaring booms of welcome. A similar welcome came from the mouths of the New Hampshire's guns, then from every ship in the harbour.

Amid the shower of this thunder came the Indomitable, her decks manned and her yards dressed. Slowly she swung into her berth between the Albemarle and the Exmouth. The hoarse roar of the anchor chain through her hawsehole was yet distinct when from the French flagship were heard the strains of the British national anthem.

The vessels were now anchored. Around them came launches and boats of every description bearing messengers of two republics and their admirals together with the representatives of Britain and Canada. As soon as the gangway was lowered, the Admirals and Captains of the Atlantic fleet accompanied by Rear-Admiral Kingsmill of the Canadian Marine Department went on board to pay their respects to the Prince of Wales.

Following this naval contingent, His Excellency the Governor-General and Field-Marshal the Earl Roberts attended by Col. Hanbury-Williams and Capt. Newton were conveyed from the King's wharf to the Indomitable. After an interval of five minutes a launch containing Sir Wilfrid Laurier, Mr. Joseph Pope, Under Secretary of State, Col. Sherwood, A.D.C., and Lt.-Col. Roy, A.D.C., boarded the Prince's ship. The next group to pay their respects to His Royal Highness were Vice-President Fairbanks and Rear-Admiral Cowles of the New Hampshire. Following these came the French naval commanders who were in turn succeeded by the Lieutenant-Governor of Quebec province, Sir Lomer Gouin, the Chairman and members of the Battlefields commission, Major-General Lake, and Brigadier-General Otter.

THE LANDING OF THE PRINCE OF WALES

On the King's Wharf with the Indomitable at Anchor in the Distance

The scene was a remarkable one. The gaily decorated launches bore their cargo to and from the immense war engine. The bands of the various ships

THE ROYAL LAUNCH

Approaching the King's wharf.

played national anthems. The booming of the cannons was incessant. Flags fluttered to the breeze and all were waiting for the debarkation of the Prince.

After the official visits had ceased, there was a pause, an air of expectancy and then realization. The Prince descended the gangway and entered a little green launch, the swiftest in the navy. At its peak flew the Royal Standard denoting the presence of His Royal Highness. The course of the little launch to the wharf was marked by the incessant and deafening salutes fired by all the ships in the harbour and from the citadel, the reports resounding for miles around.

Several minutes later, the Prince stepped on Canadian soil. The Royal Standard floated over the King's wharf; the band of the forty-third Regiment of Rifles, forming the guard of honour, played the national anthem; the guard presented arms and, led by Sir Wilfrid Laurier, the gathering on the wharf cheered enthusiastically. The Prince, conducted by His Excellency Earl Grey, was led to the marquee nearby. With soldierly instinct he turned however from the brilliant assemblage there to the guard of honour which he inspected along with His Excellency Earl Grey and followed by the staffs.

This over, the party returned to the marquee, the Prince stationing himself before the seat of honour. Sir Wilfrid Laurier, Premier of Canada, surrounded by the members of his Cabinet stepped forward and read to His Royal Highness the address of welcome on behalf of the Canadian people. The address read both in French and in English follows—

Sir Wilfrid Laurier's Address

To the Most High, Most Puissant, and Most Illustrious PRINCE, GEORGE FREDERICK ERNEST ALBERT, Prince of Wales, Duke of Saxony, Prince of Cobourg and Gotha, Duke of Cornwall and of Rothesay, Earl of Chester, Carrick and Dublin, Baron of Renfrew and Lord of the Isles, Great Steward of Scotland, Knight of the Most Noble Order of the Garter, etc., etc., etc.

May it Please Your Royal Highness :—The members of the Government of Canada desire, in their own name, and in that of the Parliament and people of the Dominion, to offer to Your Royal Highness a respectful and cordial greeting.

We are deeply sensible of the honour which Your Royal Highness has done us in making this special visit for the purpose of gracing by your presence the glad occasion which we are assembled to celebrate. We rejoice to welcome, in the person of Your Royal Highness, the representative of our beloved Sovereign, whose never failing interest in all that pertains to the welfare of this country, has had no small share in stimulating those feelings of devoted attachment towards His Majesty's person and government, which animate His Majesty's Canadian subjects from one end of the Dominion to the other.

Three hundred years ago, almost on this very spot, the heroic Samuel de Champlain laid the foundations of this ancient city, and with admirable constancy and courage, laboured for many years, in the face of privations and hardships innumerable, in the noble work of implanting in the heart of a savage wilderness the

H. R. H. THE PRINCE OF WALES

Ascending the gangway leading to the King's Wharf.

blessings of Christianity and civilization. His equally undaunted successors carried on his work after him, until at length their prophetic vision was realized, and the grain of mustard seed has grown into a great tree whose branches overshadow the land.

Your Royal Highness, who we are glad to know, is no stranger to Quebec, will not fail to recall the rich memories of its storied past. How during a century and a half New France gradually rose into being —how Canada became the theatre of the old world conflicts—and how the fortunes of war, long trembling in the balance, at length decreed that it should pass under British rule.

We cannot doubt that Your Royal Highness will

gracious and winning personality has endeared her to all Canadians.

We trust that Your Royal Highness may enjoy your all too brief stay amongst us, and that on your return home, you will convey to the King the assurance of our unswerving loyalty and devotion and of our united resolve to do our part to promote the interests of the Great Empire to which we are all proud to belong.

Quebec, 22nd July, 1908.

THE PRINCE, AFTER RECEIVING ADDRESS, ON THE KING'S WHARF
Walking Towards the State Carriages, to Drive to the Citadel.

agree with us in believing it fitting that the scene of these exploits, and especially the ground upon which Montcalm and Wolfe strove with equal valour for the mastery, should be set apart as a perpetual memorial by English and French Canadians, of the great deeds in which both peoples feel an equal pride.

It is to preside over this great solemnity that we have asked your Royal Highness to be with us at this time. We much regret that circumstances did not permit us to have the great pleasure of welcoming Her Royal Highness the Princess of Wales whose

The Prince, who during the reading stood motionless, his left hand upon his sword, now replied in both languages. He said :—

✳ ✳ ✳

His Royal Highness' Reply

I am greatly touched by the loyal and sympathetic words of your address with which you, in the name of the people of Canada, welcome me on this occasion of my sixth visit to the Dominion.

I am fully sensible of the honor and responsibility of my position as the representative of your sovereign, who, ever mindful of the unswerving loyalty of his Canadian subjects follows with affectionate interest everything which concerns the welfare and development of the Dominion. My privilege is therefore twofold, for I join with you both as the representative of the King, and on my own behalf, in celebrating the 300th anniversary of the founding of your famous city by Samuel de Champlain. I look forward with keen interest to the impressive ceremonies of the next few days, during which the past and present will appear before us upon a stage of unsurpassed natural beauty. And here, in Quebec, I recall with much pleasure the no uncertain proofs which I have received on my several visits to Canada, of the loyalty of the King's French Canadian subjects. Their proved fidelity in times of difficulty and danger, happily long past, is one of the greatest tributes to the political genius of England's rule, and the knowledge that they and their fellow Canadians of British origin are working hand in hand in the upbuilding of the Dominion is a source of deep satisfaction to the King, as well as to all those who take pride in British institutions.

I cordially agree with you in the propriety of setting apart, as a memorial for present and future generations, the battle ground of the Plains of Abraham, hallowed by the association of past years, and I heartily congratulate all concerned in this noble undertaking, upon the success which has attended their patriotic efforts.

I much regret that my present visit cannot be extended beyond Quebec, and also that the Princess of Wales was unable to accompany me on this occasion. We both retain the happiest recollections of our stay in Canada seven years ago, and of the kind and affectionate welcome we experienced during that most interesting and enjoyable visit.

I shall not fail to convey to my dear father the King, who takes the deepest interest in this celebration, the gratifying expressions of your loyalty and attachment to his throne and person, of which His Majesty is well assured.

Once more I thank you from my heart for your kindly greetings.

Three cheers followed for His Royal Highness, who with the Royal Party moved up the wharf and through the archway to the waiting carriages. The word to start was given. There was a clatter of hoofs and the Royal procession began. There were in the first carriage—State Postillion Landau and four horses, H.R.H. The Prince of Wales; H.E. The Governor-General, Lord Annaly. Two A.D.C.'s mounted. Second carriage—Landau and pair; Her Excellency the Countess Grey; Field Marshal, Earl Roberts; Lt.-Col. Sir Arthur Bigge, Col. Hanbury-Williams. 3.—Lady Sybil Grey, Lady Aileen Roberts, Sir F. Hopwood, Earl of Dudley. 4.—Lady Susan Dawnay, Duke of Norfolk, Lord Lovat. 5.—Lady Mary

SIR WILFRID LAURIER ON THE KING'S WHARF
Reading the Address of the Government to
H. R. H. the Prince of Wales.

THE WARSHIPS IN PORT SALUTING THE PRINCE OF WALES

Arrivals at the Naval Review

Parker, Lady Violet Elliot, Lt.-Gen. Sir E. Pole Carew, Capt. Godfrey Faussett. 6.—Mrs. Hanbury Williams, Miss Hanbury Williams, Lord Bruce, Lord Howick. 7.—Captain Newton, Mr. Leveson Gower, Mr. Sladen.

The streets were filled with people who were with difficulty kept within their limits by the militia who lined the route of the procession. At an interval of one yard from each other the soldiers stood forming a guard through the complete way from the wharf to the citadel. The advance guard and Chief of Police Trudel, mounted, preceded the royal carriage and its outriders. Mounted police and Royal Canadian Dragoons formed the rear. The drive was a rapid one and was accompanied with the hearty cheering of the multitude whose sole desire seemed to be concentrated in obtaining a view of the Prince.

His Royal Highness passed on the way to his headquarters in the Citadel, Champlain's Abitation. He saw and noted carefully the fac-simile of the founder's first palisade and residence, surrounded by a rough picket fence. No less attentive was his observation of the monument recently erected to Mgr. Laval, soon passed, bringing before the Prince's gaze the monument of Champlain. St. Louis Street was hastily crossed and within a few minutes the Citadel gate was reached.

The crowds were satisfied, They had observed, though hurriedly, the future King of England. With a rush they now began to disperse, which was far from easy, on account of the narrow streets and throngs of people.

The Prince had come and the celebrations assumed a new appearance.

✹ ✹ ✹

Vice-President Fairbanks Arrives

Vice-President Fairbanks arrived in the morning, the official representative of the United States at Quebec's Tercentenary celebrations.

It had rained heavily through he night and the signs of the weather were by no means auspicious, as the sun's rays stole quietly over the shades of the gloomy night. The bright appearance was but temporary for soon the clouds of the Cerberus sky again wept their burthens to the ground marring the effect of the brilliant welcome which had been arranged for Mr. Fairbanks.

It was a few minutes before eight o'clock when the special train conveying the Vice-President, Mrs. Fairbanks, General Arthur Murray, Chief of the United States Coast Artillery Service and Major T. E. B. Mott, of the Field Artillery, arrived at the Levis station. Here the United States representative was met by Rear-Admiral Cowles and Captain Winslow, of U.S.S. New Hampshire, by Lt.-Col. Hanbury-Williams who represented His Excellency the Governor-General and by other distinguished officers and dignitaries.

The trip across to Quebec, a distance of over a mile was made in the launch of the New Hampshire

greeted by Earl Roberts. Mr. and Mrs. Fairbanks then left for Spencerwood where they were the guests of Lieutenant-Governor Sir Louis Jette during their stay in Quebec.

✤ ✤ ✤

Royal Society Meets

At the request of Sir J. G. Garneau, Mayor of Quebec city, the Royal Society of Canada held two special meetings in honour of Champlain. Both were held on Wednesday in Laval University.

Four new members were received by the learned body at the morning session. They were Sir Francois Langelier, Prof. P. B. Mignault of Laval University, Montreal, Prof. Wrong, the eminent historian of Toronto University, and Mr. Adjutor Rivard, whose

A MAN-OF-WAR LAUNCH,

With "Le Don de Dieu" in the distance.

which was highly decorated. As it glided through the mist, the guns of the British, French, and United States war-vessels gave the usual demoniacal salutes which seemed to shake the very fog overhanging the river. From amid the noise, the tune of "The Star Spangled Banner" was heard proceeding from the bands of all the ships. Arrived on the King's Wharf, a new welcome was extended to the distinguished-looking statesman by Capt. Pickering, aide-de-camp to Earl Grey, Col. Wadmore and other official persons.

Escorted by two companies of the Royal Canadian regiment, all drove to the Citadel. Despite the early hour and inclement weather many were on the streets to salute the tall smiling man who soon made himself popular in the ancient city.

At the Citadel, the distinguished visitor met with a cordial reception from Earl Grey and was warmly

excellent work for the preservation of the French tongue in Canada through the Societe du Parler-Francais helped to bring him this distinction.

His Excellency the Governor-General and many of the official guests were present at the meeting. Professor J. E. Roy, who presided, welcomed these in felicitous terms and was replied to by Earl Grey in a few well-chosen words.

The session was rendered memorable by the reading of two poems written on the occasion to commemorate Quebec's three hundredth birthday party. Their authors are Rev. F. G. Scott, and Mr. L. P. Lemay. Both poems breathed the spirit of loyalty, patriotic optimism and large hopes for the future of the Dominion.

The evening session was devoted to the eulogy of Champlain.

The audience contained men renowned in every science and art. Among them were:—Sir Sandford Fleming, Rev. N. Burwash, Judge Routhier, Hon. Thomas Chapais, Sir Francois Langelier, Prof. Baker, of Toronto University; Prof. Adams, of McGill University; L'Abbe Camille Roy, Mgr. Laflamme, Senator Poirier, Mr. P. B. Mignault, Adj. Rivard, Dr. Ami, Dr. Wilfred Campbell, Dr. A. DeCelles, Col. Geo. Denison, Mr. J. H. Coyne, Frere Charland, of Fall River, Mass; Mr. W. D. Lighthall, Prof. Wrong, Dr. Dionne, Mr. Adolphe Poisson, and many others, including the secretary, Dr. James Fletcher.

Among the important features of the meeting was the presentation of special diplomas given by the Royal Society to Messrs. Eugene Rouillard, Ernest Myrand, Abbe Amedee Gosselin, P. B. Casgrain, Phileas Gagnon, H. J. J. B. Chouinard, Pierre Georges Roy, Abbe Arthur Scott, J. B. Lacasse,

Abbe Lortie, L. P. Carrier, and Mr. Zidler, all of whom have contributed to the literature and history of Canada. It may be noted that the special diploma awarded to Mr. H. J. J. B. Chouinard was so given as a mark of thanks to the originator of the Tercentenary. It was Mr. Chouinard who first planted the germ of the idea to make Quebec's Tercentenary the great celebration that it proved to be. This was advocated by him in an article which appeared in the special Christmas Number published by the Daily Telegraph of Quebec, in 1904.

A delegation from the Ontario Historical Society was present at the meeting. Its president, who acted as spokesman, eulogized the founder of Quebec and the Tercentenary celebrations. Its purpose in coming was to join with the Quebec brethren in the joys of the Tercentenary. That both races should join hands at this epoch was natural and that the

EARL GREY AND THE DUKE OF NORFOLK
Driving through the Streets of Quebec.

THE ILLUMINATION OF THE WARSHIPS IN THE HARBOUR

French Canadians themselves, the descendants of the hardy Normans should extend a fitting welcome to the Prince of Wales in whose veins flowed also Norman blood, was to be expected.

Two addresses analyzing the work of the man whom all were then honouring were delivered. Both were masterful and well worth reading before the most learned body of Canada.

The first paper was read by Judge Routhier who is well-known as a French-Canadian litterateur and orator. His discourse was a masterpiece of rhetoric. It was effulgent with beautiful comparisons and charming in its well-shaped appeals for the unity of the two races in Canada and the firmer strengthening of the entente cordiale. Choice phrases redounded throughout, but they were not mere empty phrases. Behind their flowery language lay wisdom and strength couched in words that left no doubt as to their real meaning.

The Tercentenary was not to honour Champlain alone, said the speaker. It stood not for the glorification of one man or one city. There was a grander motive. Three hundred years of growth and progress, the result of the seed of 1608 was the true reason for joy and celebration. It was not the act of a score of Frenchmen setting up a fortification in Quebec that furnished food for a Tercentenary celebration. It was the foundation of Quebec which meant the beginning of that movement of exploration and colonization which spread east and west and resulted in the formation and cementing of the Dominion of Canada.

The city of Quebec was eulogized and a good appreciation of it given. It was destined to be the home of French Canada in the future as it was in the past. "What Rome was to the Roman, Mecca to the Mussulman, and Jerusalem to the Jew, Quebec must be to the Canadian." Three nations were taking part in the celebrations, but not alone for the purpose of welding friendship as imagined by most people. It was the rejoicing of the parents in the welfare of the common offspring.

The value of the pageants was referred to by Hon. Judge Routhier. Their worth was in their historical value and in the teaching of past events which moulded a people. They not only charm the eye but leave a lasting impression. The pageants represented facts and not fables. They were not based on mythology as was the story of some other peoples but on historical happenings. Dollard, Montcalm and the rest of the Canadian heroes were facts and not in a category with King Arthur and Romulus. A plea for fraternization between the French and English elements of Canada ended a great oration.

Different was the paper read by Rev. Dr. Burwash, Chancellor of Victoria College, Toronto. Champlain and his work alone were dealt with. The subject was treated in a scientific way. The address was not a blind flow of eulogy of Quebec's founder. His character and actions were analyzed in detail, his purposes truly depicted, and his convictions laid bare.

A century which bears a new world must be strong. Its men must be giants. Those who colonize and explore are not the weak ones but represent the strength of the land. These men must possess courage, determination and faith, and such a man we find in Champlain. He chose the St. Lawrence for his work, a demonstration of the judgment and foresight of the nation-builder. He saw here the great resources that the land could offer. His sagacity was surpassed by his ideals for it was by his moral conduct towards the Indians that he won them over. Other white men cheated them. He dealt with them kindly and honestly.

Champlain wanted not only a waterway. He wanted fields. He was a poet and wanted beauty. He was practical and wanted material advantages. What better choice could he make than Quebec?

The Royal Society adjourned. Its work at Quebec was at an end.

* * *

Bands Play in Public Places

The symphonic ode "Christophe Colomb" which was performed at the Drill Hall the previous evening was repeated. The rain which began in the morning fortunately kept off during the remainder of the day and only resumed its downward course in the evening. Open air concerts had been arranged for all the public places in the city, but only a few bands and small audiences dared the weather.

The Terrace and river below were again the scene of splendour. The promenade was decked with pleasure-seekers whose emergence from sheltered houses into the rain was amply repaid. To their view was presented a spectacle on the river below, not often witnessed. Nine warships were brilliantly illuminated. Thousands of electric lights lined the decks and funnels of the ships, whose usual gloomy and forbidding forms were outlined above the river covered with mist. The sombre surroundings heightened the scene. The effect of the bright lights seemed to be augmented rather than diminished. The whole affair was a kind of phantasy heightened by the dismal rain and the occasional boom of a gun's salute.

The band on the Terrace ended the concert. "O! Canada" and "God Save the King" were played, and the admirers of the scene walked homeward.

The fourth day of the celebrations was at an end.

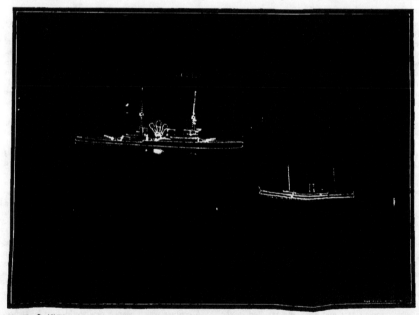

H. M. S. INDOMITABLE AND THE CRUISER CANADA ILLUMINATED

Fifth Day, Thursday, July Twenty=Third

The Don de Dieu Arrives

THURSDAY was set apart as the day especially dedicated for the honouring of Champlain. It was Champlain day.

Once again the hardy explorer sailed up the St. Lawrence River, held a palaver with the Indians, and anchored before the rocks of Quebec.

Quebec's founder, carried out in a real and effective way.

The crowds of the preceding day which had gathered to see the arrival of the Prince and the mighty Indomitable were again in their stations as eagerly and with more fascination waiting for the arrival, not of a wonderful battleship this time nor that of a royal personage. No! A different spirit now breathed through the spectators. They would again see

THE ARRIVAL OF THE DON DE DIEU

The events of three centuries ago were repeated with all the realism possible. In a modern way, honour was also given to Champlain by distinguished men at the foot of his monument.

The day was a fine one. It was the great day of the Celebrations and nature lent its aid in making it such. The Tercentenary had involved other ideas which were marked in the celebrations. On Champlain Day there was but one—the honouring of

Champlain arrive at Quebec in the little ship, the Don de Dieu. Again would they see him parley with the astonished Indians and again settle in the Abitation. They would look back three hundred years and revert in mind and in vision to 1608. And they did.

A ship! a ship!

From around the curve at St. Joseph de Levis was seen to emerge a small play-like vessel. She was rigged with sails and presented a strange appearance.

The word immediately went around. The Don de Dieu had come!

And just as three hundred years before, so to-day, the vessel that bore Quebec's founder visitd the scene which was destined to become transformed from a bare rock to the neuclus of an important colony. A fac-simile of Champlain's vessel had been built, and so well had the idea been executed that the arrival of Champlain at Quebec in 1608 was perhaps the most realistic incident of the Tercentenary fetes.

Designed by Mr. Lawford Dale, and built by Mr. Gagnon, the fac-simile was an excellent imitation. With but little to guide the designer, for there is no model or picture of any kind of the little vessel in existence, the task was a difficult one but was well ac-

CHAMPLAIN IS SEEN ON THE RIGHT-HAND SIDE,
Walking with one of his officers.

complished, and the ship was built in the remarkably short period of about ten weeks. The design of Mr. Dale which was the selection of the executive committee of the Tercentenary from among many others that were submitted, was based to a large extent upon the French merchant vessel of Henry IV's day.

The fac-simile has a flat bottom built of seven inch elm. The ribs are of new spruce six inches square, lengthened to provide for the additional height of the Don de Dieu. The deck is of two inch timber as is also the side planking. The stem and stern posts are solid pieces of twelve inch timber curved to shape. The raised forecastle, though of lighter construction than the lower parts of the ship, is one and three-quarter inch spruce backed by five inch ribs. The raised poop is constructed in the same manner, every tim-

ber of both the poop and forecastle being curved and Lent as is all the timber in the ship by steaming.

The deck beams from side to side of the ship are ten inches by three except near the masts where there are solid beams of timber nearly nine inches square. The poop contains two cabins abaft of which is the captain's cabin. On either side of these run passages giving access to two guns, one on each side of the stern. The rudder is of the old pattern and of solid oak, being three inches thick and of three timbers strongly fastened together. The steering is done by an ordinary tiller and rope tackle, there being no "wheel." The masts and bowsprit are each of a single stick, the main mast being seventy-three feet long, the foremast sixty-five feet, and the mizzen mast forty feet, step to truck. These masts are fitted with shrouds furnished with rat-lines, stays, "tops" to fore and main masts and all the gear needed for the working of the sails of the ship. The necessary belaying pins are in their proper places. In fact, the vessel is fitted in all respect as if to pass the usual Board of Trade examination for seaworthiness.

The vessel is provided under the forecastle head with a powerful windlass for heaving up the anchors, of which she has two, port and starboard, and with the necessary chain cables. The bulwarks are fitted and constructed in all respects in the usual way of wooden ships and are provided with hawse-holes for anchors and mooring ropes.

The fac-simile of the now famous Don de Dieu sailed from Levis to Quebec on her own sails and without any aid. The only thing that was carried under deck was stone ballast as in Champlain's day and old steel rails, the best sort of ballast but hardly that of 1608.

As this rather remarkable conveyance sailed into the harbour, much interest was displayed by those eager to view the curious spectacle. On the ship were seen strange men—with clothing of old patterns, pretty and of various colours. It was Champlain and his crew.

The Don de Dieu of 1608 minds not the rows of houses on shore, the lofty public buildings, the guns pointing toward it, the thousands of persons gazing at it, the immense war vessels in the harbour, the busy launches around. It sees but the bare rock on which is to be built Quebec. Its famous occupant sees not 1908. He again gazes on a natural stony fortress. He has visions of a New France, the extension of the glory of King Henry IV and the spread of Christianity. He sees not the half hundred thousand faces that peep at him from every nook and crevice.

A VIEW ON THE TERRACE
Around Champlain Monument on
Champlain Day.

He beholds but a half dozen canoes filled with tanned savages painted in colours and with heads bedecked with feathers. The Don de Dieu is again in 1608 and with the fleur-de-lys flying from her two masts, the white oriflamme of France hanging in the rear, her sailors gazing intently on the huge rock and on its dusky inhabitants, pursues its course until she arrives opposite the Citadel and anchors.

The Indians are surprised. What means this strange fleeting sail? Why are her sailors white, and whence come they? Half fearing, half threatening they paddle up. Champlain hails his hosts. A parley takes place. Terms are made and agreed to. Champlain debarks and sets his foot on soil, destined three hundred years later to be a multitudinous city and the centre of a new country.

What more natural than that Champlain revisiting the scene of his actions should again visit his old

home, the first white man's house in Quebec. The executive committee, on the alert for Champlain's comfort, had rebuilt his old home to which he now resorted for several minutes.

The fac-simile of the old house, L'abitation, was perfect in its design and modelled after the drawing left by Champlain himself of his first home here. The rude fort was erected on a spot near the wharves, perhaps on the site where stood the Abitation, and certainly not far away from it.

All the building's peculiarities were observed. The moat in front of the fort was again in its place. The old cannons again assumed the foreboding look of 1608—mere playthings of to-day. The old rough palisade was again surrounded with a gate of pointed and high pines—all a memory of 1608 and a most real one. Here Champlain, revived, sojourned for some time until he was to take his place in the historical procession which had been arranged.

* * *

At the Champlain Monument

During all this time while the founder of Quebec again appeared on the spot of the old palisade, another ceremony was being enacted in the upper part of the town, which though of different character had a similar purpose. In the lower town there was a living appearance of the hero, a revivification as it were of Champlain and his day. In the upper town there was no attempt at retrospection. Men of today gathered by the monument of Champlain and paid him homage. This gathering was especially remarkable, thousands upon thousands of people having assembled to somehow witness and join in the act of honoring Champlain.

The 48th Highlanders, of Toronto, furnished the

THE INDIANS IN THEIR CANOES

Escorting Champlain to the Shore from the Don de Dieu.

guard of honor and surrounded the monument. The sixty-fifth French-Canadian battalion from Montreal held the place of honour nearest the monument. The Royal Military College Cadets, the Ninety-first, and the Queen's Own Rifles provided the units who lined the route from the Citadel along St. Louis street to the Terrace. The Prince was accompanied by a field officers' escort. Once arrived at the monument, the Prince was led up to the especially erected pavilion at the foot of the monument. There a great spectacle awaited him, for on either side was a grand stand in

which sat many of the distinguished visitors of the Tercentenary. Their arrival, especially that of Sir Wilfrid Laurier had caused much cheering and handclapping. Flags were hauled up on the grand stands as the Prince arrived and the Highland pipers played the national anthem. On the platform were H.R.H. the Prince, while on his right sat Earl Grey and Vice-President Fairbanks; on his left, Lady Grey and Admiral Jaureguiberry. Behind the Prince sat Lord Roberts and other military dignitaries.

A scarcely less distinguished spectacle was that presented by the guests who began arriving at three o'clock. Conspicuous among these was Mr. Fairbanks, a most impressive and yet most unassuming man. Among the other guests were the Duke of Norfolk, Field Marshal Earl Roberts, Lord Dudley, Lord Lovat, Lord Bruce, Major-General Pole Carew and Lady Carew, Sir L. A. Jette, Sir Wilfrid Laurier and Lady Laurier, Major Mott, acting A.D.C., to Vice-President Fairbanks, Sir Arthur Bigge, Sir Chas. Fitzpatrick, Sir L. Gouin, Sir J. Whitney, Lady Whitney and Miss Whitney, Sir George Garneau, Mayor of Quebec, and Lady Garneau, Sir Francois Langelier and Lady Langelier, Marquis de Levis, Marquis de Levis Mirepoix, Count de Montcalm, the Lord Bishop of Quebec and Mrs. Dunn, Mgr. Roy, Mgr. Mathieu, C.M.G., Judge and Mrs. Blanchet, Sir C. A. P. Pelletier, Judge and Mrs. H. C. Pelletier, Judge and Mrs. Carroll, Mr. and Mrs. R. L. Borden, Judge, Mrs. and Miss Cannon, Mayor Oliver, Toronto, Mayor Scott, of Ottawa, Mr. Godfrey Fawcett, Admirals and officers of the fleet now in port, members of the Senate, House of Commons, Legislative Council, and members of Legislatures of several provinces.

The Prince arrived at four o'clock amid the great shouting and cheers of the assembled thousands. He was received by His Worship Sir George Garneau who introduced the aldermen to the Prince. The civic fathers would remove their hats and stand bareheaded in the sun, but the Prince would not allow this, and prayed them to don their headgear.

The ceremony commenced without delay. Earl Grey presented the Mayor Sir J. G. Garneau who proceeded to read the civic address of welcome to the Prince. It read thus :—

THE CROWD IN FRONT OF THE CHATEAU FRONTENAC
On Champlain Day.

Mayor Garneau's Welcome.

May it please your Royal Highness :—

To-day the Canadian nation celebrates with joyous enthusiasm an eventful date in its history, the three hundredth anniversary both of its birth and the founding of this city of Quebec, by Samuel de Champlain. Our pleasure and rejoicings will be increased by the fact that, through a happy combination of circumstances, we are honoured by the presence of Your Royal Highness, specially sent by His Gracious Majesty, our much beloved Sovereign, to inaugurate in his name, the series of festivities which will commemorate these gracious events.

Yesterday, Canada and the Province of Quebec welcomed Your Royal Highness. To-day the citizens of Quebec claim the honour of offering to you, in this Ancient Capital, their warmest and most cordial greetings.

Assembled round the monument of the glorious founder of Canada, our hearts filled with the heroic memories of three centuries, the story of which seems more like an epic than a history, the French-Canadians cannot suppress an inexpressible feeling of patriotic pride and of gratitude towards the two great nations which have, in turn, presided over their destinies; to their ever beloved France, to whom they are indebted for their being and their grand traditions, and to England which has left them free to expand the full enjoyment of their faith, their language, and their institutions, and has given them a political constitution which is based upon the greatest possible extent of liberty, and is undeniably the finest and most perfect in the world.

This sentiment, moreover, must be still further heightened in all Canadians, of every origin, in the presence both of its magnificent display in honor of the immortal Champlain, and of this tribute to the young and vigorous nation, which, born as it were

THE CASKET

Presented to H. R. H.
the Prince of Wales
containing the Civic
Address of the City
of Quebec.

yesterday, has expanded with gigantic strides over an area vast enough to contain another Europe.

On this solemn occasion, which must ever remain an eminently prominent factor in our national life, we are deeply sensible of the pleasurable security which we enjoy during the prevailing peace of nations, and also of the marvelous developments we everywhere behold. Thus inspired, our thankful voices rise in a harmonious hymn of gratitude to the Almighty who has showered his gifts upon us; to the two great nations who are our mothers, and to whom we owe our national existence; to that very great and very powerful Sovereign, the arbiter and apostle of the nations' peace, who so wisely presides over the destinies of the British Empire; to Your Royal Highness, his worthy representative, who have crossed the seas to participate in our rejoicings, and to all these, our guests, come together from every quarter of the globe, to honour with us the immortal founder of Quebec and his life work, which we can to-day appreciate in all its splendor and magnificent results.

Deeply moved and touched by the readiness with which Your Royal Highness yielded to the desire of the Canadian people, and stirred to the very bottom of our hearts by the imposing nature of this great demonstration, we must ever cherish the memories of this glorious day, rendered so brilliant by your presence.

In return we ask you to convey to His Majesty the King our protestations of loyalty to his person and his Crown, and to Her Majesty, our Very Gracious Queen, our admiration for the eminent qualities with which she so conspicuously adorns the throne of Britain.

During the modest festivities of the time of Cham-

MEDALLION PORTRAIT

On the Casket.

plain, the few people of the colony, assembled round their leader, were accustomed to crown their rejoicings by the loyal cries : "Vive le Roi! Vive Monseigneur le Dauphin!"

To-day, three centuries later, the citizens of Quebec, and the whole Canadian people, faithful to their new allegiance, as were our forefathers to the old regime, welcome Your Royal Highness with the heartfelt acclaim : "God Save the King! God Bless the Prince of Wales!"

The discourse ended, the speaker placed the address in a casket of gold and presented it to His Royal Highness as a gift from the city of Quebec. The casket is of the finest frosted gold and in the form of a cigar case. It is seven inches high, eleven long, and seven and a half in width weighing altogether one hundred and fifty ounces. The address was placed in a casket made of genuine Canadian cedar which is again covered by the gold casket.

On the front of the casket are the arms of Quebec, in a medallion in coloured enamels; the cliffs, fort and ship in the background. In the central foreground of the medallion is a female figure at whose feet is seated a Canadian beaver. In her right arm she supports a cornucopia while beneath is a beehive. At the figure's side rests a shield bearing on it the semblance of a lion holding a key;—the old arms of Quebec City . A wreath of laurel around which is entwined a ribbon with the motto in blue enamel "Natura Fortis Industria Crescit" frames the medallion. Beneath the frame is a scroll bearing the words "Troisieme Centenaire de Quebec."

To the left of the medallion are the "Ich Dien"

A SIDE VIEW OF THE CASKET

Presented to the Prince of Wales, showing
the Old Coat-of-Arms.

and grey ostrich feathers of the Prince of Wales in enamel. To the right is the Prince's coat-of-arms. On the right hand side of the casket is an enamel of Champlain's drawing of the Abitation with a frame of mussel shells in gold, with gold laurel leaves and

ing "Champlain, 1608," this being surrounded by a gold laurel wreath and maple leaves.

The Prince was given an ovation as he stood up to reply. He first spoke in French with the distinct accent of the educated Englishman. He said:—

THE DON DE DIEU

ribbon. On the left in enamel is seen the Don de Dieu. On the back, in gold lettering in blue enamel inscribed in a frame of pierced old scroll work is the dedication "Adresse des citoyens de Quebec a son Altesse Royal le Prince de Galles, presentee le 23 juillet, 1908, a l'ouverture officielle des Fetes du IIIe Centenaire de la Fondation de Quebec par Samuel de Champlain."

The casket rests on feet of eagle's claws clasping a ball at each corner. Each corner is decorated from top to bottom with acanthus leaves. The top of the casket bears a medallion portrait of Champlain executed in enamel painting upon enamel over silver, surrounded by a plain frame of gold with the letter-

His Royal Highness's Reply

Mr. Mayor:—

I am touched to the heart by the warm welcome which you have offered me in your ancient city of Quebec, as well as by the loyalty of the sentiments which you have so eloquently expressed.

It gives me the most profound satisfaction to be able to join with you in celebrating the 300th anniversary of the foundation of Quebec by the immortal explorer whose statue has so justly its site on this spot, commanding a panorama which the most ardent imagination could scarcely conceive.

The history of New France is singularly attractive, as much by the moving events recorded on its pages as by the heroic personages who have made that history, amongst whom the commanding figure of the chivalrous Samuel de Champlain stands out with great brilliance. It is owing to his pen that the recital of his adventures has reached us to this day, and this story, with the modesty and sincerity which distinguish it, stamps each page with the sign manual of truth.

From the bottom of my heart I congratulate you on possessing such a hero. May his statue for ever ornament your historic capital to recall—should that

THE PLATFORM

Erected at the foot of Champlain's Monument where H. R. H. spoke on Champlain Day.

be necessary—to the citizens of Quebec, the high qualities of piety and courage, of humanity and strength of spirit which distinguished this faithful servant of his God and his King.

While to-day we are celebrating the birthday of Quebec, we must not lose sight of the fact that this celebration also interests the whole Canadian people, who are joining with you in your rejoicings. And more. It is not merely this vast Dominion which to-day is honoring the memory of the great Champlain. The Mother Country also claims the honor of associating herself in this homage, and from the most distant parts of the Empire come the assurances that

our fellow-citizens desire to celebrate the occasion, and have sent representatives whom I am glad to see here to-day amongst us.

In the same manner other lands are justly proud of the renown of Champlain, chief of whom is the great nation to whom he owed allegiance, which he loved with passionate devotion, and which has delegated as its representative here to-day one of its most distinguished citizens.

The last words which you have addressed to me have most profoundly touched me, and I most cordially thank you. I shall be happy to convey to the King, my father, the assurance of your loyalty and devotion to his person and to the Crown. His Majesty, as you well know, takes a most lively interest in all which concerns the prosperity and happiness of his French-Canadian subjects.

He continued in English to eulogize Champlain and said :—

I have now replied to the address which it has given me so much pleasure to receive, but, standing here by his monument, I desire to add a few words in appreciation of the memory of Champlain, and of satisfaction that such a distinguished Company should have assembled in his city to do honor to the birthday of Quebec.

Our minds are full of thoughts of Champlain, the founder of those wonderful events in history which have followed from his foresight and determination. But, I myself, a sailor, fresh from a voyage across the Atlantic, also like to think of your hero as the able and intrepid navigator, braving the perils of the deep, visiting new lands, and unconsciously helping to lay the foundations of the great civilizations of this Continent. His work, national in its inception, has with time proved to be of immense international importance, and it is from this interesting aspect of our proceedings that we desire the special pleasure of welcoming the distinguished representatives of France and the United States of America.

The King, whose earnest desire is always to promote the best and closest relations between nations, has specially desired me, as his representative, to convey to you, Mr. Vice-President of the United States, and to you, Monsieur l'Amiral, and to your colleagues, not only a hearty welcome, but also a warm expression of thanks, both to you and to your presence on this occasion. Your attendance is not merely an indication of your interest in the proceedings attending the celebration of the Tercentenary, it is an outward and visible sign of the friendship, concord, and goodwill, between ourselves and the two great countries which you represent with so much distinction.

We think to-day of the United States as having given the example of energy and courage in conquering and cultivating the forests and boundless prairies, which now yield harvests of illimitable wealth. We think of France, as the giver of the man whose greatest deed we are here to celebrate—one of the first of those heroes who found his way from the old world to the new, and left here an imperishable name.

We recognize that the presence of representatives of France and of the United States amongst us, testifies to the growth of the spirit of friendship between nations. On that spirit the progress of humanity depends. In it, I hope and believe, true progress will express itself more and more during years to come. The high ideal of universal peace and brotherhood may be far from realization, but every act that

Quebec on its celebrations. He first read a cable which had been sent to His Majesty by the Canadian Government, and the reply.

Exchange of Messages

Telegram to the King :—

The people of Canada assembled to celebrate the tercentenary of the founding of Quebec, present their humble duty to your Majesty and desire to thank your Majesty for the honor done them by the presence here to-day of H.R.H. the Prince of Wales. They see in this gracious act a fresh proof of the interest which

CANADIAN SOLDIERS
Saluting the French Admiral
Jaureguiberry.

promotes harmony among nations, points the way towards its attainment. This celebration is such an act, for it appeals to Canada, to the British Empire, and to the whole civilized world. I therefore rejoice to be here, to take my part with you during these memorable days, in paying homage to Champlain and doing honor to Quebec.

✤ ✤ ✤

His Excellency Earl Grey, before introducing the other speakers of the occasion, read a number of messages from different parts of the world congratulating

your Majesty has ever manifested towards your Majesty's Canadian subjects, who on this great and historic occasion hasten to renew the expression of their unalterable devotion to your Majesty's Throne and person.

* * *

Reply from the King :—

Please convey to the Mayor and the citizens of Quebec my congratulations and good wishes on the joyous celebration of the three hundredth anniversary of the foundation of their city by Samuel de Champlain. I am much gratified to learn of their cordial reception of the Prince of Wales whom I have sent to represent me on this great occasion. I received with pleasure the renewed assurances of loyalty on the part of my Canadian subjects, in whose welfare I am deeply interested, and to whom I wish an ever increasing measure of progress and prosperity.

His Excellency then proceeded to read the other messages :—

Her Royal Highness Princess Louise, to the Governor-General :—

LONDON, 22nd July.

Sincerest congratulations on the occasion of the Tercentenary celebrations in dear old Quebec, and on the great gathering your happy inspiration has called together. The enthusiasm this interesting event has evoked is fully shared by me.

(Signed)   LOUISE.

*   *   *

The Prime Minister of The United Kingdom to the Governor-General :—

LONDON, July 22.

On the occasion of the three hundredth anniversary of the founding of Quebec, I send the warm congratulations and hearty good wishes of His Majesty's Government to our colleagues and fellow subjects the Government and the people of the great Dominion of Canada. The Dominion, as it stands to-day, is living evidence of the foresight and endurance of Samuel Champlain, and it bears witness to the world that peace and prosperity are the fruits of freedom and self-government.

(Signed)   ASQUITH.

*   *   *

The Viceroy of India to the Governor-General of Canada :—

SIMLA, 20th July.

Hearty congratulations on Champlain Tercentenary, and my very best wishes to the Canadian descendants of the two great races who have together built up their magnificent Dominion.

(Signed)   MINTO.

*   *   *

The Governor of Orange River Colony, to the Governor-General :—

BLOOMFONTAINE, 22nd July.

Responsible Ministry in the name of this colony, desire on this, the three hundredth birthday of Canada, to express to the Dominion its feelings of sympathy and good will on the momentous occasion.

Besides the great bond of union between Canada and this Colony, as a part of the British Empire, which it is hoped may never be severed, there is also a valued link of brotherhood owing to many in both countries claiming descent from French forefathers, which must always cause a feeling of close kinship.

(Signed)   GOVERNOR.

*   *   *

The Governor of the Transvaal to the Governor-General :—

PRETORIA, July 22nd.

The Government and the people of the Transvaal desire to convey their hearty sympathy and cordial good will to the Government and the people of the Dominion on the occasion of Canada's 300th birthday. The Transvaal Government hope that the celebrations will be a great success, and that they will be the means of strengthening further the bonds with which we are all united under the flag of the British Empire.

(Signed)   GOVERNOR.

*   *   *

The Governor of Newfoundland to the Governor-General :—

23rd July, 1908.

On behalf of the Government and people of Newfoundland, I beg to tender to the Government and people of the Dominion my heartiest congratulations on Canada's 300th birthday, and on the presence in your midst of H.R.H. the Prince of Wales.

The Government of Newfoundland sincerely hope that the festivities may be a great success and be the means of promoting the best interests of Canada and the crown. .

*   *   *

The Governor of New Zealand to the Governor-General of Canada :—

Across Pacific, New Zealand echoes Empire's congratulations upon object lesson Canada gives to-day of pride in her glorious past, solidarity of her people and growth of her nation. May I add personal congratulations and splendid response to your proposals.

(Signed)   PLUNKET.

*   *   *

The Secretary of State for the Colonies, to the Governor-General :—

As Secretary of State for the Colonies and still more as a warm personal friend of Canada and the Canadians, I send my cordial congratulations upon the great and impressive ceremony which will take place

HON. CHARLES WARREN FAIRBANKS,
Vice-President and representative of the United States.

to-morrow. Few countries can show three centuries of history of such abiding interest and for few countries is so bright a future so earnestly desired and confidently anticipated

CREWE.

* * *

The Governor-General of Australia to the Governor-General of Canada :—

MELBOURNE, 21st July.

Australia, greeting Canada, the sister and senior of all Dominions of the Empire, welcomes the celebration of your third century of adventurous advance. In early days the triple tides of gallant pioneers from the old world, British, French and Loyalists entered into a rich heritage of rivers, lakes and forests in your eastern regions by the red routes of war. To-day, speeding westward by rail across vast prairies, towering mountains and sunny slopes, you are peopling a new world, bordering on earth's greatest ocean whose waters are on both our shores.

Australia prays that your numbers may multiply, your unity strengthen and your prosperity increase, along the all-red route of peace.

(Signed)   NORTHCOTE.

* * *

Cablegram from the Prime Minister of Cape Colony to the Prime Minister of Quebec :—

CAPE TOWN, July 22nd, 1908.

I offer on behalf of Cape Colony, hearty congratulations to Canada on the occasion of its three hundredth anniversary and I wish the Dominion a long and prosperous future.

PRIME MINISTER.

Cape Colony.

* * *

Cablegram to the Mayor of Brouage, France :—

QUEBEC, July 23, 1908.

Quebec at the foot of Champlain monument sends its cordial souvenir to the land of origin of its noble founder.

GARNEAU,
Mayor.

* * *

The Right Honorable Sir Wilfrid Laurier, Prime Minister of Canada, Quebec :—

WELLINGTON, July 21st, 1908.

Our hearts are with you on your Tercentenary. We share your pride in all that strenuous and noble past which thrice a hundred years ago began with Samuel de Champlain's planting where stands to-day your

noble city of Quebec. In your annals live forever the glory of great names and great achievements over which to-day two great mother nations must feel a thrill of mutual pride. We rejoice in all your splendid history, in all your steady rise to greatness. With loving and unenvious eyes we behold the majestic destiny that lies before you when all your vast Dominion is occupied by one great loyal people. To you, the greatest daughter of our parent land, New Zealand sends her joyous greetings, feeling more and more as the years roll on that we share with you one life, one flag, one fleet, one throne.

JOSEPH GEORGE WARD,
Prime Minister of New Zealand.

* * *

No cable was read from the town of Brouage, the birthplace of Quebec's founder. The town was represented by Mr. Brandelis, its mayor, who was introduced to the Prince and delivered orally the message of the little French town.

❊ ❊ ❊

Vice-President Fairbanks was the next speaker. He was loudly acclaimed by the vast throng present from among which many small flags of the United States were seen to float. The republic's representative, a dignified and yet most unassuming man created a good impression and made a strong plea for the closer alliance of the two American countries. He said :—

Vice-President Fairbank's Address

Your Royal Highness :—

I acknowledge with grateful appreciation the welcome which you so generously extend. The sentiments which you are pleased to express with regard to my country I receive with profound sensibility. They are renewed evidence of that respect and cordial good will which has so long existed between the United States and Great Britain, and will tend to strengthen and preserve their amicable relations.

Permit me to extend to Quebec my hearty congratulations upon the distinction which she enjoys in the presence of your Royal Highness and upon the enthusiasm with which she has welcomed you within her gates. It is indeed a signal honor which you have done her. It is a happy circumstance which brings you across the sea. The event is one which will be long treasured among the annals of Quebec.

The eyes of the western world are upon this historic city. The celebration of the tercentenary of Champlain's founding of Quebec is altogether admirable both in the comprehensiveness of its conception and in the excellence of its execution, and is an event which awakens interest not only in the Dominion of Canada but in the United States also. From this point as a base, intrepid explorers blazed the pathway of civilization through trackless forests and explored lakes and rivers in territory which is now within the jurisdiction of the United States. Names associated with the early history of Quebec are landmarks in our geography and are indelibly impressed upon our civilization.

Three hundred years is but a brief period in the history of Quebec and all of Anglo-Saxon America. Here has been written an interesting story. Here have been witnessed the victories and defeats of war and the blessed triumph of peace. The battleships of three great nations rest yonder upon the bosom of the

DUFFERIN TERRACE

And Champlain Monument.

St. Lawrence. The representatives of these powers assembled here are recalling past differences, but only to emphasize the present prevalence of a spirit of genuine friendship between them.

It is with unusual pleasure I bring you greetings from the President and the people of the United States, who rejoice with you in the progress you have made in manifold ways which make for the strength and honor of a great people. We are not indifferent to your welfare nor are you indifferent to ours. The blood of a common ancestry is in our veins. We have much in common. We glory in many of the same traditions and we have the same jurisprudence. Our standards of civilization are alike. Here, side by side, owing to allegiance to different sovereignties, we are, in God's providence, to work out our destiny.

We wish you that contentment which comes from the cultivation of the arts of peaceful industry under those political institutions which are the guaranty of justice and liberty among men.

The United States and Canada have but fairly entered upon their career. Each has vast areas either sparsely settled or unoccupied, where many will make their homes in the future. Many millions will be added to our population and to yours. We have each made much advance in the scale of civilization and are gratified with the progress we have made. Back of us lies a brief but honorable history and before us stretch illimitable opportunities. We confidently believe that we are each destined to play a large and worthy part in the progress of the human race upon the western continent. We have no rivalries except in the ways of peace. We neither covet the other's territory. We rest upon a common frontier more than 5,000 miles in length. It is crossed and recrossed by instrumentalities of commerce which tended to strengthen our neighborly ties. There are no fortifications upon our frontier and no battleships upon the waters which divide us, and we believe and fervently hope that there will never be need of any defensive preparation between us.

As we behold this majestic celebration in which the representatives of different nations participate and witness the manifestations of a genuine fraternal spirit among them, we are impressed with the thought that there is no rational reason why nations should resort to war. May we not, on this theatre of past conflicts, surrounded now by the impressive monuments of peace, venture to hope that the widespread movement which seeks to insure the maintenance of peace among the nations of the world without invoking the sword, may grow in strength and at no distant day become incorporated as a part of the fixed policy of nations. To advocate measures for the maintenance of international tranquillity, to endeavor to substitute reason for force, is not evidence of any decay in the courage or manhood of nations, but it is the proclamation of the great truth that modern civilization is not a failure if it does not substitute for force the serene and all-powerful chamber of reason and deliberation. There is such a thing as righteousness among nations. Let

H. R. H. REPLYING TO ADDRESS OF WELCOME
At foot of Champlain Monument.

them take their differences into international courts of justice and there let reason and righteousness prevail. Let nations by every honorable means which enlightened statesmanship may suggest, avoid an appeal to that court where might alone turns the balance.

We have no need to fear that the relations between the United States and Great Britain will ever again be disturbed. We have faith to believe that our flags which grace this historic occasion and which mingle together and salute each other upon the Plains of Abraham will never confront each other in conflict upon either land or sea.

I beg again to thank your Royal Highness for the gracious welcome and hospitality which you tender to me as the representative of the United States and to wish for your country and your people a continuance of the blessings of peace, progress and prosperity.

✤ ✤ ✤

The representative of France, Admiral Jaureguiberry followed with a brief address in which he emphasized the value of the entente cordiale. His discourse read :—

Admiral Jaureguiberry's Address

By sending a mission to this grand celebration, to the so impressive ceremonies now taking place in Quebec, the Government of the Republic has seized the opportunity to once more affirm the cordiality of its relations with Great Britain and to respond at the same time to the sentiments of affectionate esteem entertained by France towards Canada.

It has conferred upon me a great honor to greet in its name H.R.H. the Prince of Wales, the Government of Canada and that of the Province of Quebec.

The words pronounced a moment ago by H.R.H. will speak loud in France and will be added to the everlasting souvenir of the reception tendered by England to the President of the Republic.

I thank His Excellency the Governor-General for his words of welcome. They are addressed to a nation that is glad to show the Canadians its fraternal sympathy, a nation that rejoices with them in the coming to Quebec of H.R.H., whose presence is adding in so large a degree to the splendor and the bearing of the French-Canadian festivities.

In the name of France I render the most respectful homage to the glorious dead who have founded Quebec, who have contributed to its grandeur and who have developed the strong virtues which win its Canadians universal esteem.

From the other side of the Atlantic we applaud with ardent sympathy the union that has been realized, in Canada between two races so well in a position to understand each other, each contributing to the common work the qualities which are its own.

In France, as well as in Canada, Champlain's name is pronounced with legitimate pride as that of a valiant soldier, distinguished administrator and a very apt diplomat. His hardy initiative has resulted in the conquest of a new domain for civilization, in the creation of a new home for the sons of Great Britain and of France.

And we all, as we are assembled before this monument to do honor to the founder of Quebec, will greet with the same respect the illustrious men revived before us by this imposing celebration and who all have increased the glory of their mother country.

✤ ✤ ✤

The last speaker, Hon. Adelard Turgeon, speaking on behalf of Canada delivered a speech redounding with beautiful rhetorical phrases describing the grandeur of the Dominion. He said :—

Hon. A. Turgeon's Address

May it please Your Royal Highness, Ladies and Gentlemen :—

This monument, this rock, this grand river, this incomparable panorama of Beaupre, unfolding its succession of beautiful hill-sides, this island resting on the surface of the water like a basket of verdure, those heights of Levis, whose very name rings like a clarion blast, these plains, these fields and moats— the scenes and witnesses of century-old struggles for the supremacy of a world—all this sublime landscape charm, appeals to our imagination to give it a soul

and recalls a heroic age of noble dreams and valiant deeds.

What hour, what place, could be more solemn and more propitious for evoking the memory of him whom the voice of history and the gratitude of peoples have honored with the two-fold title of founder of Quebec and of the Canadian nation. And—as if the setting back of the hand of Time and majestic decorations were not sufficient for such an apotheosis—through concerted kindness for which we are indebted to the generous initiative of our well-beloved Sovereign, the three countries that have in turn, and at times concurrently, mingled in our national life, bring him the tribute of their respect and admiration. The spec-

HON. MR. TURGEON, QUEBEC'S FRENCH-CANADIAN ORATOR
Delivering his brilliant speech before the Prince. The Prince, Earl Grey and Vice-President Fairbanks sitting on the right.

tacle of three nations assembled at the foot of this monument, animated with the same spirit of peace, of harmony and civilization, on the very soil where in days of old they strove to decide their destinies by the sword on blood-stained battlefields, is surely unique in the annals of the human race.

The presence of the Heir-Apparent to the Throne imparts a special significance to the participation of the metropolis which we cannot misinterpret. The high consideration enjoyed by our country, and the important place it occupies among the aggregation of peoples that make up the British Empire, could not have been better demonstrated. Your Royal Highness will permit me here, on behalf of Canada, to tender the respectful tribute of our devotedness and loyalty to the person of our Sovereign and to the institutions whereof he is the incarnation. And among all Canadians whose voices swell the concert of acclamations that welcomes you, none are more enthusiastic or more sincere than those of the descendants of the companions and fellow laborers of Samuel de Champlain.

Our thanks are also due to the great Republic, our neighbor, which shares in the glory of the founder of Quebec, since the field of his action extented beyond our frontiers, and since, with his immediate successors, he left on the North American continent, from East to West, from South to North, from Newfoundland to the Rocky Mountains, from Hudson's Bay to the Gulf of Mexico, an imprint that political revolutions have been powerless to efface. Thus, at the head of all the great lakes, at the bends of all the rivers, and at the strategic points of the valleys, one can see at once, by their French names, that our distinguished ancestors were once there.

As to France, she could not help being here. Without her this memorial celebration would have been somewhat incomplete, as when in family gatherings an empty chair tells of mourning for one who has gone away. It was right that she should once more bend over the cradle of the colony which for a century and a half lived its life as a scion of France, watered by the purest of her blood and wherein, despite political storms, her language, her traditions, her mode of thought, all the flowers of her national originality still flourish.

The glory of France lies in the fact that, through Cartier and Champlain, she stands at the head of those captains, discoverers and missionaries who—roaming under every latitude and penetrating into the remotest solitudes of the North and West, into the forests full of mystery and dread legends—were the pioneers of civilization and Christianity, and left on their surroundings everywhere the impression of the manners, customs, tastes and ideas of their native land. Under whatever ethnical name they reveal themselves, those brilliant flashes have not been lost to the Canadian nation, and the first rays of our history still warm and vivify our national body. Why then should we not love France, when the purest French blood flows in our veins? We love her ardently, disinterestedly, for no political "arriere-pensees" mingles with our love. We love her naturally and without effort because she was the cradle of our infancy, the land of our fathers, "imagines majorum," and because a whole world of memories, of traditions, of struggles, of glories and of mourning, links us to the past.

But, how can such affection be reconciled with our loyalty and profound attachment to the British Isles?

Thanks be to God, the hour of tentative effort and experiment has passed and the problem has long since been solved. It has been solved by the sound political sense of our statesmen, by the broadmindedness of our English-speaking fellow countrymen, by the clearsightedness and liberality of the metropolis and its representatives. The fact has been realized that the preservation of the French element and language is not a source of danger, but a pledge of greatness, of progress, and also of security; that the Canadian Confederation is like the beehive whereof Marcus Aurelius said that what is good for the bee benefits the whole hive; that national dualism, according to Lord Dufferin's happy expression, is not an obstacle to the development of a young nation that has everything to gain from the preservation of the literary and social inheritance it has received from the two greatest peoples of Europe. Such a conception is a true one, for what is a nation? Does "nation" mean but one language? The modern nation is made up of divers elements. We have but to look at England, France, Switzerland and Belgium. Each of those countries has been a vast crucible wherein its constituent elements have become fused under the action of time and ambient influences. There is something above language, and that is : will, moral unity of mind, harmony of views, possession of the same ideal aspirations, devotedness to the same works of progress. Each element, each ethnical group, can develop itself solely by developing its natural gifts and its own qualities. Seek not to separate it from its past, to give it another soul as it were, because then you will have naught but uprooted trees, according to a justly celebrated expression.

Animated with that spirit, Canada pursues her way towards the highest destinies. She has barely emerged from the mists of the unknown, and already the older civilization, like the Wise Men in days of yore, is asking who is that child born in the West, whose name fills the world? Westward the star of empire holds its way. The Mediterranean was long the centre of commercial and politcal activity; then the discoveries of the 15th and 16th centuries gave the preponderance to the Atlantic. In our time the greatest human currents are changing their course, and some day the Pacific Ocean will infallibly play the most important role in the general life of the human race. Cast an eye on the map and tell me if Canada does not occupy a privileged position? The dream of Champlain and of Jacques Cartier is realized. Midway, and by the shortest route between Europe and Asia, our country is the true "road to Cathay," the true road to China, which discoverers sought and which was their fixed idea by day, their dream at night.

O Canada! land of valor and of beauty, I would that

my voice were as far-reaching as Roland's magic horn to carry the accents of my love and pride into the homes of all! Land that thrills with life, with its lakes and springs, its rivers fertilizing the plains or mirroring the trees of the great forests on their banks! Land rocked to sleep by the melody of torrents and the songs of streams, irridescent with the powdery spray of cascades, watered by the St. Lawrence, "of all famous rivers, the only one unchangeably pure" (Reclus) Land invigorated by our winters that breathe powerful energy and gayety over fields bespangled with sparkling crystals, sheltered by splendid

a permanent entente-cordiale, love of civil and political liberty, force of tradition, poetry of effort, chivalrous generosity, thirst for justice and for the ideal. We love it, in a word, because it is our country, that so well expresses all the sweetness of one's fatherland.

* * *

This ended the second great event of Champlain day when another followed immediately after. The Prince and his staff after the ceremony on the Terrace departed and entered their carriages waiting by the entrance to the Chateau Frontenac hotel. There

THE HISTORICAL PROCESSION
Marching up Mountain Hill.

mountain tops, and rich in the glowing health of its plains! Land wherein memories sleep and hopes are at rest! Land redolent with the poetry of fields, stars and souls! While still in the bloom of thy virgin energies, well might thine immortal founder utter in admiration that exclamation never yet surpassed and that we repeat to-day: "It may be said that the country of New France is a new world, and not a kingdom, beautiful in every perfection." (Champlain.)

Of that land, we love not only its natural beauty, but also its moral features, the complexity of its soul, diversity of its races mingling their mutual virtues in

was however no attempt at proceeding. The Prince sat in his carriage witnessing a grand spectacle. The historical procession was passing.

* * *

The Historical Procession

During the course of the events of the afternoon on the Terrace, preparations were made for the procession which proved to be one of the main features of the celebrations. As the Prince sat in his carriage in the Place D'Armes, the historical personages passed by in review. It was no mean sight to witness over three thousand persons all representing characters which loomed in the history of the making of a country. The ages of the past as it were defiled before the result of their efforts.

First came the mounted heralds and men-of-the-watch. What more natural than that public announcers precede the cavalcade of history? Then came Jacques Cartier and his sailors, following a wooden cross placed by him in Stadacona nigh four hundred years ago. Indians in the apparel of their ancestors whom the first white man in Canada surprised in 1534 came next.

King Francis I accompanied by his queen and followed by the members of his court next pass in review before the Prince. Under his regime the idea of a New France was first conceivable. It remained, however, for Henry of Navarre to give that commission which resulted in the making of a nation. He and his court are then seen passing on in the procession of time—and of men. Before the lined streets then comes Champlain and his crew. He walks by the Terrace, gazes at the monument nearby —and passes on.

Then comes a gap of half a century in the winding procession. The scene changes. Noble courtiers and hardy sailors have now gone by. The land is now thinly settled. White man has begun his fight with the red man, and Dollard des Ormeaux presents himself before us. He is closely followed by his sixteen noble and brave comrades. The period of fighting soon ceases. The colonists now begin to explore and found cities. Before us pass La Violette, Maisonneuve, d'Iberville, de Bienville, LaMothe, Cadillac, La Salle, Joliette, Marquette, de Duen and de la Verendaye. Following these come Marquis de Tracy and four companies of the Carignan-Sallieres regiment. Duluth and the Coureurs de bois come next. Daumont de St. Lusson and the Jesuits who took possession of the western country for the King follow.

Sturdy and hot-headed Frontenac with his Superior councillors pass by. Madeleine de Vercheres, the Canadian Joan follows, closely succeeded by descendants of the savages whom she so bravely fought.

Time again leaps extravagantly. Montcalm and Levis, the heroes of Montmorency and St. Foye again lead their brave French and Canadian soldiers. Close behind march Wolfe and Murray once their foes. Behind these follow their regiments. Another British soldier, Guy Carleton later to be Lord Dorchester and his soldiers pass in review while de Salaberry and the defenders of Chateauguay who defeated Hampton end a procession remarkable in its composition, and valuable in its lesson.

The procession has passed. The Prince now returns to the Citadel. The soldiers vacate the streets. Champlain has been honoured.

CROWDS ON THE TERRACE
Watching the Naval Salute to H. R. H. the Prince of Wales as he leaves the King's Wharf to inspect the fleet.

* * *

Street Military Parade

In the morning took place the street military parade. The event was not on the programme but was added to comply with the request of the citizens of Quebec.

The morning like the afternoon was warm and bright. The streets were crowded with at least sixty thousand people who had gathered to witness the pick of the Canadian militia. Many were clustered on the side-walks; others were perched on lofty places; windows were all put to use. Everybody was anxious to see the parade.

The soldiers who numbered twelve thousand left the Plains of Abraham where they had collected and marched over the route mapped out which covered the most important points in the city. With bands playing and colours flying, the men kept up a steady march. The parade was on a large scale, it taking

lent impression. The force of youthful Canada was shown. It inspired respect and perhaps dread—but above all it was imposing.

✠ ✠ ✠

Prince Returns Visits

Thursday morning again heard the booming of cannon and the wild roar of guns. The Prince of Wales was repaying the visits tendered him by the Admirals on his arrival which furnished another occasion for the filling of the river with the sound of naval battle. The beautiful weather contributed to the scene making the effect a very picturesque one.

ILLUMINATIONS OF THE PARLIAMENT BUILDINGS

one and a half hours pass any point. The whole to the spectator was a continued march of steeds, men and cannons.

It was the largest muster of Canadian militia ever held. The different units were divided up into brigades commanded by Lt.-Colonel Turner, V.C., D.S.O., Cavalry; Lt.-Col. Grant, the Artillery; and Brigadier-Generals Cotton and Buchan, and Col. Gordon the infantry. The marching was well executed and evoked applause from every spot passed, for witnesses were everywhere. The parade was but a harbinger of the military and naval review that was to take place on the morrow but yet created an excel-

His Royal Highness was attended by Lord Annaly and Col. Sherwood. The guard consisted of four men of the Northwest Mounted Police, two riding in front and two in the rear. A guard of honour consisting of the 43rd regiment was drawn up on the wharf.

The party entered the royal launch when the salutes at once began. The French flagship was first visited. Cheers greeted the Prince on his ascending the gangway. These were no less vociferous when the U.S.S. New Hampshire was visited. Vice-Admiral Curzon-Howe and Rear-Admiral Jellicoe were the last to receive the royal visit,

Royal Honours Conferred

"By command of His Majesty the King I appoint you Knight Bachelor. Arise Sir Lomer Gouin."

These words, were addressed to Hon. M. Gouin while a similar honour was extended to several others; for the Prince of Wales held on Thursday a royal investiture at which Knightships and decorations were awarded to several prominent people who had played a leading role in the organization of the tercentenary celebrations.

The ceremony was held shortly before the events of the Terrace commenced. The State ball room of the Citadel was used for the occasion and by its grand outlook and historical aspect lent much effect to the investiture. The conferring of a Knighthood is one of the prerogatives of sovereignty which is carefully guarded and in His Majesty's command for honouring Canadians is seen his appreciation of the merits of those who are his subjects across the sea.

In the ball-room were present but a score or so of the celebrities who visited Quebec. The complete list of honours is as follows:—

Earl Grey, Grand Cross of the Victorian Order.

Sir John Hanbury-Williams, Knight Companion of the Victorian Order.

Sir Lomer Gouin, Knight Bachelor.

Sir James Pliny Whitney, Knight Bachelor.

Sir George Garneau, Mayor of Quebec, Knight Bachelor.

Commander of the Victorian Order—Brig.-General William Dillon Otter.

Companions of the Victorian Order—Sir George Drummond, Byron E. Walker, Adelard Turgeon and Joseph Pope, Assistant Secretary of State.

Victorian Order:—Colonel Percy Sherwood, Col. Alexandre Roy.

Companion of St. Michael and St. George:—H. J. J. B. Chouinard, City Clerk of Quebec, and originator of the idea of the Tercentenary.

The Prince stood on a dais from which he handed the insignia of the various decorations to the recipients. Earl Grey was the first to come forward in response to the call from an aide-de-camp, "His Excellency Earl Grey,'to receive the Grand Cross of the Victorian Order." As His Excellency advanced to the throne he bowed three times at proper intervals As the Governor-General is already a Knight he did not kneel. His Royal Highness passed the broad purple ribbon over the Earl's right shoulder, caught it under his left arm and attached the gold insignia. The Prince then warmly shook the Earl's hand, wispered a few words in his ear—and Canada's Governor-General was a Grand Commander of the Victorian Order.

Col. Hanbury-Williams then proceeded gracefully to the foot of the throne, knelt on a crimson footstool as an accolade was necessary, and a moment later was a Knight Companion of the Victorian Order.

Three knightships were then conferred on Hon. Mr. Lomer Gouin, Hon. Mr. J. Pliny Whitney, and on Hon. Mr. J. G. Garneau, respectively. This ceremony was very simple consisting merely of a touch upon the left and right shoulders with the naked sword of the Prince, followed by the command to arise. Thus arose Sir Lomer Gouin, Sir J. Pliny Whitney and Sir J. G. Garneau.

The other recipients of honours obtained them from

THE CROWNED ARCH

In front of the Government
House illuminated.

the heir to the throne who pinned them on to each and cemented this with a hand shake.

The ceremony gave Quebec the air of royalty which marked the celebrations. Merit was recompensed. Those who laboured for the task of honouring Quebec's founder were honoured. It was now Champlain's turn to be honoured. There was no royal investiture needed. The Prince instead repaired to the monument of the founder and there paid his respects.

MARQUIS DE MONTCALM

MARQUIS DE LEVIS

A descendant of the
victor of Ste. Foye.

Lunch to Famous Descendants

In the afternoon, a social event of unique interest took place when a luncheon was given at the Garrison Club in honour of the descendants of the men who played leading roles in the past history of Canada. Seldom has it happened that around one festive board have been gathered the representatives of different families whose ancestors all played leading parts in the great events of a nation's history a century and a half before. At the luncheon, over which Sir Charles Fitzpatrick presided, sat Mr. George Wolfe and Comte de Montcalm, descendants of the families of the two famous soldiers whose names must ever commence the tale of Canada's history.

The Marquis de Levis, the Marquis de Levis-Mirepoix and Capt. the Hon. Arthur Murray, descendants of brave men serving different masters were present. The genial Lord Dorchester had a descendant there in the person of Hon. M. Dudley Carleton. Lord Bruce, Lord Howick who represented His Excellency the Governor-General, Sir Wilfrid Laurier and others were present. The sorely-tried Haldimand, who from a Swiss soldier became a Canadian governor, had no representative at the luncheon, although a descendant, Miss Haldimand, was present during the festivities in Quebec.

English Greetings

During the day, Sir J. G. Garneau, Mayor of Quebec, received the following cable from the city of Bath :—

"City of Bath sends hearty congratulations upon your tercentenary. Sir Gilbert Parker will unveil tablets here next Wednesday to commemorate residence of General Wolfe in Bath.

(Signed) THOS. HODGSON MILLER,
Mayor."

Following is the copy of the answer :—

"Mayor, Bath, England—City of Quebec greets the city of Bath and returns hearty thanks for congratulations upon tercentenary. Tablet to one of Quebec's heroes will be a bond between us.

(Signed) GARNEAU, Mayor."

✦ ✦ ✦

Earl Grey Gives Dinner for Prince

Champlain day was a busy one. The memory of the founder had been honoured. All else was laid aside. In the evening little occurred but the holding of a dinner at the Citadel in honour of His Royal Highness, the Prince of Wales.

MR. GEORGE WOLFE.

A member of the family
to which belonged the
conqueror of Quebec.

The dinner given by Earl Grey was followed by a reception in the apartment adjoining the private terrace, all the guests being presented to the Prince. The host of the evening stood beside the royal guest of honour as the line of guests passed the dais on which he stood. The hall was prettily decorated and, with the brilliant uniforms worn, presented a charming spectacle. A buffet supper was served after the presentations.

The following guests were present :—

Vice-President Fairbanks, Vice-Admiral Jaureguiberry, Conseiller Herbette, M. de Loynes, Earl of Dudley, Sir Henry de Villiers, Earl of Ranfurly, Hon. James Pitts, Field Marshal Earl Roberts, Duke of Norfolk, Lord Annaly, Vice-Admiral Sir Assheton Curzon Howe, Lieut.-Gen. Sir R. Pole-Carew, Lieut.-Col. Sir Arthur Bigge, Rear-Admiral Sir John Jellicoe, Sir Francis Hopwood, Lord Bruce, Rear-Admiral Cowles, Brig.-Gen. Murray, Capt. Henniker Hugham, Capt. L. E. Goodenough, Capt. Clement, Capt. A. D. Ricardo, Capt. Serres, Capt. Habert, Capt. C. G. Chapman, Capt. Winslow, Capt. H. Hudelstone, Capt. King Hall, Capt. W. C. Boothby, the Marquis de Levis, the Marquis de Levis Mirepoix, M. Le Comte Bertrand de Montcalm, Mr. Geo. Wolfe, Lord Lovat, Captain the Hon. Arthur Murray, Capt. the Hon. Dudley Carleton, His Worship the Mayor

of Brouage, His Honor Sir Mortimer Clark, His Honor Sir Louis Jette, His Honor M. D. Fraser, His Honor L. J. Tweedie, His Honor Sir Daniel McMillan, His Honor Mr. James Dunsmuir, His Hon. Mr. D. A. Mackinnon, His Hon. Mr. A. E. Forget, His Hon. Mr. G. H. V. Bulyea, the Apostolic Delegate, the Most Rev. Archbishop of Quebec, the Most Rev. Archbishop of Toronto, the Right Rev. Bishop of Quebec, the Moderator of the Presbyterian Church, the General Superintendent of the Methodist Church, the Right Hon. Sir Wilfrid Laurier, the Right Hon. Sir Richard Cartwright, the Hon. R. W. Scott, the Hon. Sir Frederick Borden, the Hon. Sydney Fisher, the Hon. W. S. Fielding, the Hon. Wm. Patterson, the Hon. W. Templeman, the Hon. L. P. Brodeur, the Hon. Frank Oliver, the Hon. A. B. Aylesworth, the Hon. Rodolphe Lemieux, and the Hon. Wm. Pugsley, the Hon. G. P. Graham, the Hon. R. Dandurand, the Right Hon. Sir Charles Fitzpatrick, the Right Hon. Sir Elzear Taschereau, Chief Justice Sir Melbourne Tait, Chief Justice Sir Francois Langelier, Right Hon. Sir Charles Tupper, the Right Hon. Sir Mackenzie Bowell, Lord Strathcona, the Hon. G. E. Foster, the Solicitor-General, Admiral Kingsmill, Major-Gen. Lake, Brig.-Gen. Otter, Brig.-Gen. Buchan, Hon. Sir George Drummond, Hon. J. A. Lougheed, Hon. R. F. Sutherland, Mr. R. L. Borden,

H.R.H. THE PRINCE OF WALES AND HIS EXCELLENCY EARL GREY
Coming out of the Citadel.

THE FESTIVITIES AT NIGHT—THE ILLUMINATIONS ON DUFFERIN TERRACE
Drawn by F. de Halnen, from sketches by the Graphic's special artist, Correspondent, Frank Draig.

Mr. F. D. Monk, Hon. Sir James Whitney, Hon. Sir L. Gouin, Hon. G. H. Murray, Hon. J. D. Hazen, Hon. R. P. Roblin, Hon. R. McBride, Hon. F. Hassard, Hon. Walter Scott, Hon. A. Rutherford, His Worship the Mayor of Quebec, the Hon. Adelard Turgeon, Hon. L. A. Taschereau, Col. Geo. Denison, Mr. Byron Walker, Lieut.-Col. Hon. J. G. Hendrie, Sir Thomas Shaughnessy, Sir Montagu Allan, Sir William Macdonald, Mr. C. M. Hays, Mr. F. W. Morse, Mr. W. Mackenzie, Mr. E. S. Clouston, Mr. Pope, Col. Benson, Lieut.-Col. Sherwood, Lieut.-Col. Roy, Mr. J. J. Hill, Brig.-Gen. Cotton, Brig.-Gen. Macdonald, Capt. A. W. Ewatt, Viscount Lascelles, Lt.-Col. Sir John Hanbury-Williams, Mr. Godfrey-Fausset, Lord Howick, Capt. Newton.

✳ ✳ ✳

Illuminations and Fireworks

The evening witnessed the great pyrotechnical display, one of the most spectacular events of the many that were marked by phantasy during the celebrations

The terrace was again covered with people. It

seemed as if all Quebec had repaired to spend the evening on the famous promenade. Heads only were visible, so densely were the spectators massed. The heights above the Terrace were not visible. A moveable cover seemed to have been laid over them. Once in a while a form might be seen to stand conspicuously from amid this mass of people seated on the stony cliff. It was dangerous and almost impossible to move. The crowd seemed to be one mass of moveable parts. It was a series of patch work—colours of every description. Red-coated soldiers, ordinary garbed individuals, blue jacketed sailors, and crimson coloured historical performers sat together. It is estimated that there were fifty thousand persons on the Terrace and its vicinity that evening.

A spasmodic shower of rain would drop down now and then. This did not mar the scene. It had but the effect of solidifying the already thick mass. Discomforts may have been experienced but the trouble was worth while.

The scene which offered itself to the view was not merely spectacular. It was grand and wonderful. Nine warships in the river below were illuminated shining out from the dark and glimmering water. Levis, bespangled with bright signs, formed and admirable back ground. On the east, was darkness; on the west, a broad expanse distinguishable only by a row of lights several miles off. The river, opaque itself, was here and there illuminated. The glare overhead shone into the smooth liquid penetrating its other secrets. Rocket followed rocket. While one mass of stars and diamonds was descending another took its place keeping up a continual stream of fire. The rockets like clouds seemed to be thick and laden overhead, and like them weep their contents on the river below.

Fire in every shape was in the air. Figures of

THE PYROTECHNICAL DISPLAY FROM THE BRITISH WARSHIPS
Showing the crowd on the Terrace watching it.

depth laid bare by the powerful and brilliant searchlights.

Then came the fireworks. From Levis was showered a mass of light varying in colour, strength and effect. Rockets were shot into the air scattering in their explosion hundreds of fiery diamonds falling together into the river, which, bright for a moment, soon buried these offshoots in its bosom along with light evolved in the atmosphere and falling seemed to dance on the surface of the water. Portraits of various important personages were distinguished across the river set in frames of light. A cataract with its rushing cascades was seen in outline of fire. The whole had a wonderful effect and left an ineffacable impression.

Thus ended the fifth day of the celebrations.

Sixth Day, Friday, July Twenty=Fourth

Military and Naval Review

RIDAY, the sixth day of the celebrations bore a military air. It was the grand day for the soldiers and sailors who had gathered at Quebec. The militia of Canada, numbering about twelve thousand men, and the naval defenders of three nations numbering altogether about five thousand, passed in review before His Royal Highness the Prince of Wales.

From early morning troops had been marching through the streets until at ten o'clock the vast concourse of men, steeds and guns has assembled on the Plains of Abraham to pass peacefully before the future King of England on the same spot where a century and a half earlier stood their forefathers arrayed in battle against each other. A special stand had been erected on the grounds where sat three thousand spectators among whom were the official guests of and a brilliant concourse of men and the Tercentenary women. On the

H.R.H. THE PRINCE OF WALES
At the Military Review.

ground below were thousands of people watching the event.

The review was a memorable one, for not military grandeur alone was displayed. The very interesting and simple ceremony of handing over the deeds of the battle-fields to the Canadian people was also enacted.

The different regiments to be inspected at half past ten were in their positions waiting. The large number of spectators stood around eager to see the spectacle. Suddenly a clamouring of hoofs was heard.

A body of dragoons was seen to force its way through the crowd. The Royal Standard was hoisted over the grand stand, the national anthem played, and a moment later the Prince of Wales, clad in the uniform of a general of the British army, stood before the assembled mariners and militiamen ready to inspect them. Beside the Prince rode His Excellency the Governor-General, attired in the uniform of commander-in-chief of the Canadian army. Directly behind came Earl Roberts bearing a handsome gold tipped field marshal's baton, while beside him was General Pole-Carew. A brilliant staff of officers followed. There were:—Lord Lovat, in khaki, the uniform of Lovat's Scouts, which His Lordship raised and commanded during the South African war; Sir John Hanbury-Williams; Rt. Hon. Lord Annaly, lord - in - waiting; Lieut.-Col. Sir Arthur Bigge, Sir Chas. Cust, Captain Bryan, Godfrey Faussett, Captain the Hon. Hugh Dawnay, Cap. Pickering, A. D. C.; Lt.-Col. Sherwood, A. D. C.; Lt.-Col. Williams, Major-General Wilson, Lt.-Col. Roy, Lieut.-Col. Sam Hughes, General Macdonald, Gen. Otter, Col. Lessard, Capt. E. Panet, Capt. D. D. Young, Capt. L. S. Macoun, Major H. A. Panet, Lieut.-Col. A. T. Thompson, Lieut.-Col. O. E. Talbot, Lieut.-Col. J. L. Biggar, Col. A. B. Perry, of the Mounted Police.

His Royal Highness lelayed not, but at once, followed by his staff, passed down the lines of the drawn up soldiers and sailors. Everywhere the reviewers were greeted with a military appearance. All was spick and span and organized to a detail. Nothing was lacking. The lines of British strength were regarded with the keen eye of acute military authorities, but nothing seemed either wanting or superflous.

Having inspected all, the Prince returned to the stand, where he dismounted and ascended the stairs leading to the pavilion over the entrance to the grounds. Here took place the ceremony which came as a result of the labours and contributions of many loyal Canadians. The deed transferring the property covering the battle-fields was formally handed over to the Canadian people there represented by their Governor-General. In handing over the title deeds and $450,000 the Prince said:—

"It affords me the greatest pleasure to hand over to Your Excellency, the representative of the Crown in Canada, the sum of $450,000, which through the patriotism of British citizens in all parts of Canada and of the Empire and the generosity of French and American sympathizers, has been entrusted to me in order that the historic battlefields of Quebec, on which the two contending races won equal and imperishable glory, may be acquired for the people of the Dominion and preserved under the special supervision of the Sovereign, as a permanent shrine of union and peace. I place in your hands, as representative of the Sovereign, the charge of the sacred ground, which it is my pleasure to be able to present to you on the 300th birthday of Quebec as a gift to the people of Canada and the Crown."

Earl Grey in replying, said:—"As Governor-General of Canada and in the names of the Government and the people of the Dominion, I accept this sacred trust which Your Royal Highness the heir to the Throne has graciously placed in my hands."

The important event was over in a few minutes. It was marked by its simplicity.

The Prince again mounted and with his staff took his place before the grand stand. Before him for over eighty minutes defiled portions of the Canadian militia and detachments of the navies of France, the United States, and Britain. First came the French sailors, preceded by a drum and fife band. The senior colour sergeant of the flagship carried a small tricolour attached to the muzzle of his rifle. The detachment numbered six hundred. Three hundred and fifty bluejackets of U.S.S. New Hampshire and a hundred marines next came forward. It was now the turn of the British tars. Sixteen field guns pulled

THE SEVENTY-EIGHTH HIGHLANDERS
Marching past H. R. H. the Prince of Wales

CANADA'S ARTILLERY AT THE REVIEW

47 guns passing before the Prince of Wales.

by five hundred sturdy men came first. The crews of H.M.S. Indomitable, Minotaur, Exmouth, Albemarle, Duncan, Russel and Venus came close behind, the bluejackets marching first in watches of one hundred men each, followed by the blue and then the red mariners.

The naval brigade had passed. Next came the military. As each regiment, whether infantry or cavalry, passed the Prince it was loudly cheered by the onlooking crowds. The greatest applause was given to Earl Roberts as he rode at the head of the R.C.A. and the Queen's Own Rifles, of both of which the Field-Marshal is honorary lieutenant-colonel.

The many units of the review passed in the following order :—

Cavalry Brigade, Lieut.-Col. R. Turner, V.C., D.S.O.—6oth Hussars, 7th Hussars, 11 Hussars, 13th S. L. Dragoons, 17th D.Y.R.C. Hussars.

Field Battery, commander, Lieut.-Colonel J. Davidson—6th Brigade, C. F. A. (3rd and 21st batteries.) Lieut.-Colonel W. A. Drake, 7th Brigade C. F. A. (15th and 22nd batteries.)

Gentlemen Cadets, R.M.C. Major E. N. Mozley.

Garrison Artillery, Lieut.-Col. H. McL. Davidson —Composite Regiments (2nd and 3rd Regiments and Cobourg Company.) Engineers—Major S. Howard— 4th Field Company.

Infantry, 1st division, Brigadier-General W. H. Cotton—1st W. O. Brigade, Lieut.-Colonel J. W. Little—7th Regiment, 13th Regiment, 21st Regiment, 91st Regiment. 2nd W. O. Brigade, Lieut.-Colonel W. C. MacDonald—2nd Regiment, 10th Regiment, 48th Regiment.

Divisional troops—Corps of Guides, Captain R. W. Leonard.

No. 6 Company, C.A.S.C.—Major W. M. Tomlinson.

No. 5 Field Ambulance—Lieut.-Col. K. Cameron.

Second Division, Col. W. D. Gordon—3rd W. O. Brigade, Lieut.-Colonel J. Mason—1st composite battalion, 2nd composite battalion, 3rd composite battalion—4th E. O. Brigade, Lieut.-Col. J. Hughes —Governor-General's Foot Guards, 14th Regiment, 43rd Regiment, 4th composite battalion.

Divisional troops—No. 5 Company, C.A.S.C. Major S. E. De la Rondea, sr. 3rd Division, Brigadier-General L. Buchan, C.M.G., A.D.C. 5th Quebec Brigade, Lieut.-Colonel E. B. Ibbotson—3rd Regiment, 5th Regiment, 56th Regiment, 5th composite battalion, 7th M. P. Brigade—Lieut.-Col. H. McLean—62nd Regiment, 7th composite battalion.

Divisional troops.—No. 5 signal corps, Captain C. H. E. De Blois. No. 10 Company, C.A.S.C., Major J. N. R. Guay. Field Ambulance (Western Ontario),

Lieut.-Col. G. S. Rennie, Royal Canadian Regiment, Lieut.-Col. R. L. Wadmore. Western contingent, Lieut.-Colonel J. A. Hall.

After the Review the Prince and his guard returned to the Citadel visiting on the road Wolfe's monument and that erected to the heroes who fell at St. Foye, at each of which he deposited a wreath.

Sir Frederick Congratulated

On the same day, Sir Frederick Borden, Minister of Militia and Defence received the following letter from Sir Arthur Bigge, equerry to H. R. H. the Prince of Wales:—

"Citadel, Quebec, July 24. 1908.

"Dear Sir Frederick Borden—

"The Prince of Wales directs me to convey to you the expression of his high appreciation of the very successful review of the Canadian Militia, which His Royal Highness had the great pleasure of holding this morning. He is well aware that the work of conveying so large a body of men and horses to Quebec must have entailed much heavy work and careful organization, also that many of the troops could only have been present at considerable individual sacrifice.

SIR FREDERICK BORDEN

Minister of Militia and Defence. As he looked after Military Review.

The Prince heartily congratulates you, Brigadier-General Otter, and the staff upon the happy result of your efforts. The march past was extremely well carried out, and H.R.H. hopes that you will convey to all ranks his congratulations upon the smart soldier-like bearing on parade of the Canadian troops.

"(Signed) ARTHUH BIGGE."

On the same day Lord Roberts reported to His Majesty as follows:—"The review this morning was a great success. The troops looked well, and I was much impressed with the precisicn, order, and organization generally. There were about 12,000 under arms and there was no hitch anywhere. Canada appears to me to be dealing adequately with the problems affecting her militia, and with care and improved organization to be building up a very useful force.

BRIG.-GEN. W. B. OTTER, C.B.

In Command of the Forces during the celebration

✠ ✠ ✠

Mayor Gives Luncheon for Prince

Shortly after the review, a luncheon was given by Sir J. G. Garneau in honour of His Royal Highness the Prince of Wales at the Garrison Club. Quebec's Mayor presided having on his right the guest of honor and Vice-President Fairbanks. On his left were His Excellency Earl Grey and Admiral Jaureguiberry. The function was a most pleasant one and attended by extremely influential guests.

The list of the invited guests is as follows:—

H.R.H. the Prince of Wales, His Excellency Lord Grey, Vice-President Fairbanks, Admiral Dudley, the Count of Ranfurly, the Rt. Hon. Sir de Villiers, Hon. Mr. D. C. Fraser, Hon. Mr. Dunsmuir, Hon. Mr. McKinnon, Hon. Mr. Bulyea, Lord Roberts, Sir W. Laurier, the Duke of Norfolk, Sir F. Borden, Hon. Mr. Fielding, Vice-Admiral Curzon Howe, Hon. Mr. Brodeur, Vice-Admiral Cowles, Vice-Admiral Oliver, the Hon. R. Lemieux, the Hon. Mr. Pugsley, the Hon. Mr. Graham, the Hon. Mr. Dandurand, Sir Louis Herbette, Lord Annaly, M. de Loynes, Sir F. Langelier,

THE MILITARY REVIEW

On the Plains of Abraham.

Count de Montcalm, Mr. W. Wolfe, Marquis de Levis, Marquis de Levis Mirepoix, Capt. Murray, Lord Lovat, Lord Bruce, Capt. Dudley Carleton, the Mayor of Brouage, Lord Henrick, Lt.-Gen. Sir Pole-Carew, Sir F. Hopwood, Sir A. Bigge, Vice-Admiral Jellicoe, Major-Gen. Lake, Rear-Admiral Kingsmill, Major-Gen. Wilson, Brig.-Gen. Murray, Brig.-Gen. Otter, Brig.-Gen. Cotton, Brig.-Gen. Buchan, Capt. Clement, Commander Leon Gambetta, Capt. U.S.S. New Hampshire, Col. Sir J. Hanbury Williams, Capt. H.M.S. Exmouth, Sir Geo. Drummond, Hon. R. W. Sutherland, Sir Lomer Gouin, Capt. H.M.S. Albemarle, Capt. Godfroy, Mr. F. Faussett, Sir Thomas Shaugnessy, Sir H. Montague Allan, Capt.-Amiral Aube, Capt. of H.M.S. Indomitable, Col. Turnbull, Col. Duncan, Col. Russell, Mr. R. L. Borden, Capt. H.M.S. Venus, Capt. H.M.S. Arrogant, Capt. H.M.S. Minotaur, Wm. Power, M.P.; Sir J. P. Whitney, Hon. Mr. Murray, Hon. Mr. Hazen, Hon. A. C.

troller of His Excellency's Household, Mr. Lascelles, Mr. Frederick W. Emmett, Mr. J. A. Bellisle.

AMERICAN SAILORS PASSING IN REVIEW
Before H. R. H. the Prince of Wales on the Plains.

Dance on U. S. S. New Hampshire

The day was essentially one of social events. There was a luncheon to the Prince, an afternoon dance, and a state ball in the evening.

The afternoon dance was on board U.S.S. New Hampshire. Invitations were issued to a large number of people by Rear-Admiral Cowles and his officers. The affair was a successful one and terminated all too soon. The scene as the dancing couples gaily flitted over the deck of the profusely decorated ship was a brilliant one. All around were sombre and huge war vessels gazing sternly as it were on the coloured United States ship looking more like a pleasure yacht than a dangerous implement of war. The Admiral and his officers did everything that lay in their power to contribute to the comfort and enjoyment of their many guests.

GARRISON CLUB
Where luncheon was given by Sir J. G. Garneau.

Rutherford, Capt. Howe Ruthven, Hon. A. Weir, Hon. Rod. Roy, Hon. Mr. Taschereau, Hon. Mr. Kaine, Hon. Lt.-Col. J. S. Hendrie, Hon. H. Archambeault, Hon. Ths. Chapais, Sir Geo. Garneau, Col. Lessard, Col. Fiset, Col. Benson, Mr. B. E. Walker, Mr. Jos. Pope, Lieut.-Col. Sellers, A.D.C., Lieut.-Col. Sept. Denison, Commander Haggard, Mr. C. M. Hays, Lieut.-Col. Sherwood, Mr. Will. Mackenzie, Mr. J. M. Courtney, Lt.-Col. Roy, Dr. Doughty, Lieut.-Col. O. Pelletier, Lt.-Col. Wood, Mayor of Ottawa, Mayor of Toronto, Mayor of Winnipeg, Mayor of Victoria, Mayor of Montreal, Mayor of St. John, N.B., Mayor of Vancouver, Mayor of Levis, pro-Mayor Alderman A. Picard, A.D.C. of Admiral Jaureguiberry, A.D.C. of Governor-General, A.D.C. of United States Admiral, A.D.C. of Admiral Howe, A.D.C. of Admiral Jellicoe, Major Mott, H. J. J. B. Chouinard, City Clerk; Major Sheppard, the Con-

H.R.H. AND OFFICERS INSPECTING
The soldiers and sailors on the Plains.

Naval Sports

In the afternoon, sports at the Quebec Athletic grounds attracted most of the sailors on shore. The sports were entirely in the hands of sailors who turned every number into a jolly event. It was an afternoon of naval fun.

The sailors performed their antics with the simple-hearted mirth of children. A spirit of fairness and of naught but a desire for fun coupled with the fraternization of the English and French sailors marked the events of the occasion.

Most of the fun-makers were tars of the Leon Gambetta and the Amiral Aube. The majority of their British confreres were mere spectators evidently regretting that they did not share in the fun.

The sports opened with a hundred yards dash in which almost two hundred French light-footed runners figured. Many heats resulted, leaving the honours divided between the two French ships. The sack race was attempted with the highest glee. The naval feet of the participants served them badly, and a mass of heads and sacks was soon piled up in front of the starting-point. An international bunting contest was a success for the superior solidity of the British sailors.

A contest of tilting with padded spears among the Frenchmen provided the greatest merriment. At the starting signal, the two teams dashed into each other and a melee of steeds and riders was on the tapis. The non-participant sailors vociferously urged on the men to victory which after a valiant rush went to the

men of the Amiral Aube. A display of free gymnastics by the Cadets of the Royal Military College was excellent in its rhythm and ended a very fine programme of sports.

State Ball at Parliament Buildings

The evening witnessed the greatest social event of the celebrations—the State Ball given by the Government of the Province of Quebec in honour of His Royal Highness, the Prince of Wales. It was grand from a spectacular point of view, for the extent of the decorations and illuminations was illimitable. It was grand from the point of view of beauty, for the magnificence of the gorgeous robes of the ladies and of the official garb of the men was beyond description. It was grand from the point of view of numbers, for over six thousand invitations were issued.

The Parliament buildings were resplendent with beauty within and without. Around them in the spacious and pretty grounds were erected towers bedecked with flowers from which shone electric lights as if they were but the bulbs of glowing roses. In the centre of the grounds over-towering all the others and visible from a great distance stood an Ionic arch supported on six columns. The beauty of its design and style of the finish were hidden from view as a frame of electric lights covered it.

The building itself could be distinguished at a distance by the rows and strings of lights which covered it. From the central tower of the building depended long loops of red, white and blue lights carried to the extreme end of either facade. The walls of the structure always covered with the inlaid statues of Canadian heroes were now bright with illuminated inscriptions and famous pictures. In the centre of the driveway leading to the main entrance was especially conspicuous the canopy-pagoda beneath which trickled the pretty fountain rendered more beautiful by the masterpiece of Hebert above,—a group of Indians with bow and arrow, naturally artistic and made beautiful with streamers of lights whose sparkling shadow in the water below made a pretty spectacle.

Within the hall, the visitors trod on carpet of the reddest hue leading up the outside flight

PARLIAMENT BUILDINGS
Where the State Ball took place.

THE STATE BALL GIVEN IN THE GOVERNMENT BUILDINGS
In honor of the Prince. Drawn for the London Sphere by Signor Matania.

of stairs to a superb canopy of red velvet embroidered with gold. The broad stairway was lined with pots of ferns and palms gaily interspersed with red and green lights.

The white and golden Legislative Assembly chamber and regal crimson Council chamber which were used for dancing hardly required further embellishment. Every window was curtained with flags so arranged that the folds hid cosy recesses which looked on the scene outside. Between them hung shields bearing the coats of arms of famous Canadians. The place of honour in the chamber of the Legislative Council was decked with the folds of the flag of the ancien regime—a perfect white field thickly dotted with golden fleur-de-lys. The royal arms of the Prince of Wales flanked on either side with the royal standard, the tricolor, the Canadian flag, and the Union Jack were suspended in the centre of the draped gallery. The whole was a scene of unparalleled magnificence further enhanced by the splendour of gold lace, sashes, orders, sword hilts, medals, epaulets, stars and brilliant insignia of officialdom, the evening dress of civilians, and the artistic results of the costumer.

The guests were received by His Honour the Lieutenant-Governor, Sir Louis Jette, Sir Lomer Gouin, Hon. A. and Mrs. Turgeon, Hon. W. A. Weir, Hon. C. R. and Mrs. Devlin, Hon. J. C. and Mrs. Kaine,

Hon. L. A. and Mrs. Taschereau. Invitations were freely issued. As a result there was some inconvenience through inevitable crowding. The Prince of Wales and his staff, the Governor-General and staff, the Lieutenant-Governors of every province, the Prime Minister of Canada and his Cabinet, the members of both houses, the Premier of each Province and their ministers, the official guests, the Admirals and officers of the fleets in port, the officers of the militia, citizens of Quebec and their visitors, in short, all occupying any station were invited.

Dancing began early. The first three numbers had passed when a hush pervaded the halls. The Prince had arrived. The entrance of the Legislative Council chamber was at once the focus of all eyes. Accompanied by Sir Louis Jette, the royal guest entered and proceeded to the place reserved for him. Immediately after commenced the ceremony of special introductions. The fortunate ones were summoned to the side of the Prince and for a time installed in a chair at his right.

After a considerable stay in the ball-room during which time all feasted their eyes on him, the Prince, taking in Madame Turgeon, repaired to the special supper-room reserved for him. Her Excellency Lady Grey was accompanied by Sir Lomer Gouin, while Mrs. Kaine was led in by His Excellency the Governor-General.

Seventh Day, Saturday, July Twenty-Fifth

The Naval Review

THE seventh day of the celebrations witnessed the grand naval review. As a general of the British army, His Royal Highness the Prince of Wales reviewed the Canadian militia on the previous day. The navy of the Empire was now to be reviewed by the Prince in his capacity as British Admiral.

The weather was fine. A bright sun shone upon

SIR WILFRID AND LADY LAURIER
Going on board the ship from which the Prince reviewed the Fleet.

sonage? The belching of salutes from the cannons of a dozen leviathians, the cheers from the sailors on board, the brilliant assemblage, made the occasion a memorable one.

Shortly after breakfast, the Prince left the Citadel accompanied by His Excellency Earl Grey and staff. A guard of honour was mounted at the King's wharf where the royal sailor was met by Hon. L. P. Brodeur, Canadian Minister of Marine and Fisheries. No time was lost, and in a few moments, the Prince, Governor-General and staff and Hon. Mr. Brodeur seated in the royal launch at whose mast flew the royal standard, reached H. M.S. Arrogant which was boarded and which bore the Prince during the review. On ascending the gangway, a royal salute was fired from every warship causing the river to be covered at once with a veil of smoke growing larger in its ascent and from which was heard only the thundering peals of cannon.

The Arrogant then slowly steamed up the long line of ships. Every vessel was decorated. There could be no grander spectacle than that presented by the ships. On the main deck of each was drawn up its sailors side by side, while on the upper decks were the officers in gorgeous uniforms. The Amiral Aube

the heights of the city where again were posted thousands of people eager to witness the novel spectacle on the river below. Novel indeed,—for when else in Quebec were the battleships of the three nations mightiest on sea reviewed together by a royal per-

was the first to be passed and at once a cheer for the Prince of Wales was raised by the French sailors and did not end until it had been taken up by the men of the Leon Gambetta, the next vessel to be passed in review. With the cheer went the playing of the national anthem on board each ship. Thus, vessel after vessel was passed, its men cheered, its bands played, and the Arrogant floated on.

Her task performed, the Arrogant returned to her berth. The Prince, Earl Grey, Sir Wilfrid Laurier, Mr. Brodeur and Lord Roberts who had also been on the ship, again descended into the green launch from which flew the Royal standard. Again the river was hid by a mist which once more accompanied the noisy salutes. The review was over.

✱ ✱ ✱

Pic-Nic for the Sailors

In the afternoon about twelve hundred sailors took part in a pic-nic which had been arranged by the Tercentenary Sports Committee to take place at Lake St. Joseph. The party were the guests of the Lake St. Joseph hotel where supper was served. During the day many sporting events were gone through by the sailors. After a day's fun, the pic-nickers returned to the city in the evening.

✱ ✱ ✱

Prince Visits Pageants

The State performance of the pageants took place in the afternoon. Though the usual throngs that visited the performance were markedly diminished on account of the high prices on this occasion, the State performance of the pageants was without doubt the most important one from a spectacular point of view.

The Don de Dieu which was usually at anchor opposite the Citadel was now stationed on the river near Wolfe's cove where she was plainly visible from the pageant grounds above. The already very real scenes that were being enacted above, were emphasized by the presence of the little craft below.

The grand stand was well filled. In the royal box sat His Royal Highness the Prince of Wales, His Excellency Earl Grey and a brilliant assemblage of official guests. The scenes were all executed with despatch.

One quickly followed another. The Prince witnessed pictured before him the attempt of old France during two centuries to build up an Empire in the new land. The attempts, the struggles and failures were all depicted until finally on the battlefields which were comprised in the deed that the Prince had formally transferred to the Canadian people on the preceding day, stood the two armies of Montcalm and Wolfe, above which fluttered, side by side, the Union Jack and Fleur-de-lys.

All was now silent. Champlain's little vessel was lying easy below. The Prince and those on the grand stand were gazing with reverence at the two armies in front. The spectacle was a gorgeous one. A moment later, from a thick bush in the centre of the field, were seen to emerge a cluster of white doves—emblems of peace. They were released, but uncertain of their freedom, hesitated, then soared overhead, as if cementing the unity of the two armies below.

The large gathering at first stands dazed at the unexpected and appropriate ceremony, then as if realizing what had happened and its full meaning, applause comes from every direction and carries with it the unalloyed enthusiasm of all. The band begins the strains of "O Canada," the French-Canadian national anthem. All rise and with bared heads join in singing the patriotic song. The national anthem of the Empire follows. All including the Prince stand

THE PRINCE OF WALES

Hands over the deed of the battle-fields to Lord Grey.

bare-headed. The singing over, the French and English armies join in a loud cheer for their common King's son.

The pageants are not yet over. To the mimicking of history is added another scene crowning the pageants with a fitting episode. Side by side the armies of Wolfe and Montcalm march to the spot where the English hero fell. A hollow square is formed around the monument. One leader gives the

FRENCH SAILORS PASS IN REVIEW

Before H. R. H. and Lord Roberts on the Plains of Abraham.

command "Army of Wolfe, present arms!" the other "Armee de Montcalm, presentez les armes!" A soldier clad in the uniform of Montcalm's army advances and places on the monument's base a wreath "to the honour of Wolfe." By his side stands a soldier garbed in the old uniform of Wolfe's army. He lays a wreath by the side of the other "To the honour of Montcalm" Both salute the monument. At the column of stone the unity of two nations is pronounced. Each admires and respects the hero of the other.

Thus ended the State performance of the pageant.

✳ ✳ ✳

Concert at Drill Hall

In the evening another concert had been arranged for by the Tercentenary Committee on music. This was perhaps the most important musical event during the celebrations. The Quebec Symphony Society under the leadership of Mr. Joseph Vezina comprising one hundred instrumentalists and three hundred vocalists rendered excellent selections with that harmony for which that body of musicians is noted.

The feature of the concert was the singing of Madame Bernice de Pasquali, who is possessed of a voice of penetrating sweetness, power and rich quality. Of a charming presence and master of her art, she is one of the best contralto singers that has been heard in Quebec. Madame Pasquali sang selections from the "Chant du Mysole," from "La Perle du Bresil," from the "Inflammatus," and a cavatina from "La Traviata." "Salut a la France" and "Rule Britannia" were given as encores—happy selections during a time of common rejoicing by the two peoples of Quebec.

The reception that awaited the famous singer can only be described as a demonstration. Every number brought forward new qualities in the vocalist's superb singing which was acknowledged by storms of applause until it seemed as if a wave of everlasting hand-clapping pervaded the huge Drill Hall only to be quelled by the miraculous voice of Madame de Pasquali.

The gala concert proved an unqualified success and was repeated several days later.

✳ ✳ ✳

British Empire Dinner

In the evening took place the celebrated State dinner. It was given by Earl Grey, Governor-General of Canada to the representatives of the various British dominions who were in Quebec during the Tercentenary. Ministers and Governors of different British provinces were gathered to a sort of Imperial Conference dinner, for there every part of the Empire was represented by its most brilliant figures who discussed questions of general Imperial interest.

The guests were presented to their future King on their arrival and after a few minutes spent in conversation were led to the superb dining-room of the Vice-regal appartments overlooking the St. Lawrence river below, bearing its burden of war-vessels representing three different nations. The room was neatly decorated with trophies and stacks of arms while from the adjoining room were heard the strains of music.

The dinner was a grand one. It was attended by many celebrities and was the occasion of several powerful speeches. His Excellency Earl Grey who presided proposed the first toast—that of His Royal Highness the Prince of Wales, saying :—

Toast to His Royal Highness

I now have the privileged honor to propose a toast which I know will stir in your hearts, as it does in mine, feelings of deep and generous emotion. I give you the toast of H. R. H. the Prince of Wales.

Everyone will agree that the remarkable manifestations of enthusiasm evoked by Your Royal Highness's presence will never be forgotten by anyone who has been so fortunate as to be in Quebec during the present week, I do not believe that there is a man in Quebec; I do not believe there is a single intelligent Canadian in any part of Canada, into whose distant hut the echoes of those festivities will not reverberate, who will not feel most grateful to Your Royal Highness for your sympathy with them which caused you to leave England—that happy isle—at the very pleasantest season of all the year, and to face the discomfort of a double tossing by the rude Atlantic, in order that you might do honor to Canada on her 300th birthday and lay the wreath of your homage at the foot of the statue of Champlain.

By coming to Canada at this season of the year, when your presence is so urgently desired in England, you have given to the British race a standing lesson as to the way in which it should be the duty of every subject of the King to subordinate his personal interests and convenience to the higher interests of the Empire and the Crown.

Further, Your Royal Highness, in putting yourself to so much trouble and inconvenience in order that you might pay homage to Champlain, and do honor to Quebec, you have associated yourself for all time with Champlain, the hero of Quebec, in the hearts of the people.

Sir—the fact that this is the sixth occasion on which you have visited Canada is in itself sufficient to show how well qualified you are in heart and action to be the heir to the throne of not only Great, but

Greater Britain. In making yourself acquainted with every portion of the Empire, you have given an example which it would be well if those subjects of the Crown who have the necessary time and money would increasingly follow. Many have the necessary time and means to make themselves, like Your Royal Highness, acquainted with every portion of the British Empire. All they want is Your Royal Highness's inclination. I constantly wonder how those who jog along year after year in the same old tedious ruts, and who lavish their surplus fortunes upon foreign holiday resorts, do not, as a change sometimes cross the Atlantic in order that they may make themselves acquainted with the charms and attractions of this wonderful Dominion.

SAVARD PARK

Interior of Officers'
Marquis in Colonel
Mason's Brigade.

Just as there is no one who has been in Quebec during this wonderful week who will not be glad to revisit it, so I believe there are few Britons who have spent their holiday in Canada who will not do so again as often as they can. A trip across the Atlantic in a C. P. R. Empress or in one of the turbine steamers of the Allan Line, is in itself a holiday. I therefore believe that Your Royal Highness's example will be followed by an increasing number, as soon as people at home realise their opportunities.

The motto which has decorated this city by day and illuminated it by night "Si nous nous connaissons mieux, nous nous aimerons plus," represents a great truth of which this week has been an eloquent illustration, and which ought to be carved in imperishable letters on the doorstep of every Briton.

Sir,—The speech which you made at the foot of the Champlain Statue, and the words with which you dedicated to race confusion and peace the sacred ground

on which the two races won equal and imperishable glory, will long be remembered. Your speeches, Sir, have already won for themselves the place of household words in the life of the Empire. Never did a high-mettled horse answer to the prick of the spur more quickly than did the whole British Empire, when as the result of your travel round the world, you pointed out in your famous Guildhall speech, that the one need of the British race was to "wake up."

After you had visited India you again concentrated in the one word, "Sympathy," the greatest need of the moment in the national character. The satisfaction given by that speech to the three hundred odd million Indian subjects of the King, was evidenced by the speech of the Nizam of Hyderabad, one of the three Premier Princes of India, and the ruler of the largest state, when he said last November that "the form of government was far less important than the spirit of its administration, and that the essential thing was "sympathy," on which the Prince of Wales, with the truly royal instinct of his race, laid stress on the conclusion of his Indian tour."

To-day, Sir, you have given to us the ideals of race fusion and harmony, as the ideals to which we should endeavor to attune our national life. I am happy to believe that this Tercentenary week will do something to promote in the life of the Canadian people, and perhaps also in the life of the Empire, that fusion and sympathy on the full realization of which the character of Canada's destiny and of the Empire's depends.

Thanks, Sir, to the deep interest which you have taken from the bottom of your heart in this National and Imperial celebration; thanks to Your Royal Highness's presence, for which we shall never cease to be deeply grateful, this Quebec Tercentenary is proving itself to be an instrument for fusing the two great races of the Dominion into a more united people; for welding the provinces of the Dominion into a more consolidated nation; for strengthening the ties between Canada, the Motherland and the Sister States, so well and worthily represented on this occasion; for uniting the whole French and English-speaking world in a point of common interest at Quebec, and for strengthening the "entente cordiale" between the British Crown and our ancient ally France, and our friendly and powerful neigbor, the United States of America.

Sir, it is in the belief that history will record that the Quebec Tercentenary was a blessed instrument for achieving these high results, and that it was owing to your presence among us that this Tercentenary has been able to secure this high distinction that I venture, with feelings of deepest gratitude, most respectfully to propose the toast of Your Royal Highness.

As His Royal Highness arose to respond the band played "God Save the King," three cheers were given for the Prince, and it was some time before he was able to speak. He said:—

His Royal Highness's Reply

Your Excellency, My Lords and Gentlemen:—

I thank you all most sincerely, Your Excellency, for proposing this toast, and my other friends here for the manner in which they have received it.

Your Excellency has referred to the fact that this is my sixth visit to Canada. I cannot, I regret to say, hope to rival the hero of these celebrations, the founder of Quebec, who crossed the Atlantic no less than twenty times in the interests of his infant settlement, and even made something like a record passage for those times, passing from Honfleur to Tadousac in eighteen days. There is one difference, however, on which I cannot but congratulate myself and my companions on the voyage. Champlain's vessels were from sixty to eighty tons; our ship was nearer 20,000, and, I suspect, rather more comfortable. (Laughter and applause.) But the navigators of those days disregarded dangers or discomforts of their voyages. Their minds were fixed on great discoveries, and in speculations upon the benefits which would be thus conferred upon mankind. I am confident that Champlain, and others like him, thought less of present success or failure, than of the results which he and they foresaw would follow from their energy and enterprise. I was much struck, for instance, when reading Champlain's life, to find that he had in fact recommended the linking of the two oceans by the construction of a canal across the isthmus of Panama. (Cheers.)

We in the Indomitable—that splendid ship, the largest and most modern of cruisers, which has been so kindly placed at my disposal—tossed about in a North Atlantic gale, thought much of Champlain and his little craft, and of many great men, soldiers and sailors, who had crossed the ocean to visit Canada on errands of peace and war; of the heroic Montcalm, never to return to his beloved France, and of Wolfe, borne home to his last resting place. Even if our voyage had in any way entailed the discomfort suggested by Your Excellency, it would certainly have been more than compensated by the welcome which awaited me on my arrival. On each occasion when I have been to Canada I have found and made friends —friends whom neither I nor the Princess of Wales, who accompanied me on the last occasion, will ever forget. (Cheers.) I delight to see old friends again, and to make new ones. But apart from such personal feelings, there is the wider satisfaction of realizing how enormously Canada has prospered during recent years, thanks to the fostering care of successive governments and the wonderful enterprise of its people. I can assure you that everything which conduces to the prosperity and well-being of the Dominion is watched with the keenest interest by the Mother Country. (Cheers.)

As the representative of our King, I knew that an enthusiastic greeting awaited me in Quebec, but the marked affection of that greeting has touched me most deeply; indeed, it is not possible to express all I feel. The three hundredth birthday of Quebec has been made the occasion not of parochial or provincial, but of National and Imperial importance. (Cheers.) We rejoice that from all quarters of the globe, from the great self-governing dominions, from Australia, New Zealand, Africa, a warm interest has been taken in Quebec's Tercentenary.

In its celebration Canada undertook a magnificent work. Success could not have been achieved without considerable self-sacrifice, individual and by the State itself.

If, as Your Excellency suggests, my coming here to take part in these ceremonies may stimulate that true spirit of citizenship, then, indeed, shall I look back with pride and satisfaction upon my association with events so unique and memorable in the history of Canada.

Once more, Your Excellency, I thank you for your kind words in proposing my health, and I thank you, my Lords and Gentlemen, for the very kind manner in which you received the toast.

The Prince resumed his seat amidst great cheering. Earl Grey then made the following announcement:—

"Before I call upon Sir Wilfrid Laurier to propose the toast to the self-governing Dominions, I wish to inform you that I have ordered Australian and South African wine to be poured out to you, so that we shall have this toast of Empire honored with no foreign wine. I may add that ever since his last visit to Canada, seven years ago, His Royal Highness, while in England has used no mineral water other than Canadian, Canada's celebrated Radnor water, I believe."

Sir Wilfrid Laurier arose and delivered a great oration, breathing the spirit of Imperialism and disseminating those ideas which at the Imperial Conference of the preceding year brought him that position which he there obtained. He said:—

Sir Wilfrid Laurier's Address

May it please your Royal Highness, your Excellency, my Lords and Gentlemen:—

By the permission of His Excellency, I rise to propose a toast which I trust will meet with your approval. The toast I am privileged to propose is one that must appeal to all. As I advance in years I appreciate the more the wisdom of that British constitution under which I was born and brought up, and under which I have grown old, which has given to the various portions of the Empire their separate free governments. (Cheers.) It is our proud boast that Canada is the freest country in the world. (Cheers.)

It is our boast that in this country liberty of all kinds, civil and religious liberty, flourish to the highest degree. (Cheers.) To those who look only on the surface of things this may not be apparent. The fact that we are a colony does not alter the truth of the statement which I have made before you. The inferiority which may be implied in the word colony no longer exists. We acknowledged the authority of the British Crown, but no other authority. (Cheers.) This privilege, however, is not our's alone, but it is shared by the other great self-governing colonies which are represented here to-night, who have sent

SIR WILFRID LAURIER

In company of the Marquis de Levis and the Comte de Montcalm.

their envoys to aid us in celebrating the glorious deeds of the founders of this country, as well as the exploits of Wolfe and Montcalm, Murray and Levis. I have reason to believe that His Royal Highness made much sacrifice to come here to attend this celebration, but it must be a source of some satisfaction to him to be able to report to his father, the King, that he found in Canada a loyal and contented people. (Cheers.)

It is also a source of satisfaction to us to have our powerful neighbor, the United States, represented at this national commemoration, and represented by no less a person than their honored Vice-President.

(Cheers.) I wish to thank Mr. Fairbanks for the kind words he has spoken on this occasion, and especially treasure his declaration that nothing on earth can change the cordial relations that exist to-day between his country and England. (Cheers.)

We are also deeply gratified at the action of the French Government in sending its distinguished re presentatives to aid us in celebrating the three hun dredth birthday of our country. This act is especially grateful to the section of our population to which I belong, for while we are loyal British subjects of His Majesty, it must not be forgotten that we are French subjects of His Majesty, and while we have been se- parated from France in a political sense for nearly a hundred and fifty years, all our sympathies go out to the country to which we owe our origin. (Cheers.) Let me add that in no part of the British Empire, in no part of France or England has there been more rejoicing at the entente cordiale now happily existing between the two countries than here in Canada, where that entente cordiale has existed for years and is growing stronger with the march of time. (Cheers.) We hope that this state of affairs may continue between our old mother country of France and our powerful neighbour, the United States. Not only this, but the belief is growing on both sides that a war between England and France would be not only a calamity, but a crime against humanity. (Cheers.)

I wish to refer first to the neighboring colony of Newfoundland, which is represented here by Hon. J. Stewart Pitts, C.M.G. Newfoundland is the first sentinel of the gulf, with whom we are associated, not as closely as we would wish, perhaps, but with which we have most pleasant relations. We rejoice in her success, and with all our hearts, whatever may be the result of the forthcoming years; we wish her Godspeed.

Next comes Australia, represented here by the Earl of Dudley. We will watch her career with the deepest interest. Seven years ago she undertook to do what we did over forty years ago. She established a federation of the various states. Australia chose in establishing her constitution to imitate the United States to a greater extent than Canada. I am not at all sure that she was wise in proceeding in this manner. (Laughter.) However, if she finds anything goes wrong with the operation of that constitution she has men strong enough to apply the needed remedy. It has been my privilege on three occasions to be associated with the representatives of Australia, and among them such leading statesmen as Sir John Forrest, Mr. Reade and Mr. Lynne, of whom I formed the highest opinion.

Another country represented here is New Zealand, whose men I also hold in the highest esteem. I had the pleasure to be associated with Sir Richard Seddon, who was removed all too soon from the scene of his labors. He was indeed a stalwart—a stalwart in stature, a stalwart in mind and intellect. In his successor, Sir Joseph Ward, New Zealand has indeed been fortunate, because for ability, courage and prudence he cannot be surpassed.

Last, but not least on the list of self-governing colonies, comes South Africa, represented here by the Chief Justice of the Cape Colony, Sir H. De-Villiers. (Cheers.)

I had hoped to see here, besides the distinguished Chief Justice, the Premier of the latest British self-governing dominion. With the approval of His Excellency, I endeavored to induce General Botha to come to Canada to attend this tercentenary celebration. Premier Botha could not come, however, but he wrote me a letter which I think it well to communicate to you here this evening, and to the whole country as well. In reply to my letter he wrote as follows:

"PRIME MINISTER'S OFFICE,
PRETORIA, 22nd May, 1908

"*The Right Honorable*
"SIR WILFRID LAURIER, G.C.M.G., etc.
"*Prime Minister's Office,*
"OTTAWA, CANADA:

"*My Dear Sir Wilfrid Laurier:*—

"I was indeed very pleased to receive your letter of the 8th ultimo, with your good wishes. I feel honored at your invitation to represent South Africa at the Quebec celebrations and I assure you that it would have afforded me the greatest pleasure if I could have been present there, but I am sorry to say that it is impossible for me to go away now, I am

After the giving of self government so generously,

leaving to-morrow for Cape Town in connection with the Inter-Colonial conference to be held there and I will probably have to remain there for some time.

"You will have heard how that at the conference held in Pretoria a few weeks ago a resolution in favor of the closer union of the British South African colonies was passed—this is only the first step and many great difficulties will have to be overcome before we attain that ideal—You see therefore that very important matters require my presence in South Africa now, and besides on the 15th of next month our Parliament will be opened and I could not possibly leave the Transvaal during the session.

"After consultation with the other Prime Ministers, we agreed that South Africa could not be more suitably represented than by the Chief Justice of the Cape Colony—Sir Henry de Villiers—South Africa's most prominent jurisconsult and a man of whom every true South African is proud. He does not represent any political party and, what we considered especially appropriate, he is of French descent.

"It is a great pleasure to me to see that you are following events in South Africa with interest. It is our intention to follow in the footsteps of Canada as soon as possible.

"Please convey my kindest regards to Lady Laurier.

"Believe me, yours very sincerely,

LOUIS BOTHA."

It is remembered that the man who wrote this letter was from the Dutch point of view the hero of the war, as we have here with us to-night General Lord Roberts, who was the real hero of the war from British standpoint. (Cheers.) Only five years after the war, that gentleman has become a most loyal British subject. (Cheers.) The war was only five years old when the British nation took the somewhat doubtful alternative of granting South Africa self-government. I am tempted to use an expression which has been used elsewhere in a far different sense, and to say that England staggered the world by her magnanimity. (Cheers.) But I believe the event has proved the wisdom of the course adopted. If the state of affairs now existing is continued, if this experiment proves successful, as there is every reason to believe it will, England will have added another master stroke to the successes of that policy in which she stands unique. There are only two ways of governing a people, one by stamping out all liberties under foot, and the other to gain the confidence of the people by trusting them, and appealing to their sense of justice and liberty, the policy of conciliation. The latter has been England's policy. She employed it in New Zealand with marked success, as well as in Canada and Australia and the results have been such a. to justify those who have builded the highest expectations on the future of South Africa.

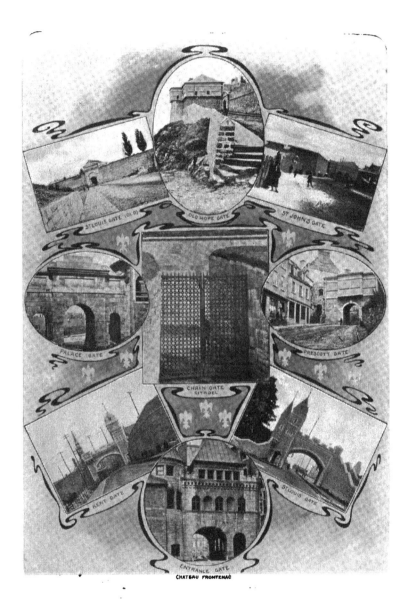

QUEBEC'S OLD AND MODERN GATES

WOLFE'S HOUSE
At Montmorency

we find the people who were at war with England a few years ago preparing to establish a confederation. "It is our intention to follow in the footsteps of Canada," declared General Botha. This means that in South Africa, as in Canada, we shall find two nations working together for the common weal, in building up a great free country under the British flag, in peace, liberty and good will.

I will therefore ask you to stand and drink to the self-governing dominions, to Newfoundland, Australia, and New Zealand, and last, but not least, and perhaps in some respects the foremost in our thoughts, South Africa.

* * *

Hon. Mr. Pitts' Reply

The Hon. J. Stewart Pitts, G.C.M.G., who bore to Quebec the greetings of Newfoundland—England's oldest colony represented at the festive board—was the first to reply to the Premier's toast, saying :—

"As the representative of the most ancient colony of the Empire, I extend to you on its behalf hearty congratulations and warmest greetings on this auspicious occasion.

The event that has brought us together is one of historical interest. If it were not so we would not observe representatives from all parts of the British Empire gathered together to unite with their Canadian brethren in this magnificent ceremonial. We should not have the high distinction of meeting here the special representative of Our Gracious Sovereign, the King—His Royal Highness, the Prince of Wales.

We commemorate to-day the 300th anniversary of the founding of this city, whose history renders her one of the most famous cities of the world. We also commemorate the battle of the Plains of Abraham, because it opened the way for the union of French and British races in the Northern Hemisphere, which has led to the present magnificence of this great Dominion

and the prospect before it so eloquently expressed by its Prime Minister, "that the 20th century will be Canada's century."

The foundation of our colonial empire was first laid in the island I have the honour to represent on this occasion, but that foundation was made secure by one of the events that we to-day commemorate.

We know of the struggle that took place on yonder heights and the gallant deeds of those who fell in the fray.

Thanks to His Excellency, Lord Grey, the battleground shall henceforth remain a national memorial to those illustrious warriors, Montcalm and Wolfe.

Very kindly reference has been made to the land I represent. The beloved land of my birth, compared with your's, is, generally speaking, not fertile. The soil does not yield those rich harvests which clothe your more fertile soil with beauty, but I may venture to assure you on behalf of my countrymen at home that we behold not with envy but with pride, your national advantages and wonderful progress. We look across a gulf which the Creator has placed between us, which has been bridged by commercial enterprise, but which has not yet been spanned by political diplomacy. At present we are content to admire at this distance, to profit by your magnificent example, and to work out our own salvation under the aegis of the British Constitution, as an independent appenage of the Empire.

* * *

Earl Dudley's Address

Responding for the Commonwealth, the Earl of Dudley, Governor-General of Australia said :—

May it please Your Royal Highness, Your Excellency, my Lords and Gentlemen.—

I beg to tender to you my most grateful thanks for so cordially drinking the toast, and I appreciate very fully the kind and grateful terms in which Sir Wilfrid

CITADEL HILL
Leading from St.
Louis St. to Citadel.

Laurier has referred to Australia. It is much to be regretted that the distinguished Premier of the Commonwealth to whom you extended so cordial an invitation was not able to avail himself of your hospitality. The wonderful experience through which we are passing would have provided a great theme for his eloquent tongue, and I venture to say that brilliant and distinguished as is the great company assembled at present at Quebec, it would have derived but added lustre from Mr. Deakin's presence. To me, however, has fallen the great pleasure and privilege of representing Australia on this occasion, and it is an occasion which I certainly shall never forget, for these celebrations will leave, I think, a deep and lasting impression upon the minds of all who have attended them. No one, I imagine, could witness the

wonder in our hearts, whether we, of our day, are still made of the same tough fibre and whether we, too, are capable of performing deeds as great as those which they accomplished. God grant that it is so. But in any case the contemplation of their lives and achievements such as this celebration affords cannot but have most stimulating and inspiring effect upon our actions. But, Your Royal Highness, these are not the only considerations which are brought home to us at this time. As we watch the scenes which reproduce so graphically the incidents of the birth of a nation, are not our thoughts irresistibly turned to the position which that nation occupies to-day? Can w: contemplate these natal celebrations without allowing our minds to dwell upon the wonderful progress and development that Canada has experienced in the

LAKE ST. JOSEPH COURSE
Where the Sailors' Pic-Nic was held.

vivid pageantry, the imposing ceremonies which are daily enacted before our eyes, without experiencing the feeling of boundless admiration for the man and for the deeds which these celebrations recall. No one as H.R.H. has so truly said, could watch the great warships lying at anchor beneath Quebec, or still less have a passage in one of them, without comparing the conditions of navigation to-day with those which existed in the time Champlain and Cartier. When one pictures to one's self the difficulty with which these men were confronted, when one thinks of their indomitable courage, their skilful seamanship, and their unflinching determination, one is filled, I think, with a great sense of humbleness. We bow to the memory of these mighty men with a feeling of anxious

three hundred years that have elapsed since her birth? Aye, and more than that. Is it not an imposing spectacle to see the great assemblage composed of men of different races and different religious beliefs graced by the presence of the heir to the throne, united by a common love of their native land, and animated by a common feeling of loyalty and devotion to their Sovereign.

Your Royal Highness amidst strife and suffering and at the cost of much valuable life, the national edifice has been constructed but these celebrations bring home to us a realization of the fact that to-day old differences are forgotten in the determination of a united people to march forward in undivided strength to the great destiny which awaits them.

My Lords and Gentlemen, it was my privilege, a few weeks ago, to be present at the opening by His Royal Highness of the Franco-British exhibition. As one walked from one part of the grounds to another one could not fail to be immensely impressed by the beautiful and substantial-looking building, by the lakes and canals, by towers and turrets, and by the many other evidences of what seemed a solid and permanent work.

But on closer examination one found that all these things were of the lightest and flimsiest description. That which seemed to be stone was, as a matter of fact, lath and plaster capable of being removed in a few days without leaving a trace behind. The national edifice of Canada, however, is not, thank heaven, of such a description. Canada stands to the world as a great Franco-British exposition, but its foundations are deep and its walls are strong. By fire have its girders been tempered. By liberty, as Sir Wilfrid Laurier has said, have its rivets been forged. It stands, as we see it, not for to-day or to-morrow, but for all time a glorious and enduring monument to the genius of two great races and to the beneficial effect of self-governing institutions."

The Earl of Ranfurly who represented New Zealand, said :—

Earl of Ranfurly's Address

Your Royal Highness, Your Excellency, my Lords and Gentlemen :—

In the first place let me thank Sir Wilfrid Laurier for the kindly manner in which he spoke of Mr. Seddon. Mr. Seddon was the Premier of New Zealand during the seven years during which I had the honor to represent my sovereign, and he was one of the greatest Loyalists, I might say Imperialists, in the British Empire. It is queer that here you are celebrating the Tercentenary of the foundation of the country, while I had the privilege of being present at the fiftieth celebration of the raising of the British flag in the southern colony, New Zealand. Mr. Seddon had been in Parliament for forty years of that period. When anyone asked him about New Zealand he was wont to answer "It is God's country." After an experience of seven years in that country I do not know that I would care to say that he was far wrong. New Zealand's message, which it is my duty to deliver to you to-night, takes that practical form for which the Dominion and its people are noted. There is no portion of His Majesty's dominions where his subjects take a greater interest in the history and welfare of the Empire :—

"To duty firm, to conscience true,
  However tired and pressed;
In God's clear sight high work we do,
  If we but do our best."

She was thus ready to give liberally of her sons when their active services were needed. In an equally practical manner, when famine and fire caused disaster, she sent large contributions in the first case to India and in the second case to Ottawa. Now to-day, as their representative, I have the great honor of handing to His Excellency the Governor-General, a cheque for £1,000 as a small contribution, showing practically the sympathy of the people of New Zealand in this great movement of His Excellency the Governor-General for acquiring the battle-grounds of Quebec and thus honoring heroes whose names must ever remain green.

New Zealand desires me, in handing you this cheque, Sir, to convey its heartiest congratulations on the past and its best good wishes for the future of the Dominion of Canada.

The next speaker, Sir H. de Villiers, Chief Justice of Cape Colony who represented the South African Colonies spoke in a very interesting manner on confederation in South Africa, saying :—

Sir H. de Villier's Speech

Your Royal Highness, My Lords and Gentlemen :—

I greatly regret that the Prime Ministers of the self-governing Colonies of South Africa are not personally present to respond to the toast which has been so eloquently proposed by Sir Wilfrid Laurier. I know that nothing would have pleased them more than to come in response to the invitation addressed to them, but as all the South African parliaments are now in session, this was impossible. More especially would it have been a pleasure to General Botha, the Premier of the youngest self-governing colony, to renew the acquaintance, or rather the friendship, which he struck up with your Premier, Sir Wilfrid Laurier, during the recent Colonial Conference in London.

While regretting the absence of those who could so appropriately have responded to the toast of South Africa, I highly appreciate the distinguished honor which the different South African Governments have done me, on the first occasion on which they had to come to a joint decision, in asking me to represent them on this great occasion, and the equally distinguished honor of being asked to reply to this toast on behalf of South Africa. Unfortunately I cannot speak of or for a constitutionally united South Africa. We have four separate self-governing colonies, each independent of the other; the only bond of union being that they all now form part of the British Empire, and the problem now before us is how to unite upon terms that shall be fair and fit to each colony and to every section of its population. The first and most important step has been taken in the appointment by the different parliaments of delegates to a convention which is to meet in Natal in October next. It is a good omen for the success of the convention and for the spirit in which the discussion will be carried on that the selection of delegates has not been made upon party lines, but that every shade of political opinion will be represented. Men of English and Dutch descent, the ex-President of the Orange Free State, Generals like Botha and Smuts, who took an equally gallant part in the war with the Boers and even men who had been sentenced to death for high treason, but reprieved under the South African republic, will all peacefully meet together, and will, I trust, in a fair and impartial spirit discuss the terms of the South African Union. They will have before them the great example of Canada, which has flourished by the happy union of the provinces in a manner exceeding

have adhered to the old faith, but the same French blood flows through our veins. As to the Dutch of South Africa, their conduct during the recent war shows that they have not degenerated through being transplanted from the damp Netherlands to the sunny climes of South Africa. With the blend of three such races as Anglo-Saxon, French and Dutch there is no need to despair of the future of South Africa. Difficulties such as the native question, which you have been free from, will have to be met, but we hope to surmount those difficulties just as you have surmounted your's.

The greatness of a task must always be in proportion to the difficulties to be overcome and we hope

THE RETURN TRIP

From St. Joachim in automobile

the wildest dreams of the fathers of our confederation. They will profit by your experience, but they will of course have to suit their constitution to the needs of their own country.

We have not your rivers and lakes, but we have European races as virile as your's, and after all, the greatness of a country depends as much upon the character of its people as upon its physical features. A large proportion of our people is descended from French Huguenots and they have retained the faith of their forefathers just as your French-Canadians

that the practical statesmanship and spirit of conciliation which animated your statesmen, will also animate our's. It must ever be a satisfaction to Canada that she has been privileged to show the way to the constitutional development of the British colonies. She was the first to obtain responsible government and she was followed by Australia and New Zealand, and afterwards by the South African colonies. In Confederation also she has shown the way and has been followed by Australia; but South Africa, although fairly on the way to it, has not yet reached this stage of development. It should not be forgotten that the settlement of the Cape by European peoples began nearly 50 years after the settlement of the French in Canada under the auspices of your great Champlain. Just as he, with the keen eye of a great pioneer, fixed upon this grand site as the cradle of the nation still to be born, so did the Dutch Van Rubeik fix upon the finest strategic site in the world as the spot from which civilization was to be spread northwards among the barbaric tribes of South Africa.

We have not a mighty St. Lawrence flowing at our feet, but we have a bay of unrivalled beauty, guarded, as it were, by the grand old Table Mountain, under whose shadow so many historic scenes have been enacted. Nearly three hundred years ago the possession of that peninsula was considered to be the key to India, and I feel sure that His Royal Highness who has twice honored South Africa with his visits, will bear me out that, notwithstanding the making of the Suez Canal the Cape is still one of the most important naval posts of the British Empire. It is a pleasant dream to think that 50 years hence our children, having learned or read of the Quebec celebration of 1908, may be fired by the ambition again to follow in your footsteps by celebrating the Tercentenary of Van Rubeik's arrival and by inviting representatives from Canada, and other parts of the Empire to take part in their rejoicings. It is pleasant to think that by that time there will be a great and growing dominion of South Africa in close communion with other parts of the Empire, and having a Governor-General at its head. Most pleasant of all it is to hope that he may be able to take the leading and important part in the celebrations which has been taken by your present Governor-General, and that he may conduct all the proceedings with the grace, the tact and urbanity which, by the admission of all, have distinguished His Excellency Earl Grey. And should the dream ever become a reality then there is one prediction I may safely make, and it is this: that however great and numerous the South African people may then have become, they will never be able to eclipse the Canadians of the present day in the kindness which they have shown towards their visitors from all parts of the world, or in the magnificence and complete success of their celebration.

Your Royal Highness, My Lords and gentlemen, South Africa has of recent years passed through a terrible ordeal, but she is slowly recovering from the effects of the ruinous war. Only those who lived there and had friends and relatives fighting on both sides, can realize what that war meant to us. It was undertaken for the purpose of obtaining equal rights for all, but for some time after peace was established it looked as if political rights would be withheld for an indefinite time from the new subjects of the King. At

length, however, different counsels prevailed. A policy of trust in the people was adopted with the usual result that sullen and discontented people were transformed as if by magic into loyal and law abiding subjects. From that quarter no danger need be apprehended for the future; on the contrary, if ever any foreign power should attempt to wrest South Africa from the British Empire you may be quite sure that history will repeat itself, and just as the French-Canadians were foremost in defending their country against attacks from without, so the Dutch inhabitants will fight shoulder to shoulder with their Anglo-Saxon fellow subjects for their King and country.

On behalf of South Africa, I thank you, Sir Wilfrid Laurier, for the terms in which you have proposed the toast, and I thank you all for the manner in which you received it.

❖ ❖ ❖

Sir Lomer Gouin, Premier of the Province of Quebec proposed the health of the visiting Premiers of the other provinces in the following speech:—

Premier Gouin's Address

Your Royal Highness, Your Excellency, my Lords and Gentlemen:—

I rise to offer you a toast naturally suggested by the one which you have just so warmly honored at the request of Sir Wilfrid Laurier. With that rare eloquence, of which he alone is the master, that distinguished statesman, who so ably presides over the destinies of this great Dominion, has given you the toast of the "Self-Governing Colonies." Now, it is with the utmost pleasure that I propose to you that of the men who, in the different provinces which make up the present Dominion, are so powerfully seconding him in the work of national development. I refer to the provincial Prime Ministers, some of whom have come from long distances to join with us in the present celebration and to add to its splendor and significance. I deem myself specially privileged as

LE ROYAL ROUSILLON
Of Montcalm's Army.

the representative of this old province of Quebec in extending to them the most cordial welcome to its capital, the birthplace of that Canada which now stretches from the Atlantic to the Pacific, to this grand old city founded by the illustrious Champlain, whose memory to-day we specially reverence. It is my agreeable duty also to thank them as publicly as possible for the generous, the handsome contributions which through their instrumentality their several provinces have made towards enhancing the eclat of the grand spectacle that Quebec naturally presents. That spectacle is so unique as to attract the attention and command the admiration of the whole civilized world. It is one which has united the two great races composing the people of Canada, their mother countries of France and Great Britain and their friends of the great Republic adjoining, in one of the most remarkable entente cordiales to do honor to the heroic past. In fine, it is one which has won for us the sympathy of that beloved sovereign, who has sent us his son and heir in the person of His Royal Highness, the Prince of Wales to grace it with his presence and to place upon it the stamp of his high approval.

And, in taking occasion to thank the Prime Ministers of the different provinces, let me express further the legitimate pride we feel at the prosperity of these provinces, their ever increasing greatness and wealth, and their powerful aid to the upbuilding of the Canadian nation. They are the elements which make for Canada's greatness and assure its future, and in the persons of their Prime Ministers I greet them as worthy partners of national development, and as fellow laborers in the great work of national development. I thank them not only for their active sympathy with Quebec in the present instance, but for the splendid effect which that sympathy, both moral and material, will further have in consolidating the Dominion. It has deeply touched the hearts of the people of my race, who constitute so considerable an element of its population. It has demonstrated that difference of origin makes no difference in this country, that the heroes of the Canadian past are regarded as common property, that all are united in paying respectful homage to their memory to whatever race they belong, and in preserving those historic monuments and spots which should be so sacred to us all. In fact, there is nothing that more strikingly shows how far the national idea has developed and progressed in the Dominion than the present union of hearts and hands to forget the conflicts of the past and to remember only the things which do honor to both races and which are worthy of perpetual veneration.

And just here let me respectfully call the attention of Your Royal Highness and generally of this distinguished gathering to what was and is beyond question the most powerful of all the factors that have led up to this greater union of sympathies and feelings in Canada and that are making for the present and future grandeur of the Dominion. Among the divisions of Greater Britain beyond the seas, there is none which rightfully takes higher rank than the Dominion of Canada. Now, in considering the various causes and elements which have contributed to its wonderful development and expansion, the one which strikes the beholder most is the marvellously beneficial results which have flowed from Confederation. The adoption of the Federal system which preserved the autonomy of the provinces and increased their liberty and power of action, was the means of snatching them from their former condition of isolation and weakness and making them contended, self-reliant, strong and prosperous, as well as a shining example of the advantages of union for the promotion of mutual development and the upbuilding of a common nationality. We rejoice to see

THE CITY HALL OF QUEBEC
During the Celebration.

that our fellow-subjects of the Great Australian colonies have followed in the path in which Canada has led the way and we wish their Commonwealth the same success as we do also to our brothers of South Africa in the new political departure which they are apparently about to make.

Need I say how delighted we all are to welcome Your Royal Highness once more in our midst and especially on a memorable occasion like the present. The agreeable impression left here by your former visits has ever kept alive among us the desire for their renewals and for opportunity to assure you of our unalterable attachment to the crown of which you are the exalted representative.

I would solicit one favor at your hands. That is that when you return to England you will tell them that this great country is more prosperous and loyally devoted than ever to the Crown and person of its sovereign as well as to those institutions with which it is blessed, and that you left us in an all pervading atmosphere of peace, contentment and rejoicing. I specially couple with this toast the name of my esteemed friend, Sir James Whitney, Premier of Ontario, because at his patriotic suggestion that province was the first to set the example of a generous contribution to the creation of an everlasting monument which will knit closer together the different elements of the present generation and transmit to posterity the memory of the valor of their common ancestors.

In reply, Sir James Whitney, Premier of Ontario, said :—

Premier Whitney's Address

I esteem it an honor indeed to be asked to respond to the toast proposed in such happy and eloquent terms by my friend and confrere, Sir Lomer Gouin. The people of the provinces other than Quebec join heartily in the celebration of the great and momentous event of three hundred years ago. They desire to do so because they realize that they are joint beneficiaries in the great heritage of civil and religious liberty and self government which has come to them as one of the results of these events.

One and forty years ago the great federal experiment known as the creation of the Dominion of Canada took form and shape. The Provinces which were then united were widely separated, their people were practically strangers to each other and were of different races and religious beliefs. Under these circumstances he who anticipated disaster could hardly

be described as unreasonable, but what has been the result? In my opinion the dispassionate observer must testify that having regard to the conditions I have named, the success which has attended the Canadian union has been not only remarkable, but indeed almost phenomenal. True, a little friction has occasionally occurred, but merely as ripples upon the silent summer sea of our political contentment and progress, and it would have been strange indeed if the result of such a governmental experiment had under the circumstances been simply stagnation. This friction, which hardly deserves mention, and the difficulties which do exist are of no consequence, and prove nothing except perhaps :

We are separate as the billows are separate, yet one as the sea.

We, sir, of the other Provinces respect and love our fellow subjects of Quebec for their intrinsic worth and for their attitude and aid in times of stress and peril. We cannot forget the answer sent when they were urged to join hands with a foreign power against the British Empire.

We cannot forget Chateauguay, where the gallant de Salaberry performed the most scientific military feat of the war of 1812.

Sir, within a mile of my birthplace, on the historic field of Chrysler's Farm, was done what Sir Nigel Loring would term a "comfortable feat of arms." And we cannot forget that there and then a Company of French-Canadian voltigeurs reddened the soil of Upper Canada with their blood in defence of British institutions and British connection.

Nor can we forget the memorable words of Sir Etienne Tache, when he declared that "the last shot fired in Canada in defence of British connection will be fired by a French-Canadian."

Sir, we could not forget these things if we would, and on behalf of the other Provinces I make bold to say also that we would not forget them if we could. We revere the memories of the great men of Quebec, of Tache and Lafontaine, of Morin and Cartier, Chapleau and Dorion, among the dead, and offer our tribute of respect and honor to Laurier among the living. We stand side by side with our friends from Quebec with reference to this great celebration, and I am proud indeed to be in a position to say that the appropriation made by Ontario to the scheme of nationalization of the battlefields was the spontaneous act of both parties in our Legislature, and has received only favorable criticism.

In this city of memories, this landing place of the great pioneers of exploration and discovery, this land of Jacques Cartier, Champlain and LaSalle—in this city, whence the mellowing and ennobling influences of Christianity were spread abroad by the illustrious men who, bearing aloft the banner of the cross, went forth to certain suffering, disaster and death — in this city of memories, I am glad and proud to say to the illustrious heir to the throne, the son of the great peacemaker of the twentieth century, and indeed of all centuries—that here, on this continent, we, the men of French and English nationalities, the people of this great auxiliary kingdom within the Empire, are affording an object lesson of the benefits of free, representative government under the British system; that we stand for the continuity of the Empire and all that that implies, and that we hope to so work out the problems which will confront us from time to time that those who come after us will have no reason to feel ashamed of our record.

I congratulate heartily all concerned on the great success which has attended these functions, and desire to express what I am sure is the general appreciation of his Excellency the Governor-General, who has now forged another link in the golden chain of our love and admiration which binds us to him.

One word now of a personal nature. I desire in this presence to express my very hearty appreciation of the more than generous hospitality extended to my family and myself by the government of the Province of Quebec, and which my colleagues and myself hope to return some day. I have heard, sir, that a great French-Canadian statesman, now deceased, described himself to the late Queen Victoria, as an English-speaking Frenchman, and now as I breathe this atmosphere of kindly hospitality, charged and saturated as it is with the memories and traditions of long ago, "Je suis Canadien-Francais parlant Anglais."

His Royal Highness the Prince of Wales then arose, and amid the acclamations of all, presented in these words the toast to Earl Grey, the Chairman :—

Prince's Toast to Governor-General

If it were possible to propose the toast with which I am now entrusted to the whole population of the Dominion, it would, I am sure, be certain of a welcome no less enthusiastic, no less affectionate, than will be accorded to it by this distinguished company,

LORD STRATHCONA AND HIS GRANDDAUGHTER
Miss Howard at the Military Review.

for it is 'the health of my noble friend, the Governor-General.' We thank him heartily for his splendid hospitality of this evening. But a deeper feeling of gratitude goes out from our hearts to him as the presiding genius over the memorable and magnificent events of this week.

These gifts, so happily combined in Lord Grey, of sympathy, tact, imagination, energy, power of organization, have enabled him to initiate and carry to a successful issue the celebrations to which we all rejoice to be associated. We heartily congratulate him upon this happy outcome of all his labors and anxieties. I know you will also join with me in offering our congratulations to His Excellency upon the honors conferred upon him by the King in creating him a member of His Majesty's Privy Council, and in the bestowal upon him of the highest class of the Order which is in the personal gift of the Sovereign.

May he long be preserved to enjoy those honors, to continue his useful life in the service of his country, and to infuse among his fellow men the sympathy and enthusiasm of his large-hearted nature.

His Excellency's Reply

In a touching way, the Governor-General answered:

Your Royal Highness,
My Lords and Gentlemen:—

To say that I am touched to the depth of my heart by the more than kind expressions which Your Royal Highness has used in proposing this toast, would be only a feeble expression of my feelings at this moment. If I have, through the promotion of the Tercentenary earned the approval of His Royal Highness, and through him, of my Sovereign, I have my reward. If, as His Royal Highness seems to suggest I have earned the approval of the people of Canada, I again have my reward, and if I am correct in my belief, that the influences which will radiate from this Tercentenary week will tend to the unification of the Empire and to the strength and glory of the Crown, I shall have an abiding and abundant cause for thankfulness that I have had the privileged opportunity of helping this Tercentenary to be a success. I wish, however, to inform His Royal Highness, who has credited me with far too much merit, that the success of this celebration is due to the unstinted, ungrudging and splendid assistance from everyone, both government and individuals, who have vied with each other in their endeavors to secure the success of the Tercentenary Celebration.

"I cannot sit down without thanking the Government of New Zealand, through my friend Lord Ranfurly, for their m st generous contribution. New Zealand's population is not one-half that of Ontario, and that New Zealand, whose gift I had not known of until Lord Ranfurly announced it, has contributed so generously, shows the interest which the people of that country take in the work of securing the battlefields of Quebec as Imperial and sacred ground. I shall be grateful if Lord Ranfurly will convey to New Zealand our sincere thanks. The celebration in which we are partaking in Canada is not only a national but an Imperial affair. I have no doubt that when the other countries hear of what has been done by New Zealand, there will be a scramble to emulate the good example thus given."

* * *

The Prince of Wales then handed to His Excellency a cheque for £10,000, England's contribution to the battlefields fund. After Earl Grey had thanked His Royal Highness for this additional proof of his interest in the battlefields project, the gathering broke up, and the dinner, which was perhaps the most notable event of the Tercentenary celebrations came to an end.

The guests present at the dinner were:—

Vice-Admiral Sir A. Curzon-Howe, Rear Admiral Sir John Jellicoe, Commodore King Hall, the Earl of Dudley, the Earl of Ranfurly, the Right Hon. Sir Henry de Villiers, Hon. James Pitts, Field Marshal Earl Roberts, their Honors Sir Mortimer Clarke, Sir Louis Jette, Mr. D. C. Fraser, Mr. L. J. Tweedie, Sir Daniel McMillan, Mr. Jas. Dunsmuir, Mr. D. A. Mackinnon, Mr. A. E. Forget, Mr. G. H. Bulyea, the Right Honorables Sir Wilfrid Laurier, Sir Richard Cartwright, the Honorables R. W. Scott, Sir Frederick Borden, Sydney Fisher, W. S. Fielding, W. Patterson, W. Templeman, L. P. Brodeur, Frank Oliver, A. B. Aylesworth, Rodolphe Lemieux, Wm. Pugsley, G. P. Graham, R. Dandurand, the Right Hon. Sir Charles Fitzpatrick, Chief Justice Sir Henri Taschereau, Chief Justice Sir Melbourne Tait, Chief Justice Sir Francois Langelier, the Right Honorable Sir Charles Tupper, Right Honorable Sir Mackenzie Bowell, Lord Strathcona, the Hon. G. E. Foster, the Solicitor-General, Rear-Admiral Kingsmill, Major-General Lake, Brig.-Generals Otter, Buchan, Macdonald, Cotton, Major-General J. F. Wilson, the Hon. J. A. Lougheed, Hon. R. F. Sutherland, Mr. R. L. Borden, Mr. Bergeron, Sir James Whitney, Sir Lomer Gouin, the Hons. S. H. Murray, J. D. Hazen, R. P. Roblin, R. McBride, F. Hassard, Walter Scott, A. Rutherford, Sir J. G. Garneau, Sir Geo. Drummond, Adelard Turgeon, Lt.-Col. J. S. Hendrie, L. A. Taschereau, Lt.-Col. Geo. T. Denison, Mr. Byron E. Walker, Sir Thos. Shaughnessy, Sir Montagu Allan, Mr. Joseph Pope, Sir Wm. McDonald, Mr. C. M. Hayes, Mr. F. W. Morse, Mr. W. Mackenzie, Mr. D. Mann, Mr. E. S. Clouston, Col. James, Hon. S. N. Parent, Mgr. Mathieu, President Falconer, Mr. J. M. Courtney, Principal Peterson, Principal Gordon, Sir Sandford Fleming, Viscount Falmouth, Hon. Clifford Sifton, Sir Wm. Van Horne, Sir Charles Rivers-Wilson, Dr. Doughty, Mr. Chouinard, Mr. Wm. Macpherson, Mr. Price, Lt.-Col. Wood, Dr. Parkin, Mr. F. Lascelles, Mr. Marcil, Mr. MacKinder, Lt.-Col. Sherwood, Lt.-Col, Roy, Engineer Capt. Chase, Flag-Lt. Hardman Jones, Flag-Lt. Buxton, Mr. Julian Corbett, the Duke of Norfolk, Lort Lovatt, Lt.-General Sir R. Pole-Carew, Lord Bruce, Capt. Hon. H. Dawnay, Hon. Angus McDonnell, A.D.C. to G.O.C.

Open-Air Concert

Open air concerts in most of the public places of the city ended the day's events. The usual scene on the Terrace was presented. Its galaxy of costumed promenaders was not diminished, while the decorations seemed ever to become thicker and more resplendent. Thus, as on every other evening, the Tercentenary throngs walked up and down the promenade, admiring the scene, gazing at the ships and listening to the music until "Vive la Canadienne" and "God Save the King," turned their walk homeward—and the Terrace was once more dark and deserted.

Eighth Day, Sunday, July Twenty-Sixth

State Service at English Cathedral

SUNDAY was a day of thanksgiving. All the elements which had united in celebrating the three hundredth anniversary of Quebec observed the day as that set apart on which all should join in offering thanks for the events that helped to build up the city of Quebec and the Dominion. Each denomination followed its own services, but all pointed toward the one goal.

In the English Cathedral of the Holy Trinity which was built by a member of the Hanoverian line, a specially appointed State service was held at which were present His Royal Highness the Prince of Wales, His Excellency the Governor-General, Countess Grey, Lady Sybil Grey, Earl Roberts, Lady Pole-Carew and most of the other guests at the Citadel. The Prince of Wales was escorted to the Church by four of the Royal North-West Mounted Police, while in the Cathedral carriageway, a guard of honour was lined up.

The Royal party was met at the door by the surpliced choir, with the Lord Bishop, preceded by the crozier-bearer, and attended by a number of ecclesiastics. Preceded by these, the Royal party walked up the aisle while the hymn "All people that on earth do dwell" was sung. The Prince occupied the front pew on the right-hand side. On his right was the Governor-General while on the outside sat Countess Grey. Among those present were many military and naval officers clad in uniform, adding magnificence to the simple and dignified scene.

The usual service was held. Following the customary prayers, the Jubilate Deo, Psalm C., and the Laudate Dominum, Psalm cl., were sung. The lesson was King VIII 54-62. The Benedictus, St. Luke 1. 68 was sung as the canticle. The Apostle's Creed, the prayers and responses, followed by the collects came next. The choir well rendered 'Glory be to the Father" which was succeeded by prayers for the Royal family and the Governor-General. Before the sermon, the hymn "For all the Saints who from their labours rest" was sung with good effect, it being noticed that the Prince joined heartily in the singing.

The sermon which was delivered by the Right Rev. Andrew Hunter Dunn, D.D., Lord Bishop of Quebec, was remarkable for its simplicity and effectiveness. There was no striving after effect, no pretentious

attempt at oratory. It was a quiet, appropriate talk marked by simplicity and dignity.

The text was Joshua XXIV, 25-27—"And Joshua took a great stone and set it up there under an oak

THE ENGLISH CATHEDRAL
In which the special state service was celebrated.

that was by the Sanctuary of the Lord. And Joshua said unto all the people. Behold, this stone shall be a witness unto you." The history of the Ancient Regime and its meaning were briefly given. The battle which changed Canada's destiny was spoken of in its historical light. The wisdom of the conqueror in giving to his new subjects the right of freely exercising their religion and the use of their laws was emphasized, for from this sprang the goodwill existing between the two elements of the population and their espousal of a common cause.

"And as to the general spirit of our lives in this old city of Quebec," continued the preacher, "I would simply remind you of the fact that when the first English bishop, Dr. Jacob Mountain, after a voyage of thirteen weeks across the Atlantic, arrived in

I am thankful to say we have been living together ever since."

The French and English in Canada had once fought for mastery. It was now but right that these fields on which was freely spilled the blood of both, be set

WATCHING THE PRINCE OF WALES
Come out of the English Cathedral after the Special Service.

Quebec, the French Bishop of that day, Mgr. Briand, went down to the quay, and kissing him on both cheeks, said, 'It is high time, monsignor, that you came out to look after your people.' And it is in the same kindly spirit of charity, of Christian love, that

apart "to be the hallowed outward sign or sacrament of the fact that we are now glad to live together side by side in peace."

Just, therefore, as Joshua of old took a great stone and set it up there under an oak that was by the sanctuary of the Lord and said to all the people, 'Behold, this stone shall be a witness to us for all the days,'—out of this truly grand contribution of many nations so are we setting apart these battle-fields to the honor of the great generals engaged, and to the untold advantage of both the races concerned now, henceforth and forevermore.

And since it is only by the love and mercy of God that out of so much darkness and difficulty there has arisen all this courtesy and friendship and strength, let us to-day, as we praise the great God for his goodness, determine that we will henceforth show to our neighbors even greater courtesy and consideration

cessional hymn, "Lest We Forget." As a special act of thanksgiving, a solemn "Te Deum" was sung. The benediction and the singing of the national anthem, followed by the recessional hymn, "Now thank we all our God," ended the stately service.

Messe Solennelle on the Plains

Less stately though more imposing was the "Messe Solennelle" by the Roman Catholic portion of Quebec on the Plains of Abraham. Held at the same time as

PLAINS OF ABRAHAM AND WOLFE'S MONUMENT
Where the " Messe Solennelle " was celebrated.

than we ever yet have done, remembering that those who do this are the best friends to Canada, are the firmest supporters of the Empire, as well as the truest and highest soldiers and servants of him who while he is ever proving himself to be more and more the Lord of Heaven and Earth, hath especially revealed himself unto us all as our dear Lord and Saviour, Jesus Christ, the helper of the helpless, and the Prince of Peace.

The sermon, which throughout breathed a spirit of thankfulness and a plea for a closer union of Canada's two peoples was followed by Kipling's famous re-

was the Service in the English Cathedral, the object was a similar one—offering thanks for the common welfare of two peoples and for the events which brought about this state. The thanksgiving service held on the ground which but two days before was dedicated as a national park in commemoration of the battles fought thereon was a true indication of the friendly spirit existing between the two sections of the population.

The morning was a beautiful one. A strong sun overhead cast its brilliant rays upon the natural setting below. There was not the gentle influence that is lent

REPRESENTATIVES OF CHURCH AND STATE

His Excellency Mgr. Sbaretti, Papal Legate to Canada talking
with His Grace the Duke of Norfolk.

Mirepoix, Sir Wilfrid Laurier, Sir Charles Fitzpatrick, Sir Lomer Gouin, Hon. Adelard Turgeon and many other well-known members of the Roman faith. To the left of the altar stood a detachment of men dressed in the uniform of Montcalm's army; to the right, the De Salaberry guards; facing the altar were the Zouaves with their bugle band. The whole scene coupled with the solemn ritual of the Catholic service was imposing and admirable.

The appointed hour for the service had now arrived. The guard had formed in. The orchestra added charm to the scene by sending its strains over the field. All was expectancy. Suddenly the blare of trumpets was heard. The strains of the "War March of the Priests" from Mendelsohn's "Athalie" were pealing across the turf, while in stately procession came forward a number of ecclesiastical dignitaries clad in gorgeous robes used only on ceremonial occasions. In slow procession preceding them came acolytes in their white surplices in red and blue sashes, a priest bearing a cross of gold, and Canons in purple and crimson robes. The Heralds and men-at-arms came next, while leading up the van came Monseigneur Begin, Archbishop of Quebec bearing a huge golden crozier, and surrounded by his ecclesiastical officers, attendants bearing his train.

Taking his position on the highest step of the altar, the Archbishop gave his blessing to the assembled multitude which received it kneeling. From the right then came the song of several hundred choristers accompanied by the orchestra. The service proceeded in its customary way with the rhythmic movements of the priests, the soft music, the gentle chorus and the final act of Elevation of the Host.

The Gregorian Mass, ever a splendid and solemn spectacle, was on this occasion remarkable for its spiritual grandeur, and for the veneration which it inspired.

Thus, the eighth day of the celebrations was marked by devotional ceremonies. Little else of importance transpired during the day. Quietness pervaded everywhere despite the large number of people about. Quebec's way of observing Sunday was not altered except in the addition of more grandeur and solemnity.

by a deep nave, nor the pleasant dignity afforded by a softly illumined chancel. There were not the pale marbles that inspire respect, nor the wonderful pictures that teach of the past. There was not the lofty dome nor steeples towering as if about to topple over. There was but the bright sky overhead, the gliding river several hundred feet below, and the plain green sward under foot. Around stood the pageant grand stand, while facing it was built an altar beneath a crimson and gold canopy.

The stand was filled with more than ten thousand people among whom were the Duke of Norfolk, Lord Lovatt, Marquis de Montcalm, Marquis de Levis-

Ninth Day, Monday, July Twenty-Seventh

Prince of Wales at Chateau Bellevue

IS Royal Highness, the Prince of Wales had now been in Quebec for five days. Each was marked by official ceremonies. Hedged in by official duties he had not been able to act as he would nor to visit where he pleased. He would now cast off all pomp and official bearing and lay aside his royal state.

To spend a day in such a quiet manner, it was decided to visit the Chateau Bellevue at Petit Cap, thirty miles from Quebec. The edifice is the summer retreat of the priests and teachers of the Seminary of Quebec. Built on the property which was acquired by Bishop Laval more than two hundred years ago for the Seminary which he founded, the spot is historically interesting. It was here that the first Bishop of French Canada repaired for a rest. Ever since, the teachers of the school founded by him have done similarly. The Prince chose the same retreat eager for a rest.

The trip was an informal one and gave to his Royal Highness not only a rest but an opportunity to see at closer range the French Canadian subjects of Britain. He could now gaze at the habitant and his family. The pacific and contented nature of him whose loyalty to his Church and faithfullness to his King were his outstanding glory and whose bonhomie and hospitality have made him renowned were readily and easily beheld. In his true light, which but emphasizes his well-deserved prestige, the descendant of the old Norman, whose lineage to the French-Canadian is still strongly visible in the latter's love of oratory and law, was perhaps for the first time directly seen by a future King of Britain, whose subject he has now been for a century and a half.

The building visited was erected in 1779 by Mgr. Briand, then Bishop of Quebec. Little change has been made in it since. The old raftered ceilings, the heavy doors and bolts still mark the old solidity of the home of teachers and ecclesiastics. The chapel is in a state of complete preservation. Nothing has been changed and where a century and a quarter ago prayed the teachers of French-Canadian youth, rest was sought at one time by Canada's first Bishop, since by his successors, and now by the Prince of Wales.

The Prince, who reached the spot in a special car, was accompanied by their Excellencies Earl and Countess Grey, the Duke of Norfolk, Lord Strathcona, Lord Dudley, Sir Wilfrid Laurier, Hon. Rodolphe Lemieux, Lord Annaly, Sir Thomas Shaughnessy, Sir Charles Fitzpatrick, Sir Lomer Gouin, Sir John Hanbury-Williams, Lord Lascelles, Lord Bruce, Lord Lovat, Sir George Garneau, Mr. Joseph Pope, and Mr. E. B. Shaughnessy, Lady Hanbury-Williams, Hon. Mary Parker, Miss Gladys Hanbury-Williams, Miss Adine D. Taschereau, Miss Corinne Fitzpatrick and Miss Kathleen Sladen.

At the Chateau he was welcomed by Mgr. Sbaretti, Papal legate, Mgr. Begin, Archbishop of Quebec, Mgr. Laflamme, Mgr. Mathieu of Laval University and by other eminent Roman Catholic ecclesiastics. After the presentation of a number of priests to the

MGR. DE LAVAL
First Bishop and Founder
of the Quebec Seminary.

Prince, an informal luncheon was served under the trees marked by the simplicity and lack of ceremony which had been especially desired. Yet French-Canadian hospitality was not lacking and a pleasant afternoon was passed.

After luncheon several hours were passed in leisurely strolling about the grounds of the property and inspecting the well-kept farms whose caretakers freely conversed with the Prince in going through the old Chateau in company with its priests admiring antiquities and in talking with many of the peasants who came to catch a glimpse of the royal visitor.

The return trip was made in automobiles. The route was decorated by the rural inhabitants who flocked to the public roads to see and cheer for the Prince. Work and cares were put aside. The best was donned. The snug cottages with long white roofs were bedecked with colours. Stops were made at several places where the Prince freely conversed with the habitants.

At Ste. Anne de Beaupre, a halt was ordered by the Prince who would see the famous shrine. The church and chapels were visited; the piles of crutches intently gazed upon and everything admired. Four parishes were traversed on the way. At each a stop was made in order that the Prince might talk to the cure, and to its principle figures. At one, an old woman who had passed the century mark was presented to the Prince. All along the thirty miles of road, cheers were lustily given for the Prince, who returned to the city in time to witness the naval regatta on the river.

✷ ✷ ✷

Fleet Holds Regatta

In the afternoon, the Tercentenary fleet held its regatta.

The day was not a pleasant one. Clouds concealed the bright sky above, although the rain held off until near the finish. It was windy. The water was not calm, but was disturbed by a sharp breeze which piled wave on wave. The spectators were driven away from the points of vantage by the gusty wind and foreboding sky.

Competition was keen. Every ship sent forth launches, rowboats, gigs, pinnaces and vessels of every description. There were races for all. None would lie quiet, but skimming over the waters rushed and dashed here and there, now urging on a fellow racer, now offering advice, and now themselves pursuing the climbing waves in their endeavour to first reach the finish boat—a huge and plain sand scow. Near by lay the Don de Dieu—Champlain's vessel—adrift as it were in an age not her own.

The struggles were between boats of the same fleets, and between those of the three assembled. An international race in which were represented England, France and the United States furnished much rivalry and excitement. The race was a hard one and resulted in a British victory. The three mile race meant severe rowing against the wind and was also won by the British crew. The men of H.M.S. Russel were awarded the victory of the pinnace race. Other races of a different type took place, all attended with the same keenness that had marked the others.

✷ ✷ ✷

Reception by French Admiral

During the afternoon a reception and dance were given on board the Leon Gambetta by Vice-Admiral Jaureguiberry and his officers. Fifteen hundred invitations had been issued. The scene was one of pleasant animation. Boats were continually arriving by the French flagship depositing their load of guests, among whom were Their Excellencies Earl and Lady Grey, Lady Laurier, Vice-President Fairbanks, Count Dudley, Sir H. de Villiers, Marquis de Levis, Marquis de Levis-Mirepoix, Comte de Montcalm, the Admirals of the United States and British fleets and numerous others.

The decks which served as dancing-floors were protected from the wind and were gaily decorated. During the afternoon the orchestra played at various points while those on board danced until the sun's rays were gradually being dimmed by the sombre hues of advancing night.

✷ ✷ ✷

Reception to Levis' Descendants

An event of historical significance occurred at Levis opposite Quebec during the afternoon, which had a direct bearing on the Quebec celebrations. A reception was being given by the town facing Quebec to the descendant of the famous French general from whom Levis derived its name. With the Marquis de Levis, Marquis de Levis-Mirepoix and Comte de Montcalm were officially received by the Levisites in the town-hall.

Mayor Bernier, of Levis, read an address to the descendants of the celebrated soldiers in which many historical allusions were made relating to the family of the Marquis de Levis who thirteen years earlier had been made a citizen of the town. Replies by the Marquis de Levis and the Marquis de Levis-Mirepoix ended the reception at which many were present.

A STRIKING WATER SCENE IN THE PAGEANT:

The Arrival of Champlain. Drawn by F. De Haenen, from Sketches by
the London Graphic's Special Artist Correspondent, Frank Craig.

Earl Grey's Dinner

In the evening was held the last dinner at the Citadel given by His Excellency the Govenor-General at which His Royal Highness the Prince of Wales was present. Those invited were :—

H.R.H. the Prince of Wales, H.E. the Governor-General, Earl of Dudley, Earl of Ranfurly, Sir Henry de Villiers, Sir James Pitts, His Honour Sir Louis Jette, His Honour D. C. Fraser, His Honour Mr. Bulyea, His Honour Mr. J. Dunsmuir, His Honour Mr. Mackinnon, Field Marshal Earl Roberts, V.C. ; Rt. Hon. Sir Wilfrid Laurier, Duke of Norfolk, Hon. R. W. Scott, Hon. W. S. Fielding, Hon. R. Lemieux, Hon. F. Oliver, Hon. L. P. Brodeur, Hon. G. P.

Sir William Van Horne, Mr. Joseph. Pope, Mr. Byron Walker, Lt.-Col. James, Lt.-Col. A. Denison, Lt.-Col. Wood, Lt.-Col. Roy, Capt. Boothby, Capt. Godfrey-Faussett, Mgr. Mathieu, Col. Sir J. Hanbury-Williams, Hon. S. N. Parent, Engineer Capt. Chase, Mr. W. Mackenzie, Mr. C. M. Hays, Mr. W. M. Macpherson, Mr. D. Mann, Dr. Parkin, Lord Bruce, Mr. Julian Corbett, Mr. Mackinder, Mr. W. Price, Dr. Doughty, Lt.-Col. Sherwood, Mr. J. M. Courtney, Mr. Moreton Frewen, Capt. Hon. A. Hore-Ruthven, V.C. ; Mr. Callan, Mr. F. Lascelles, Mr. Ivor Castle, Mr. Forestier, Mr. Henri Julien, Mr. Chouinard, Hon. Angus Macdonell, Lord Howick, Capt. Panet, Capt. Hon. H. Dawnay, Flag.-Lt. Baxton, Flag.-Lt. Hardman-Jones, Mr. Sladen, Mr. Leveson-Gower, Lord

THE LUNCHEON
Under the trees at St. Joachim.

Graham, Vice-Admiral the Hon. Sir Assheton Curzon-Howe, Hon. R. Dandurand, Rt. Hon. Sir Charles Fitzpatrick, Sir Francois Langelier, Lord Lovat, Lord Annaly, Sir Francis Hopwood, Lt. Gen. Sir R. Pole-Carew, Rear Admiral Sir John Jellicoe, Hon. Clifford Sifton, Major-Gen. Lake, Major-Gen. Wilson, Hon. R. Sutherland, Rear-Admiral Kingsmill, Brig.-Gen. Otter, Brig.-Gen. Cotton, Brig.-Gen. Macdonald, Brig.-Gen. Buchan, Lord Strathcona, Lt.-Col. Sir Arthur Bigge, Hon. Sir Lomer Gouin, Hon. Sir J. P. Whitney, Hon. A. Turgeon, Hon. A. Rutherford, Hon. J. D. Hazen, Hon. L. A. Taschereau, His Worship Sir J. G. Garneau, Mr. R. L. Borden, Commodore King Hall, Lt.-Col. Hon. J. H. Hendrie, Sir Sandford Fleming, Sir Thomas Shaughnessy, Sir Montagu Allan,

Lascelles, A.D.C. ; Captain Newton, A.D.C. ; Capt. Pickering, A.D.C.

After the dinner the guests together with those who had been invited for the after reception repaired to the bastion whence an excellent view could be obtained of the fire-works and the torpedo attack on the river below. The Prince of Wales whose last night it was to be in the Citadel during his visit had a kind word for all and was conspicuous for the urbanity with which he conducted himself toward those who came to honour him.

On Monday night came the climax of all that was spectacular during the Tercentenary celebrations. Fireworks were again presented on the elaborate scale of the previous week. To these was added a searchlight display in which took part the whole of the Atlantic fleet stationed at Quebec and a sham torpedo attack on the war vessels.

The night was a dark one. From the Terrace and the heights above where eighty thousand people had gathered nothing could be distinguished on the river below or on the opposite shore. To the left, the cliffs of Montmorency and the Beauport shore were but distinguished by a row of lights placed thereon. Across in complete darkness was the Island of Orleans. Levis could be seen at times through the glimmer and flicker of lights which lay at rare intervals on its shore. All else beyond was utter darkness. The

Royal Highness the Prince of Wales and those who had been invited to meet him.

The darkness was suddenly interrupted by a glare of light which coming from the centre of the river, leaped up as if to penetrate the gloom overhead. It shone, then flickered, and gradually dying away descended into the waves below, its brightness gone, its glare decayed as if darkness was victor and the attempt to penetrate it were futile. This was but the signal to start.

Immediately the searchlights began their work. Every ship was equipped with several of them. With their sure sight, they detected everything. The pow-

THE HABITANTS WAITING

On the country roads to see H.R.H. the Prince of Wales pass on his way to St. Joachim.

river's dark waters were seen bearing their darker burthens of war from which not a light was visible, nor a sound heard. Below all was quiet. Only now and then could one scan the frame of a barge or freight-steamer gliding quietly over the waters—a mass of darkness moving on a surface itself bedecked with gloom and gentle stillness.

Such a spectacle met the thousands who had gathered on the terrace and above, itself rendered dark by the thick masses upon it. On the private terrace on the Citadel sat watching the same spectacle, His

erful lights were pointed in every direction. As each circled the vicinity, there were exposed the streets of Levis, hitherto dark. On its heights were scanned the faces of many watching the opposite shore. Next came in sight the distant island, its magnificent landscape dotted with white cottages. The heights of Montmorency were no longer hidden from view. Dashing down from them in the descent were seen the foamy water of the river. The shore of Beauport, but a broad base as it were for the lofty steeples which rise from it, is then seen. The artificial rays of light penetrate the city and its heights, illuminating the masses of spectators upon all the higher levels, as well as the massive warehouses of the Lower Town.

For several minutes the irresistible beams play freely with the surrounding country. They seem to mock the dim stars above and put to ridicule the lights on shore. But their work soon ceases and again all is dark.

With darkness, quietness. The night air is however disturbed. From amid the stillness on the river is heard a throbbing, a muffled sound. No light is seen and soon all is quiet again. The ever wakeful men-of-war have heard the noise and in a moment,

that the torpedo boats have been repulsed and the fleet is safe.

Another wait and the fireworks begin. A red fold of light glares up from a ship. Further up, a white flame brightens the darkened vessel. A few hundred yards further the sky is tinged with blue. All this is done instantaneously, and before the vast multitude is painted in colours of fire the tricolour of France.

A swarm of many coloured rockets next fills the air. As from a volcano they are sent up, where, their heavenly course ended, they explode, and a continual shower of glowing diamonds falls on the river where they are embedded. Dark night of a short while

A BUSY SCENE IN THE HARBOR
The Day of the Regatta.

out flash the searchlights scanning every nook in the shore, hastily examining the surface of the river, until the cause of the noise is seen. At some distance, squirming and turning here, proceeding there and writhing as in torture are seen several small torpedo boats which have come to destroy the huge warship. They have been detected, and in a moment are scattered by the terrific shells of the mighty guns on board. The lights are not extinguished for fear the enemy lurk around. The river has however been cleared. A shot is fired from the flagship announcing

before has given way to a mad rush of fire, and over the masses of dark come streams of coloured light.

The warships were illuminated. Their weird forms were outlined by frames of light which for some time glowed brilliantly. Above H.M.S. Minotaur was suspended in electric lights the figure of the classical being which gave to the vessel its name.

The lights were soon shut off. The evening sky was again left to its still gloom, while the twinkling stars were no longer challenged by rival shafts of light.

GENERAL JAMES WOLFE

Tenth Day, Tuesday, July Twenty=Eighth

Prince of Wales at Victoria Park

TUESDAY was the Prince of Wales' last day in the city. It was marked by many events, most of which His Royal Highness attended, thus making the day one of activity for him.

In the morning a ceremonial tree planting took place at Victoria Park, by the grandson of her, in whose honour was named the beautiful and spacious garden. The weather was fine and enhanced the splendor of the event which was cherished by the humbler classes of Quebec, for it was in the district of the working classes where the elm—a souvenir of the Prince's visit to Quebec, was planted.

Several thousand people were present at the park to witness the ceremony. The locality chosen for the silent otherwise out of respect to His Royal Highness. An ebony-handled spade bearing the arms of the city was presented on the occasion to the royal personage by the city. At the park the Prince was conspicuous by his gracious manner and by the urbanity which led him to greet and converse with the wives of labourers who had donned their best to come to see the visitor. After the ceremony several presentations took place. This ended, the party returned, cheered on the route by thousands of persons and at the convents, many of which were passed on the road, by the young inmates who greeted the passing Prince with song and salute.

The afternoon was a busy one. There were several events which interested every class irrespective of station in life or age.

For the soldiers and sailors there were the sports.

THE PRINCE OF WALES SPEAKING
To Mayor Sir J. G. Garneau, in Victoria Park.

plantation is a small green piece of land surrounded by trees so that the spot is almost enclosed by a palisade of greenery, except at one nook where a statute of Queen Victoria faces it. It was in front of this that the Prince, in commemoration of his visit, threw three shovelfulls of earth into the excavation wherein was placed the young elm.

The ceremony was simple to the degree of beauty. Despite the large gathering, the quietness was disturbed only by the voices of the young French-Canadians whose patriotic songs and French rendering of the national anthem re-echoed over the green park,

The military and naval gymkhana was the great sporting event of the celebrations. His Royal Highness the Prince of Wales, His Excellency Earl Grey, Lady Grey, Lord Roberts and other distinguished guests were present during a part of the afternoon.

The programme contained events of various descriptions, such as sack races, calisthenic drills and tugs-of-war. The musical ride of the North-West Mounted Police, the drive of the Royal Canadian Horse Artillery, and the field gun display by British sailors, were the main features. The number executed by the Mounted Police received much applause. The men and steeds went through the series of the musical drill with exactitude and grace. Nothing was wanting to the picturesqueness of the scene as the men, holding aloft lances from which floated small Union Jacks, rode the horses as richly caparisoned as their popular khaki-hatted riders.

The drive by the R.C.H.A. bore a more warlike aspect but was as beautiful in its effect and as exact in its movements. Although heavy guns were dragged behind the horses, the circumscribed spaces in which the evolutions were performed with skill and precision were duly respected.

More novel was the naval field-gun display. Squads of sailors dragging guns weighing nearly half a ton over a small field, separating their different parts and again connecting them with incredible haste and leaping over five foot walls carrying with them heavy armament and performing other marvellous feats, displaying the system with which preparations for warfare are made, were the astounding deeds of the afternoon's programme. They were applauded again and again until the noise of dragging the heavy guns across the field was no longer heard dimmed by the greater noise, the result of admiration and wonder.

Tuesday was the children's day. In the afternoon, the Plains of Abraham were entirely given up to them and what is usually deemed the ground of heroes, battle and reverence now became that of mirth, children's pranks, balloons, paper horses, and elephants.

The grand stand built for the accommodation of the pageant spectators was filled with children who were accompanied by parents and relatives—all again children, watching what was going on as eagerly as their charges. The seats were soon vacated by the juvenile gathering when the display of daylight fireworks commenced.

Rockets soared into the air where the interesting scenes began. It was on their explosion that the hidden treasures emerged from them. For no sooner was the report of the bursting of the rocket heard than its varied contents were showered upon the ground below. Muslin figures of men, women, cats, hares, bears, cows, hyenas and other members of the animal tribes; flags of every nation, balloons, to which were attached multi-coloured parachutes, paper dolls, unicorns and other amusing specimens—in short, anything that could conceivably be drawn and designed on muslin and paper. Often in their descent these objects precipitating headlong would turn in their course to be steered by the wind hundreds of yards away, but a similar fate awaited all. Armed with long poles thousands of children were on the sward and as each parachute was about to reach its destination, it was grabbed by the point of a stick or by several of them. It was a lively scramble, but perfectly good humoured.

The spoil was fairly divided and often when on one spike was fastened a mounted muslin rider and a monkey did the neighbouring child receive its share of the drawings from above.

The glee of youth and mirth of children was scattered as it were over the Plains and seemed to be disseminated among all present for everybody was again a child. Everybody shared in the fun from the tot eagerly clambering for a balloon to its grey-haired grandfather directing it in its struggle.

His Royal Highness the Prince of Wales, while driving by on his way to Spencer Wood stopped and entered the pageant enclosure to witness and join in the children's fete. He was received by the children clad in pageant costumes, who as fauns of the court of Henry IV and as the children of the old settlers of Quebec in Champlain's day greeted the Prince by singing the national anthem and cheering in a manner which if not stentorian was at least spontaneous.

With Earl and Lady Grey, Lord Roberts, Duke of Norfolk and other distinguished guests, the Prince spent half an hour at the fete, all the time enjoying the scene with that glee and open mirth which characterized all.

A similar event occurred at Victoria Park on the following day when quite as large a number of children were present.

* * *

Garden Party at Spencerwood

From the children's fete, the Prince of Wales drove to Spencer Wood where His Honour Sir Louis Jette, Lieutenant-Governor of the Province of Quebec and Lady Jette gave a garden-party in his honour.

The beautiful grounds of Spencer Wood were resplendent with the strong rays of the bright July sun that made a glorious summer afternoon. The natural greenery required no decorations. Nor were any there—save a tower of welcome erected at the entrance to the mansion—so often the scene of splendid social events during the celebrations that marked Canada's birthday. The grounds which overlook the river below were dotted here and there with marquees where guests could take shelter from the heat. Bands discoursed both popular and classical music.

The hosts were aided by Vice-President and Mrs. Fairbanks in the reception of the guests, for over eighteen hundred invitations had been issued. The Prince of Wales who drove up to the gates in state was greeted by a guard of honour while the national anthem was played. He drove up the grounds very quietly and mingled with the other guests before the news of his arrival had been spread. After walking over the grounds for an hour, the Prince returned to the Citadel. Those who were invited are:—

SHIPS

H.M.S. Exmouth—Vice-Admiral the Hon. Sir Assheton G. Curzon-Howe, K.C.B., C.V.O., C.M.G., Commander-in-Chief; Flag Commander, Vernon H. S. Haggard and Officers, Staff of Vice-Admiral the Hon. Sir Assheton G. Curzon-Howe; Captain Arthur J. Henniker-Hughan; Commander Judge D'Arcy and Ward-room Officers; the Gun-room Officers.

H.M.S. Albermarle—Rear-Admiral Sir John R. Jellicoe, K.C.V.O., C.B.; Flag Lieut. Bernard Buxton; Secretary, Walter Gask; Captain Wm. E. Goodenough; Commander Chs. D. Johnson and Officers.

H.M.S. Russell—Captain Arthur D. Ricard; Commander Arthur G. Smith and Ward-room Officers; the Gun-room Officers.

H.M.S. Venus—Captain Cuthbert G. Chapman, M.V.O.; Commander Hugh B. LeFann and Officers.

H.M.S. Arrogant—Captain Ralph Hudleston; Commander Henry W. Osburn and Officers.

U.S.S. New Hampshire—Rear Admiral Cowles and Mrs. Cowles and Military A.D.C., Major T. Bentley Mott; Lieut.-Col. D. L. Sillers, A.D.C.; Mr. George B. Lockwood, Private Secretary to Mr. Fairbanks; Capt. C. McR. Winslow; Lieut. Commander Roger Welles and Officers.

France, Leon Gambetta—Vice-Admiral Jaureguiberry, Capt. Clement and officers; Capt. Habert, Capt. Seres and officers of the Leon Gambetta; Capt. Seres, Commander of cruiser "l'Amiral Aube"; Capt. Le Gouzde de Saint-Seine and officers.

H.M.S. Duncan—Capt. Arthur W. Ewart; Commander C. S. Townsend and Ward-room Officers; the Gun-room Officers.

H.M.S. Indomitable—Capt. Herbert G. King-Hall, C.B., D.S.O.; Commander W. W. Fisher and Officers.

H.M.S. Minotaur—Capt. Wm. O. Boothby, M.V.O.; Commander Walter E. Woodward and Officers.

CORPS

Lt.-Col. A. Roy, and Officers District Staff; Col. Benson and Officers R.C.A.; Major A. O. Fages and Officers R.C.R.; Lt.-Col. Ashmead and Officers Q.O.C.H.; Lt.-Col. Martineau and Officers 6th Regt. C.A.; Major Laliberte and Officers Field Arty.; Lt.-Col. W. Wood and Officers 8th R. Rifles; Lt.-Col O. Evanturel and Officers 9th Regt. V.Q.; Lt.-Col O. E. Talbot and Officers 17th Regt.; Lt.-Col. Laurin and officers 87th Regt.; Major Brousseau and Officers P.A.M.C.; Lt.-Col Morin and Officers C.O.C.; Major G. G. Turcot and Officers A.M.C.; Major Houliston and Officers R.C.E.; Major R. Guay, Intendant 16th Compy. Canadian Militia and Officers; Lt.-Col. J. P. Landry and Staff, 11th Brigade; Lt.-Col. G. E. A. Jones and Staff, 20th Brigade; Lt.-Col. V. C. Turner, D.S.O. and Staff, 3rd Cavalry Brigade; Lieut. E. C. Dean and Officers, P.A.S.C.; Lt.-Col. B. A. Scott and Staff, 10th Brigade; Lt.-Col. R. K. Scott, D.S.O. and Officers C.O.C.; Lt.-Col. H. Burstall and Officers R.C.H.A.; Colonel Jones and Officers P.A.M.C.; Major G. A. Dodge and Officers C.P.A.S.C.; Lt.-Col. Wadmore and Officers R.C.A.; Lt.-Col. Williams, P.A.S., A.D.C. and Officers R.C.D.; Brig.-Gen. W. H. Cotton and Officers under his Command; Col. W. D. Gordon and Officers under his Command; Brig.-Gen. L. Buchan, C.W.G., A.D.C. and Officers under his command; Brig.-Gen. Otter and Officers Headquarters Staff; B.S.M. and Gentlemen Cadets Royal Military College; Commissioner Perry and Officers R.N.W.M.P.

A

Mrs. and Miss Allard, Mr. A., Mrs., Misses and Mr. G. S. Ahern, Dr. and Miss Ahern, Mr. T. C., Mrs. and Miss Aylwin, Mr. and Mrs. E. Archer, Mr. and Mrs. J. Archer, Mr. and Mde. W. Amyot, Miss Amyot, Mr. and Mrs. Jos. Allaire, Miss and Messrs, Alleyn, Mr., Mrs. and Miss Audette, Mr. and Mrs. J. R. Audette, Mr. C. P., Mrs. and Miss Angers, Hon. Jules and Mrs. Allard, Mr. E. Aube, Rev. O. Audet, Mr. G. E., Mrs. Mr. and Miss Amyot, Miss Y. Arsenault, Mr. and Mrs. H. C. Atkinson, Mrs. and Misses Atkinson, Mr. and Mrs. V. W. F.

SPENCER WOOD

Gubernatorial residence where Garden Party took place.

Atkinson, Mr. Rene Adam, Mr. and Mrs. M. J. Ahern, Miss Ahern, Lt.-Col. J B., Mrs and Miss Amyot, Major and Mrs. G K Addie, Miss Almon, Mr. and Mrs. A. Alleyn, Mr. and Mrs. Gustave Audette, Mr. and Mrs. A. J. Auger, Mr. and Mrs. A.G. Auger, Mrs. and Misses Anderson, Mr. Donald C. T. Atkinson, Dr. and Mrs. Auger, Lord Annaly, Lord-in-Waiting to H.R H., Mr. and Mrs. Hugh Allan, Miss Emily Ashford, Mr. and Mrs. Aymur, Mr. and Mrs. Robt. Archer, Mr. Chs. Arnoldi, Mr. A., Mrs. and Misses Allan, Sir Montagu and Lady Allan, Mr. Bryce Allan, Major and Mrs. Audam, Mr. and Mrs. F. W. Ashe, Dr. and Mrs. Atwood, Hon. H. and Mrs. Archambeault, Capt. and Mrs. Agar Adamson, Major, Mrs., Miss and Mr. H. C. Ashdown, Miss Aylmer, Miss Atwater, Mr. and Mrs. J. E. Aldred, Miss Audette.

B

Mrs. C. and Miss Baillarge, Rev. H. R. and Mrs. Bigg, Mr E. A., Mrs. and Misses Bishop, Capt and Mrs J. A. Benyon, Mrs. and Misses Burstall, Mr. W. A., Mrs. and Mr. S. Bignell, Mr. and Mrs. J F Burstall, Mrs. Bayand, Mr and Mrs. A. R. M. Boulton, Mr. G., Mrs. and Miss Breakey, Judge, Mrs. and Mr. S. Blanchet, Mrs. Jas. Bowen, Mr St G., Mrs. and Misses Boswell, Mr. Godfrey and Misses Brown, Mrs., Misses and Messrs. Boswell, Mr. and Mrs. Vesey Boswell, Mr. J., Mrs., Misses and Messrs. Breakey, Venerable Archdeacon Balfour, Mr. G. H. and Miss Balfour, Mr. W. J. Banks, Mrs. S. J and Misses Bennett, Dr. and Mrs. A. Bourdeau, Mr. and Mrs. A. E. Boisseau, Mr. J. B. Bernier, Mr. and Mrs. J. de S. Bosse, Mgr. Begin, Judge, Miss and Mr. H. G. Bosse, Lieut.-Colonel and Mrs. L. T. Bacon, Mr. and Mrs. A Brosnan, Mr Cleophas, Mrs and Miss Blouin, Major and Mrs. Brousseau, Mr and Mrs. H. D. Barry, Mr. and Mrs. Geo. Bellerive, Mr and Mrs. L. F Burroughs, Major, Mrs. and Miss Benoit, Mr. F. X., Mrs. and Miss Berlinguet, Lt.-Col., Mrs., Miss and Mr H. O. Boulanger, Mr. A., Mrs. and Miss Bolduc, Mrs. Elz. and Mr. Baillargeon, Dr. and Mrs Brochu, Mr. and Mrs. Ludovic Brunet, Misses Barry, Revd. Cure Beaudoin, Mr. and Mrs. Neuville Belleau, Mr and Mrs Noel Belleau, Mr. and Mrs. W. D. Baillairge, Mr. L. Eng. Barry, Mr. and Mrs. E Beaudet, Mr. and Mrs W. M. Bancroft, Mr. W. and Miss Bender, Mrs. and Miss Bucknall, Mr. McGill and Misses Burroughs, Mr. L. A. Broot, Mr. and Mrs. D. Breakey, Mr. and Mrs. Reginald Beckett, Mr. Louis Bruneau, Major T. Bernier, Miss Bond, Col. and Mrs. Benson, Mr. and Mrs. A Bernier, Mr. and Mrs. Colin Breakey, Mr. and Mrs. H. B Bignell, Mr. and Mrs. F. A. Borden, Mr. and Mrs. C Branchoud, Mr. and Mrs.C. M. Barclay, Miss M. L. Beaulieu, Revd. A E. Burgett, Miss Maude Brewer, Mr. and Mrs. Guy Boyer Mr. and Mrs. C. E. Brodie, Lt.-Col. and Mrs. Burstall, Lt.-Col. Sir Arthur Bigge, Private Secretary to H.R.H., Mr. Brandelis, Mayor of Brouage, Lord Edw. Bruce, Hon. Mr. Boscawen. Brig.-Gen. and Mrs. Buchan, Mr. Hugh Boswell, Capt. and Mrs. W. S. Buell, Miss Bennett, Miss Bowie, Lt.-Col. and Mrs. Biggar, Capt. J. G. Burnham, Mrs. Bowditch, Mr. H. A. Bromley, Secretary to Lt.-Gov. Dunsmuir, Mr. S. Montagu Burrows, Lt.-Gov. G. H. V. Bulyea, Mr. and Mrs. Beausse, Mr. and Mrs. Brown, Miss Claudia Bote, Mrs. Baxter, Lt.-Col. J. W. and Mrs. Bridges, Lt.-Col., Mrs. and Miss Belton, Miss Busch, Miss Bethune, Mr. H. Biermans, Dr. Geo. and Misses Beauchamp, Mr. and Mrs. G. W. Benedict, Sir John and Lady Barran, Hon. L. P. and Mrs. Brodeur, Mr. and Mrs. L. N. Borden, Mr. and Mrs. Frank Beard, Miss Bovey, Miss Bosworth, Lt.-Col and Mrs. Burland, Miss Beaudry, Mrs. E. P. Brewer, Mrs. Bird, Miss Benson, Dr. G. A., Mrs. and Miss Brown, Mr. T. H. Bullock, Mayor of St. John, N.B., and Mrs. Bullock, Sir Fred. and Lady Borden, Mr. D. H. Burns, Mr. R. J., Mrs., Misses and Mrs. H. M. Bradley, Miss Bate, Miss M. Black, Mr. J. T., Mrs. and Miss Boyd, Mr. H. C. Bosse, Mr. and Mrs. Beaubien, Mrs John Burroughs, Misses Barnard, Mr. and Mrs. Donald S. Barton, Mr. Robt. Benson, Miss E. P. Bissell, Mr. and Mrs. J .W. Black, Mr. N. P. and Miss Bryant, Dr. and Mrs. R. Bowie, Capt. and Mrs. A H. Borden, the Misses Burnham, Mr de Gaspe Beaubien.

C

Capt. W. H , Mrs. and Misses Carter, Dr. and Mrs. W. L. Carter, Mr. and Mrs. L. G. Craig, Mr. and Mrs. F. J. Cockburn, Mr. Frank Carrel, Mr. E. T. D., Mrs. and Miss Chambers, Mr. and Mrs. Noble Campbell, Mr. A, H., Mrs. and Misses Cook, Mrs.

W. Darling Campbell, Mrs. Chapman, Mr., Mrs. and Mr. W. Champion, Mr. and Mrs. E. E. Code, Miss and Mr. T. J. Carbray, Dr. and Mrs E. J. C. Chambers, Dr., Mrs., Miss and Mr. P. Catellier, Hon. P.A. and Mrs. Choquette, Mr. and Mrs. A. J. Chauveau, Mr. and Mrs. L. A. Cannon, Hon. Judge and Mrs. Chauveau, Mr. J. A., Mrs. and Misses Charlebois, Dr. and Mrs. Coote, Mr. E., Mrs. and Miss Chinic, Lady and Misses Casault, Mr. and Mrs. Alex Chateauvert, Mr. P. B., Mrs. and Miss Casgrain, Mrs. F. Cannon, Mr. and Mrs. H. J. J. B. Chouinard, Hon. Judge and Mrs. Carroll, Revd. Pere Champagne, Mr. Geo. Carrier, Mr. and Mrs. J. Emile Carrier, Dr. and Mrs. C. E. Cote, Revd. A. Cloutier, Mr. and Mrs. J. R. Chalout, Mr. and Mrs. W. L. Carkner, Mr., Mrs. and Miss Levingstone Crosby. Mr. E. Clement, Lieut. L. W. S. Cockburn, Mr. and Mrs. Aug. Carrier, Mr. W., Mrs. and Misses Cook, Hon. T. and Mrs. Chapais, Mr. Chs. Chapais, Lt.-Col and Mrs. C. A. Chauveau, Mr. and Mrs. P. V. Chaloult, Judge, Mrs. and Misses Cimon, Mr. Omer Chaput, Miss Chapais, Mr. and Mrs. Alex. Cinq-Mars, Mr. Alfred Carrier, Mr. J. Rich. Clancy, Major-Gen. Sir F. and Lady Carrington, Commander Sir Chs. L. Bt. Cust, Equerry to H.R.H. Captain. Hon. Dudley Carleton, Rear Admiral and Mrs. Cowles, Mr. and Mrs. Thos Craig, Judge, Misses and Messrs. Cannon, Mr. and Mrs. C. S. Cossit, Mr. and Mrs. F. B. Cossit, Mr. and Mrs. W. H. Cornstock, Sir Mortimer and Lady Clark, Mr. and Mrs J. W Cook, Miss Enid Campbell, Mr. Nugent M. Clougher, F.R.G.S., Mr. and Mrs. J. M. Courtney, Revd. Mr. and Miss Caffin, Mr. Julian Corbett, Mr. L. Bt. Cust, Miss Clouston, Lt.-Gen Sir R. and Lady Beatrice Pole-Carew, Dr. E. Couillard, Mrs. Clinch, Miss R. B. Colfer, Mr. Carter, Mr. and Mrs. G. Cooke, Mr. Walter Callan, Private Secretary to Lord Dudley, Mr. W., Mrs. and Misses Clint, Mr. and Mrs. J. Cumberland, Lt.-Col. Montgomery Campbell, Mr. and Mrs. J. Carling, Mrs. and Miss Crombie, Misses Chadwick, Mr. C. J. Chaplin, Mr. Howard Clouston, Mr. Fred. Cook, Mr. A. and Miss Creelman, Capt. J. J. and Mrs. Creelman, Hon. T. Chase and Mrs. Casgrain, Dr. R., Mrs. and Miss Coulter, Hon. J. P. B., Mrs. and Miss Casgrain, Mr. Whitney G. Case, Mr. Ivor Castle, Rt. Hon. R. and the Misses Cartwright, Lt.-Col. and Mrs Cob, Mr. Cole, Mr. Frank Craig, Miss Clement, Miss Lily Clement, Mr. A. B. Clabon.

D

Mr. and Mrs. W. M. Dobell, Lord Bishop, Mrs. and Miss Dunn, Mr. T. W. S. Dunn, Mr. and Mrs. F. M. Duggan, Mr. and Mrs. E. J. and Mr. A. de Lotbiniere, Major A. C. Dobell, Mrs. Astell Drayner, the Misses Drury, Capt. and Mrs. A. E. Doucet, Mr. M.P., Mrs., Miss and Mr. M. P., Jr., Davis, Mr. J. T., Mrs. and Miss Davis, Mr. and Mrs. W. H. Dunsford, Mr. Jos. Dumont, Mr. and Mrs. C F Delage, Dr., Mrs. and Mrs. Chs. Delagrave, Lt.-Col. Mrs. and Miss Duchesnay, Mr. and Mrs. P. B. Dumoulin, Mr. A., Mrs. and Miss Dessane, Miss Defoy, Lt.-Col. and Mrs Desjardins, Dr. and Mrs. N. E. Dionne, Mr. Henri Delage, Revd. J. F. Dupuis, Dr. F. X. Jules Dorion, Hon P. B. and Mrs. de la Bruere, Mr. Albert Demers, Mr. G. F. C., Mrs. and Miss de Lery, Miss Dufresne, Mr. and Mrs. L. G. Demers, Mr. C., Mrs. and Misses Duquet, Mr. and Mrs. A. F. d'Eschambeault, Mrs H. Duchesnay, Viscomte and Viscomtesse de la Grandville, Mr. and Mrs. Chs. Deguise, Mr. and Mrs. E. L Denoncourt, Capt. C. H. E. deBlois, Mr. Roland Dion, Mrs. G. M. Dechene, Revd. Pere Daisy, Mrs. and Miss Delorme, Mr. and Mrs. d'Hellencourt, Miss Deville, Mr. F. X., Mrs., Miss and Messrs. Drouin, Mr. and Mrs. Albert Dunn, Miss Denechaud, Mr. and Mrs. O. Drouin, Mr. and Mrs Alf. Duberger, Major E. P. deBlois, Miss B. Dufresne, Mr. Arthur Dery, Dr. and Mrs. F. A. Dussault, Mr. S. W., Mrs. and Miss Drum, Mr. and Mrs. A. R. Decary, Miss Drolet, Hon. Sir Henri deLotbiniere, Miss C. Duchesnay, Miss Devlin, Mr. H. R. and Miss de St. Victor, Mrs. L. N. R. Dufresne, Mr. P. DeCazes, Mr. and Mrs. A. R. Drysdale, Miss Dickey, Miss Muriel Day, Mr. Mrs. and Miss de Loynes, Misses deKastner, Mrs. and Miss LeMoyne deMartigny, Mr. and Mrs. G. D. Davie, Right Hon. Sir J. H. de Villiers, K.C.M.G., Right Hon. Earl of Dudley, le Marquis de Levis, le Marquis de Levis Miropoix, le Comte Bertrand de Montcalm, Capt. Hon. Hugh Dawnay, D.S O., Mr. E. J., Mrs. and Mrs. Duggan, Lieut.-Colonel J. S., Mrs. and Miss Dunbar, Misses Rachel and Nancy Dawes, Admiral Sir A. L. Douglas, G. C.V. O., K.C.B., Lt.-Gov. J., Mrs. and Misses Dunsmuir, Lt.-Col. G. T. Mrs. and Miss Denison, Hon. Sir G. and Lady Drummond.

MRS. JETTE,

Wife of Sir Louis
Jette, Lieutenant-
Governor of Que-
bec Province who
was among the
Ladies present to
receive the Prince.

Hon. R., Mrs. and Miss Dandurand, Miss Dean, Mr. and Mrs. Dyer, Mrs. Dr. Douglas, Mr. and Mrs. de Sunichrast, Miss L. Douglass, Mrs W. Denoon, Dr. L. B. and Mrs. de la Bruere, Lt.-Col. H. R. Duff, Lieut.-Col. Septimus Denison, Lady Susan Dawnay, Dr. A. G. and Mrs. Doughty, Mr. and Mrs. R. Davidson, Mr. and Mrs. H. F. Dyke, Rev. E. A. and Mrs. Dunn, Mr. and Mrs. R. W. Dunsmuir, Mr. Wm. Downey, Mr. and Mrs. M. de la Bruere, Mr. A. E. Dyment, M.P., Mrs. and Miss Dobie, Lieut. E. F. Dawson, Marchioness of Donegal, Mr. Kenneth G. Dunstan, Mr. and Mrs. Thornton Davidson, Miss Dyer, Mrs. J. W., Miss and Mr. Digby, Mr. B., Mrs. and Miss deslles, Miss Domville, Hon. C. R. and Miss Devlin, Mr Justice, Mrs. and Mr. Hugh Davidson, Mr. and Mrs. Peers Davidson, Lieut. and Mrs. E. C. Dean, Mrs. Desbarats, Mr. and Mrs. E. B. Devlin, Mr. and Mrs. R. C. Desrochers, Miss Duplessis, Major Duffus, A.D.C., Mr. J. H. Dunn, Mr. A. L. deMartigny, Mrs. and Miss E. Drury, Mr. Leon J., Mrs. and Miss Dessane, Miss David, Mr. and Mrs. Emile Desjardins, Mr. Forbes Denis, Mr. and Mrs. G. E. Drummond, Mr. and Mrs. Thos. Drummond, Miss Du Barry, Mr. and Mrs. J. G. Davies, Mr. and Mrs. Jack Davie, Mrs. J. and Miss A. Dowd.

E

Mr. and Mrs A. J. Elliot, Mr. L., Mrs., Miss and Mr. Evans, Mr. and Mrs. Gustave Evanturel, Mr. and Mrs. Eudore Evanturel, Mr. and Mrs. Aug. Edge, Dr. Alex. Edge, Lt.-Col. and Mrs. English, Col. G. T. A. Evanturel, Lt.-Col. O. Evanturel, Lady Violet Elliot, Mrs. J. S. Elliot, Mr. Fred. W. Emett, Major and Mrs. Eaton, Hon. W. C., Mrs. and Miss Edwards, Capt. and Mrs. A. Evanturel, Miss and Miss G. Ely.

F

Mr. W. J., Mrs. and Miss Fraser, Lieut. and Mrs. J. J. Fitzpatrick, Mr. and Mrs. H. C. Foy, Mr. G. M., Mrs. and Misses Fairchild, Mr. and Mrs. Cecil Foy, Mr. N. and Misses Flood, Dr. J. E., Mrs., Miss and Messrs. Fortier, Major and Mrs. A. O Fages, Mons. Faguy, Hon. E. J., Mrs. and Miss Flynn, Chevalier O. Frechette, Mr. and Mrs. Elz. L. Fiset, Mr. S. Fortier, Col. and Mrs. J. B. Forsyth, Mrs., Miss and Messrs. Fremont, Dr. and Mrs. L. N. J. Fiset, Dr. and Mrs. E. R. Fortier, Revd. W. G., Mrs. and Misses Falconer, Mr. J. A. Freeland, Mr. A. Fitzpatrick, Mrs. Elz. Fiset, Chief Justice Sir C., Lady and Misses Fitzpatrick, Mrs. and Miss Fraser, Mr. Geo. Fane, Miss K. Van Rensselear Fairfax, Hon. C. W. Fairbanks, Vice-President U. S. A., and Mrs. Fairbanks, Mr. and Mrs. L. E. Fontaine, Mr. H. Rushton Fairclough, Capt. Bryan G. Godfrey Faussett, Equerry to H.R.H., Lord and Lady Falmouth, Mr. M., Mrs. and Miss Foley, Hon. W. S., Mrs., Misses and Mr. H. C. Fielding, Hon. D. C. Fraser, Lt.-Gov. of Nova Scotia, Lt.-Gov. A. E. and Mrs. Forget, Mrs. F. Falkenberg, Major C. F. O. and Mrs. Fiset, Mr. Morton Frewen, Lady Augusta Fane, Sir Sandford Fleming, Mr. Frominge, Dr. and Mrs. L. Frisel, Mrs. G. T. Fulford, Mrs. Henry Farrer, Mr. G. A. Followes, the Misses Fitzpatrick, Miss Isabel Foote, Mr. and Mrs. F. Featherstonhaugh, Mr. and Mrs. Roswell Fisher, Sir Keith Fraser, Miss Fowler, Mrs. Fisk, Mr. C. F. Finnis.

G

Lt.-Col. and Mrs. Gaudet, Major G. F. and Misses Gibsone, Mr. H. G. Goodday, Mr. and Mrs. H. R. Goodday, Mr. J. U. Gregory, Mrs. J. D. and Mr. Gilmour, Major and Mrs. Kenneth Gilmour, Mr. H., Mrs. and Miss Gowen, Mayor and Mrs. J. G. Garneau, Hon. E. B., Mrs. and Mr. E. L. Garneau, Mr. and Mrs. Gustave Grenier, Mr. and Mrs. A. Genereux, Hon. N. and Mrs. Garneau, Mr. C. E. Mrs., Miss and Messrs. Gauvin, Mr. and Mrs. F. E. Gauvreau, Dr. S. and Mrs. Grondin, Hon. Judge, Mrs. and Messrs. Gagne, Revd. Abbe Gignac, Dr. and Mrs. C. O. Guimond, Hon. Lomer Gouin, Monsgr. C. O. Gagnon,

SIR LOUIS JETTE, K.C.M.G.,

Lt.-Governor, Province of Quebec, one
of the First Quebecers to welcome the
Prince.

Mr Leonidas Gingras, Mr. J. A. Gobeil, Revd. B. Garneau, Mr. and Mrs. Jules Garneau, Misses Garneau, Miss M. L. Gagnon, Capt. and Mrs Donat Gendron, Mr. and Mrs. Gustave Gagnon, Mr. E., Mrs. and Misses Gagnon, Mr. H., Mrs. and Misses Gagnon, Mr. H., Mrs. and Miss Garneau, Mr J. A. Albert Gauvin, Messrs. J. E. and Em. Goulet, Miss Hortense Gagnon, Mr and Mrs. S. T. Green, Lt.-Col., Mrs., Miss and Mr. Gray, Mr. F., Mrs. and Misses and Mr. F. K. Glass, Mr. Frank Gourdeau, Mrs. C. Gethings, Mr. and Mrs. D. H. Goggie, Mr. Leon Garneau, Mr. C. Leveson-Gower, Miss Genest, Mr. and Mrs, A. Guilbault, Mr Ernest Guimont, Mr. Maurice M. Grondin, Misses Gibsone, Mr. S. E. Gregory, Mrs. E. N. and Miss Vivian Gregory, Mr. and Mrs. Gilman, Mrs Grosvenor, the Misses Gibert, Mr. A., Mrs. and Miss Green, Mr. and Mrs. Albert Gilmour, Mr. Perry Graham, Mr. F. A. Gendron, M.P.P., Mrs. and Miss Gendron, Mr. D. R. Griffiths, R.A.A., Col. W. Gwatkin, Hon. G. P. and Mrs. Graham, Mrs. W. D. Gwynne, Lt.-Col. and Miss Garrett, Mr. and Mrs. W. A. Griffith, Mr D. E. Galloway, Mr. and Mrs. Gordon Grant, Mr. J. E. Gaudet, Lt.-Col., Mrs., Miss and Mr. A. E. Gooderham, Mr. M. S. Gooderham, Mr. S. Gooderham, Mr. Jas., Mrs., Misses and Messrs. Goggie, Miss B. Gilbertson, Mr. H. H. Gadsby, Mr. and Mrs. Hugh Graham, Mr. Alex. and Misses Gauvreau, Miss Cecile Gouin, Mrs. Scott Griffin, Miss Graddon, Mr. and Mrs. P. Gagnon, Mr. Leon Mercier Gouin, Mrs. Jas. Gibsone.

H

Mr. and Mrs. W. G. Hinds, Mr. J., Mrs. and Misses Hamilton, Mr. and Mrs. W. A. Horne, Mr. and Mrs. J. W. Hamilton, Mr. W. C. J., Mrs. and Misses Hall, General and Mrs. Henry, Miss Henry, Mr. and Mrs. Jas. Holliday, Miss Hunter, Mr O. Heroux, Mr. and Mrs. Ernest Hamel, Mr. Alp. Huard, Lt -Col L. D. and Mrs. Hudon, Mr. and Mrs. Lomer Hamel, Mrs. H , Misses and Mr. Paul Hamel, Monsgr. T. E. Hamel, Mr. Theo., Mrs. and Miss Hamel, Misses and Mr. P. Hebert, Mr. and Mrs Jules Hone, Jr., Mr. and Mrs. Gaspard Huot, Mr. Alex , Mrs and Miss Hardy, Mr. and Mrs. J. A. Hudon, Revd. Pere Hage, Capt. S. A. Heward, R.C.A., Dr. A. C., Mrs. and Miss Hamel, Mr. E. A., Mrs. and Miss Hoare, Mr. and Mrs. J. B. Hance, Mr. and Mrs. F. L. Hutchinson, Mr. and Mrs., C. L. Hervey, Mr. and Mrs. H. E. and Miss G. Huestes, Miss Hartnedy, Lieut.-Col. and Mrs. C. Greville Harston, Mr. Wm Amherts, Mrs. and Misses Hale, Mr. and Mrs. E. C. Hale, Mr. and Mrs. E. Russell Hale, Mr. F. and Miss Holloway, Mr. and Mrs. Jules Hamel, Mrs. and Misses Hunter, Mr. Angus Hooper, Miss Henry, Mr. Louis Herbette, Sir Francis Hopwood, staff of H.R.H., Lord Howick, Miss G. Huestis, Miss Holland, Mrs. Darcy Hutton, Mrs. and Miss Hecker, Mr. and Mrs. Chas. Hosmer, Mr. E. Hosmer. Hon. J. P. and Mrs. Hazen, Lt.-Col. Hon. J. S , Mrs. and Miss Hendrie, Mr. C M., Mrs. and Misses Hays, Miss Holland, Mrs. John Hope, Mr. and Mrs. Alfred Hawes, Mrs A. C Hardy, Miss Howell, Mr. and Mrs. G. D. Hall, Mrs. and Misses Hughson, Mr Harivel, Miss Higginson, Miss and Mr. D Howard, Miss Jean Hervey.

I

Lt.-Col. and Mrs Imlah, Miss G. A. Irvine, Lieut A. D. Irwin, R.C.A., Col., Mrs. and Mr. Irvin, Dr. Henry Iovers.

J

Mr. A., Mrs. and Miss M. Joseph, Mr. M., Mrs , Miss and Mr. A. P. Joseph, Lt.-Col. and Mrs. G. E. A. Jones. Mr. J. A , Mrs. and Miss Jordan, Dr. and Mrs. Albert Jobin, Mr. Alf. L. Jolicoeur, Dr. and Mrs. J. A. Johnston, Miss Corinne Jones, Miss A. Jackson, Mr. W. A. Jolicoeur, Dr. G. W. and Mrs. Jolicoeur, Mr. Ed. C. Joseph, Mr. Leonard Chester Jones, l'Admiral Jaureguiberry, Lt.-Col. G. C. and Mrs. Jones, Lt.-Col G. West and Mrs. Jones, Capt. Hugh B. H. Johnston, Capt. R. O. Jones, the Misses Joseph, Mrs. A. J. Jarvis, Mr. Alex. Johnson, M.P., Miss Jones, Mrs. and Miss Jayne, Mrs. Stonewall Jackson, Dr and Mrs. Johnson.

K

Mr. and Mrs. Harold Kennedy, Hon. J. C. and Mrs. Kaine, Mr. J. A., Mrs. and Miss Kirouac, Mr. W. A. Kingsley, Rear Admiral and Mrs. Kingsmill, Revd. E. A. W. and Mrs. King,

Miss Rita Kent, Major and Mrs. Kilborn, Mrs. Kakas, Colonel Kitchener, Miss Kennedy, Miss Krause, Mr. and Mrs Walter Kernan, Hon. J. K., Mrs. and Miss Kerr, Mrs. W , Miss and Mr. J. K. Kavannagh, Miss Kavannagh, Mr. J. W. Killam, Miss Madina Kerr, Mr. S. C S Kerr, A.D.C., Mr N. S. King, Miss Knudsen, Mr. and Mrs. W. Raleigh Kerr, Rev. A. R., Mrs. and Miss Koby.

L

Mr. H. J. Lemesurier, Mr. W J., Mrs , Miss and Messrs. Lemesurier, Sir James and Miss LeMoine, Capt. and Mrs. W. P. Lindsay, Mr and Mrs. Archie Laurie, Lt.-Col. C., Misses and Mr. Lindsay, Capt. and Mrs. F. A. Lyster, Mrs. J. Langlois, Mrs. Lawrence, Mr B., Mrs., Miss and Mrs. J. K. Leonard, Dr. and Mrs Jas. Laurie, Mr. Bene Leduc, Mr. and Mrs. J. W. Lebel, Mr. S , Misses and Mr J Lesage, Mr and Mrs C. and Miss G. Lanctot, Hon. C. and Mrs. Langelier, Dr. and Mrs. A. Lavoie. Chief Justice Sir F. and Lady Langelier, Judge, Mrs. and Miss Larue, Mr. J. L., Mrs. and Miss Lavery, Dr. and Mrs A. Lantier, Dr. and Mrs. A. Langlois, Mr. and Mrs. J. C. Langelier, Mr. and Mrs. Romeo Langlois, Mr. J. A., Mrs. and Miss Lane, Mr. L. Lemieux, Mrs. C E Lemieux, Mrs J. C. Laflamme, Mr. and Mrs. F. X. Lemieux, Mr. and Mrs. Gaspard Lemoine, Mr. and Mrs. L Levasseur, Mr. and Mrs. J H. Lachance, Mr. M. A. Lemieux, Mr. and Mrs Rene Lemoine, Lieut.-Colonel and Mrs. L. N. Laurin, Mr. G. and Miss Lamothe, Revd l'Abbe Lortie, Mrs Alex Lindsay, Capt. L Leduc, R.C.R., Miss Ladriere, Mr. and Mrs. St. G. Legendre, Mr. and Mrs. Henri Lemieux, Mrs N. Legendre, Mr. Ed., Mrs. and Miss Lortie, Miss Lemieux, Mr. and Mrs. H. E. Lavigueur, Mr. and Mrs. P. C Lacasse, Mr. and Mrs. Arthur Larue, Mr. C. J. P. Langlois, Mr. Ernest Lefebvre, Lt -Col and Mrs. J. P Landry, Major N. Le-Vasseur, Lt. Col. Hon. Ph. Landry, Mr. and Mrs. A. Lachance. Judge, Mrs., Misses, and Messrs. Lemieux, Mr. and Mrs. Arthur Legendre, Mr. and Mrs. A. Lantier, Rev. A. T., Mrs., Miss and Mr. G. F. Love, Dr. and Mrs. J. N. Lemieux, Mr. Roger, Mrs., Miss and Messrs. Larue, Dr. and Mrs. E. A. Lebel, Misses Lessard, Mr. and Mrs. Francis Lennan, Mr. and Mrs. Armand Lavergne, Miss Yvonne de S. Laterriere, Mr. Edmond Lemoine, Mr. Antoine Lesage, Mrs. and Messrs. J. W. and Chs. Lynch, Mr. Frank Lascelles, Mr. and Mrs. John Laird, Mr. J. and Miss Lloyd, Mrs. W H. and Mr. Barclay Lee, Mr E J. Lemaire, Sir Wilfrid and Lady Laurier, Hon. Rod. and Mrs. Lemieux, Lord Lovat, C.V.O., C.B., D.S.O., Mr. Geo. B. Lockwood, Major-Gen. and Mrs. Lake, Mr. D. O. Lesperance, Col. F. L. and Misses Lessard, Mrs. E. LeMoine, Rt. Hon. Lord Lascelles, A.D.C., Miss Lamontagne, Dr. E. A. and Mrs. LeBel, the Misses Llost, Major and Mrs. Norman Leslie, Mr. Macp., Mrs. and Misses LeMoyne, Mr. W. Lemesurier, H. J. Logan, N P., Major and Mrs. W. E. Lyman, Dr. Alp., Mrs. and Miss J. Lessard, Mr and Mrs. P. V. Low, Mrs. E. and Mr. C. Lamontagne, Hon. Francis and Mrs. Lindley, Major and Mrs. Lafferty, Mr. A. C., Mrs. and Mr. H. H. Lyman, Mrs. Lockwood, Miss LeBouthillier. Mr. and Mrs. E. D. Lafleur, Dr. C. J. Lemieux, Mr. and Mrs. Ulric Lafontaine, Miss Laidlaw, Mrs. Janvier LeDuc, Dr. and Duc, Dr and Mrs. A. Laroque. Mrs A. Laroque.

M

Mr. G. Martin-Zede, Mr. C. M. Mowat, Lt.-Col. J. A. and Mrs Morin, Mr F. X. Morency, Dr. and Mrs. L. J. Montreuil, Mr. Robt Martin, Mr. Marriott, Mr. and Mrs. T Cory Musgrove, the Misses Machin, Dr. F. Mrs. and Misses Montizambert, Mr and Mrs. G. F. Maguire, Dr. and Mrs. Maguire, Capt. Hon. Mr. Arthur Murray, Mr. F. and Miss Morweel, Mr. W M. Moore. Mr. and Mrs. Arch Murray, Mrs. Townsend MacCann, Lt.-Col. C. Macdougall, R.C.R., Mr. T. M. Maguire, Mrs. and Miss D. Kent Macuse, Dr. and Mr J A MacDonald, Mr. H. J. Mackender, Hon. G. H and Mrs. Murray, Mr. W., Mrs. and Misses Mackenzie, Miss Florence MacLeod, Miss Molson, Brig.-Gen and Mrs. A. Murray, Mr. L. Morency, Mr. E. A. Macdonald, N.P., Mr. A. K. Maclean, N.P., Colonel Macdonald, Major and Mrs. Miller, Major and Mrs. Mozley, Miss B Murray, Miss Mackay, Mr. Arthur Moisan, Mrs. G. Plunkett Magann, Mr. and Mrs. Mason, Major and Mrs. M. Mitchell, Mrs. Dinham Molson, Mrs. L R. Masson, Brig.-Gen. A. Murray, Mr. and Mrs. Angus Machurchy, Mr. Ed. Michael, Lt.-Col. D. A. Mackinnon, Mr. and

Mrs. Chs. Meredith, Miss Maclean, Miss Heloise Meyer, Mr. and Mrs. Mann, Mr. Wm., Mrs. and Misses Mackenzie, Mr. and Mrs. Mathews, Judge and Mrs. McCorkill, Mr. and Mrs. J. M. McCarthy, Mrs. and Miss McGreevy, Mr. and Mrs. H. S. McGreevy, Mr. Wm. McLimont, Mr. H. J. McLimont, Mr. and Mrs. J. C. McLimont, Mr. and Mrs. W. G. McConnell, Mr. and Mrs. T. McDougall, Mr. D. and Miss McGie, Mr. and Mrs. D. R. McDonald, Mrs. John McLean, Capt. M. and Mrs. McMillan, Lt.-Col. Mrs. and Miss McLean, Miss M. L. McDonald, Mrs. M. McKay, Miss McMillan, Mr. and Mrs. Francis McLennan, Hon. Angus McDonnell, Miss McPherson, Dr. K. C. and Mrs. McIlvraight, Capt. C. W. McLean, Mrs. McCarthy, Mr. Bartlett McLennan, Miss Margery McGreevy, Mr. E. G., Mrs. and Misses Meredith, Mr. and Mrs. Rex Meredith, Mr. and Mrs. Arch. Miller, Mr. and Mrs. Geo. Mitchell, Lt.-Col. and Mrs. W. M. Macpherson, Rev. Cure A. E. Maguire, Mr. and Mrs. H. T. Machin, Mr. and Mrs. J. J. Murphy, Mr. D. and Misses Mitchell, Mr. Kenneth and Misses Molson, Mr. T. J., Misses and Mr. Molony, Mr. J., Mrs., Misses and Mr. F. Macnaughton, Mr. and Mrs. W. Monaghan, Miss Murphy, Judge A. and Mrs. Malouin, Miss Malouin, Mr. and Mrs. J. S. Matte, Mr. and Mrs. J. B. Morin, Mgr. Mathieu, C.M.G., Mr. G. Morisset, Mr. Ernest, Mrs. and Miss Myrand, Dr. and Mrs. J. M. Mackay, Mr. and Mrs. B. Michaud, Major L. Z. Marsan, Mr. and Mrs. J. N. Matte, Capt. J. B. Matte, Mr. A., Mrs., Miss and Mr. Henri Montminy, Mr. and Mrs. Horace Malouin, Dr. and Mrs. A. Marois, Mrs. and Miss Marois, Mgr. Marois, V.G., Mr. Aug. Malouin, Mr. J. E., Mrs. and Miss Martineau, Mr. T. E., Mrs. and Misses Martin, Dr. and Mrs. V. Martin, Capt. and Mrs. J. E. and Miss Pansy Mills, Mrs. A. Moore.

N

Mr. and Mrs. Norman Neilson, Miss Neilson, Capt. Newton, D. O.C., A.D.C., Col. and Mrs. H. Neilson, Mr. and Mrs. Byron Nicholson, Mr. Chs. Neel, Duke and Duchess of Norfolk, Major and Mrs. Nelles, Mr., Mrs. and Mr. C. R. Nordheimer, Lt.-Col. and Mrs. Nattress.

O

Mr. and Mrs. J. J. O'Flaherty, Mr. D. D., Mrs. and Miss O'Meara, Mr. and Mrs. J. S. O'Meara, Capt. and Mrs. Geo. O'Farrell, Miss O'Farrell, Mr. Harry O'Sullivan, Mrs. G. and Miss Odell, Mr., Mrs. and Misses Obalski, Mr. and Mrs. Norman Ogilvie, Major and Mrs. A. T. Ogilvie, Mr. and Mrs. Paul G. Owen, Miss Ogilvie, Mr. Lorne Ogilvie, Brig.-Gen. W. D. and Mrs. Otter, Rev. G. and Mrs. Orchard, Hon. Frank, Mrs. and Misses Oliver, Major Finbar and Mrs. O'Farrell, Miss E. Power, Miss Anna Oliver, Mr. G. L. Ogilvie, Judge and Miss Ouimet.

P

Major G. R. Poole, Mr. and Mrs. Wm. Price, Mr. G. W., Mrs. and Miss Parmelee, Mr. H. M. and Miss Price, Mr. H. F. and Mrs. Price, Mr. and Mrs. A. J. Price, Mr. C. E., Mrs. and Misses Porteous, Mr. E., Mrs. and Misses Pope, Mr., Mrs. and Miss Parkin, Mr. and Mrs. J. B. Peters, Mr. Albert Peters, Miss Price, Mr. and Mrs. H. E. Price, Mr. W., Mrs., Miss and Messrs. Power, Major and Mrs. G. H. Parke, Mrs., Miss and Major Petry, Mr. H. E., Mrs., Miss and Messrs. Peters, Mr. and Mrs. T. Poston, Miss Pentland, Major and Mrs. J. B. Pym, Miss Pym, Sir A. and Lady Pelletier, Mr. and Mrs. A. J. Painchaud, Mr. Alph., Mrs. and Miss Pouliot, Major and Mrs. A. deL. Panet, Mr. Geo. Parent, M.P., Judge H. C., Mrs. and Miss Pelletier, Rev. Abbe Plante, Mr. and Mrs. A. D. Pruneau, Hon. E. T. and Mrs. Paquet, Hon. L. P. and Mrs. Pelletier, Rev. Abbe Plaisance, Monsgr. L. A. Paquet, Mr. L. E. Parent, Dr. C. R. and Mrs. Paquin, Mrs. E. and Miss Pacaud, Mr. and Mrs. Lucien Pacaud, Rev. Abbe Pelletier, Capt. and Mrs. E. T. Paquet, Hon. J. and Mrs. Prevost, Mr. and Mrs. H. A. Pacaud, Rev. Frere Pascal, Mr. and Mrs. L. E. O. Payment, Mr. J. E., Mrs. and Misses Prince, Mrs. Peebles, Capt. Pickering, A.D.C., Mrs. Provencher, Mr. T. Nap. Pelletier, Mr. and Mrs. B. E. Parent, Mr. and Mrs. J. Camille Pouliot, Mr. J. Leon Pouliot, Mr. and Mrs. C. J. Pigot, Mr. and Mrs. C. Pentland, Lady Mary Parker, Mr. and Mrs. D. Pottinger, Mr. and Mrs. Jos. Pope, Mr. St. Denys and Misses Prevost, Mrs. E. Pourtier, Mrs. W. Pentland, Mrs. Jas.

Piddington, Hon. Jas. Chs. Pitts, Major H. A. and Mrs. Panet, Mrs. W. H. and Miss Y. Paget, Lt.-Col. O. and Mrs. Pelletier, Mrs. and Miss Pickering, Mr. and Mrs. V. Pelletier, Mr. and Mrs. Geo. H. Perley, Miss Alice Pattee, Capt. A. H. H. Powell, A.D.C., Mr. G. R. and Miss Parkin, Capt. E. deB. Panet, Mr. Ferd. and Miss Peass, Lt.-Col. Sir Henry and Lady Pellatt, Commissioner A. B. Perry, N.W.M.P., Capt. and Mrs. A. Z. Palmer, Hon. W. and Mrs. Pugsley, Mr. C. L. Panet, Major Arthur H. Panet, C.O.C., Lieut. F. deL. Passy, R.C.E., Major and Mrs. Penchen, Mr. Ls., Mrs. and Miss B. Parent, Misses Phinney, Mrs. C. O. Palmer, Miss L. Powell, Mrs. and Miss H. Peck, Capt. and Mrs. J. A. Porter, Dr. and Mrs. E. Pelletier, Captain Panntney, Mrs. Pennington, Miss Parker, Dr. and Mrs. P. Pelletier, Messrs, Raymond and Harry Pease, Miss Porter, Mr. L. N. Patenaude.

R

Hon. Rodolph Roy, Hon. A., Mrs. and Miss and Mr. G. L. Robitaille, Mrs. F. E. Roy, Hon. A. B., Mrs. and Miss Routhier, Major T., Mr. R. Mackay and Misses Rinfret, Mr. and Mrs. Ernest Roy, Mr. J. Benj. and Miss Rousseau, Dr. and Mrs. Arthur Rousseau, Mr. and Mrs. C. E. Roy, Mr. and Mrs. Ferd.

VICE-PRESIDENT FAIRBANKS

Mrs. Fairbanks, General Art. Murray of the U. S. Army and Mrs Hurlbert at the Lieut.-Governor's Garden Party.

Roy, Major G. P., Mrs. and Miss Roy, Mgr. T. G. Rouleau, Rev. Abbe C. Roy, Mr. and Mrs. Alf. and Misses Robitaille, Dr. A. and Miss Robitaille, Lt.-Col. A., Mrs. and Mr. H. A. Roy, Capt. J. W. Roy, Mr. and Mrs. Armitage Rhodes, Mr. and Mrs. J. T. Ross, Lt.-Col. and Mrs. W. J. Ray, Mr., Mrs., Miss and Messrs. Rattray, Miss Rockett, Mr. A. and Misses Russell, Mr. and Mrs. J. F. Reeve, Mr. F., Mrs. and Mr. F. W. Ross, S. G. Mgr. E. Roy, Miss Russell, Mr. and Mrs. Stuart Ritchie, Mr. Leon and Misses Rouillard, Mr. Robert and Mrs. Rocher, Mr. and Mrs. J. M. Ritchie, Miss Marie Bertha Roy, Mrs. A. D. and Miss Dorothy Ross, Mr. and Mrs. J. E. Roy, Miss Grace Robertson, Rt. Hon. Earl of Ranfurly, Field Marshal Earl and Lady Eileen Roberts, Mr. Gordon Richardson, Mr. and Miss Ritchie, Hon. A. C. and Mrs. Rutherford, Dr. and Mrs. R. Ricard, Mr. C. Panet, Mrs., Miss and Mr. R. Raymond, Mr. C. R. Rhodes, Mrs. F. H. Rosengarten, Mr. and Mrs. W. R. Russell, Miss L. Richards, Miss Fritz Randolph, Miss Riley, Mr. Robt. H. Reid, Capt. Hon. A. H. Ruthven, Col., Mrs. and Misses Rutherford, Mr. Percival F. Ridout, Miss Ritchie, Miss Roper, Miss Louise Robb, Miss Ross, Mr. A., Mrs. and Miss Ross, Mr. and Mrs. Hayter Reed, Hon. Mr. Justice and Mrs. Ritchie, Hon. J. D., Mrs., Misses and Mr. O. Rolland, Messrs. J. B. and P. Rolland, Mr. and Mrs. R. W. Reford, Mr. Elz. Roy, Miss May Riley.

S

Hon. J., Mrs. and Mr. S. Shehyn, Mr. and Mrs. J. E. Samson, Mr. and Mrs. A. Saint-Jacques, Misses and Messrs. Simard, Dr. and Mrs. A. Simard, Misses and Messrs. Simard, Dr. and Mrs. C. O. Samson, Mr. E. A. S. Smith, R.C.R., Lt.-Col. and Mrs. B. A. Scott, Mr. and Mrs. Harcourt Smith, Mr. I. G., Mrs. and Messrs. Scott, Rev. Canon and Mrs. F. G. Scott, Mrs. P. A. Shee, Mrs. E. L. and Miss Sewell, Mr. and Mrs. Wm. Sharples, Lt.-Col. E. G., Mrs. and Messrs. Scott, Mr. and Mrs. F. S. Stocking, Mr. H., Mrs., Miss and Messrs. Staveley, Mr. E. B. and Mrs. Staveley, Capt. and Mrs. J. J. Sharples, Mrs. R. Stocking, Mrs. P. A. and Misses Shaw, Mr. and Mrs. A. E. Scott, Mr. and Mrs. L. G. Scott, Col. C. C., Mrs. and Miss Sewell, Mr., Mrs. and Miss Stain, Capt. and Mrs. A. E. Swift, Mr. and Mrs. F. W. Smith, Miss M. Sewell, the Misses Stevenson, Mr. and Mrs. Arthur Smith, Hon. J. and Mrs. Sharples, Mr. and Mrs. L. Stein, Mr. and Mrs. Geo. C. Scott, Mr. and Mrs. G. G. Stuart, Miss Stuart, Miss Shehyn, Mr. Albert and Mrs. Sevigny, Mr. and Mrs. Paul Sise, Mrs. Chs. Sharples, Mr. L. P., Mrs. and Misses Sirois, Mr. and Mrs. J. A. Scott, Mr. and Mrs. E. Slade, Miss Sims, Mr. and Mrs. C. C. Scott. Mr. and Mrs. Arthur Sladen, Sir T., Lady and Miss Saughnessy, Mr. and Mrs. H. H. Sharples, Mr. and Mrs. Archie Sharples, Miss Simpson, Mr. R. G. Sare, Mr. and Mrs. W. B. Scott, Mrs. Geo. E. Smart, Lt.-Col. and Mrs. Offley Shore, Mr. and Mrs. C. S. Smith, Lt.-Col. and Mrs. R. K. Scott, Miss Scarth, Capt. Kincaid Smith, Lt.-Col., Mrs. and Miss Sherwood, Hon. Jas. and Mrs. Sutherland, the Misses Spry, Mr. and Mrs. Sanderman, Miss Hope Sewell, Mr. and Mrs. R. C. Scott, Prof. and Mrs. Sumichrast, Mr. and Mrs. E. F. Surveyer, Mrs. Stroud, Mrs. G. A. Sherreff, Mrs. W. E. Sanford, Miss M. Stewart, Mr. R. C. and Mrs. Smith, Mr. Ernest and Mr. C. Stuart, Mrs. Sweny, Mr. and Mrs. Jas. Smellie, Mr. and Mrs. H. M. Sewell, Hon. R. F. Sutherland, Miss Sutherland, Mrs. Sergeant, Miss Saunders, Miss Selwyn, Miss M. B. Slade, Mr. and Mrs. A. A. Smith, Mr. and Mrs. Russell Spaulding, Mr. B. Schriver, Miss G. Symonds, Hon. R. W. Scott, Mr. and Mrs. Collingwood and Miss Fletcher Schreiber, Rt. Hon. Lord Strathcona, Miss Smylie.

T

Mr. Paul Tardivel, Mrs. Alf., Misses and Mr. S. Turcot Hon. A. and Mrs. Turgeon, Lt.-Col. and Mrs. R. E. W. Turner, Hon. R. Mrs., Miss and Messrs. Turner, Mr. and Mrs. G. H. Thomson, Mr. and Mrs. Jack Thomson, Mr. and Mrs. Joshua Thompson, Colonel F. Turnbull, Mr. and Mrs. G. V. Tessier, Mr. and Mrs. Ant. Taschereau, Judge Aug., Mrs. and Miss Tessier, Mr. Gust. Turcotte, Hon. Jules and Mrs. Tessier, Mr. L. Trepanier, Mr. and Mrs. Félix Turcotte, Mrs. Edouard Taschereau, Mr. and Mrs. C. E. Taschereau, Mr. Ernest Taschereau, Mr. and Mrs. Alleyn Taschereau, Dr. E., Mrs. Misses and Messrs. Turcot, Mr. Cyr., Mrs. and Mr. J. des R. Tessier, Mgr. H. Tetu, Mr. Eugene Trudel, Mr. and Mrs. A. M. Tache, Mr. Geo., Mrs. and Mr. Ed. Tanguay, Rev. Pere Turgeon, Messrs. Henri and Emile Tessier, Hon. A. and Mrs. Taschereau, Mr. E. E., Mrs. and Miss Tache, Mr. Adjutor Turcotte, jnr., Capt. and Mrs. G. A. Taschereau, Mr. B. A. Turner, Mr. A., Misses and W. H. Thomson, Judge and Mrs. Tracy, Mrs. I. W. Timmer, Miss Taschereau, Mrs. and Miss Townshend, Miss Tillon, Miss Towers, the Misses Tanguay, Miss Taft, Chief Justice Sir H. and Miss Taschereau, Mr. C. V. M. and Miss and Mr. Temple, Mr. and Mrs. Chs. Tylee, Miss Thomson, Mr. and Mrs. R. Travers, Mr. Ernest and Miss Tremblay, Major Thacker, Mr. and Mrs. J. R. Thomson, Mr. Chs. S. Thompson, Mrs. Thomson, Mr. and Mrs. A. J. Turner, Mrs. Frederic Tudor, Dr. and Mrs. G. Tasse, Miss Fredwell.

V

Rev. Canon and Mrs. Von Iffland, Mrs. and Misses Van Felson, Dr. And Mrs. Chs. Verge, Mr. Alf. Valliere, Miss C. Vallerand, Mr. and Mrs. Adolphe Veilleux, Mr. L. A., Mrs. and Misses Vallee, Mr. H., Mrs. and Miss Verret, Mrs., Miss and Messrs. Vallee, Mr. and Mrs. L. P. Vallerand, Mr. Walter F. Venner, Mr. and Mrs. A. B. Van Felson, Mr. and Mrs. Van Bruyssell, Capt. G. Van Felson, Miss J. Vezina, Capt. and Mrs.

Hector Verret, Mr. R. L. Von Iffland, Mr. R. B. Viets, Sir Wm. Lady and Miss Van Horne, Miss M. Vallee, the Misses Valliere de St. Real, Dr. and Mrs. W. Verge.

W

Mrs. W. J. Whitehead, Mr. Wurtele, Mrs. and Miss Wurtele, Maj.-General and Mrs. J. F. Wilson, Mr. and Mrs. A. Wheeler, Very Rev. Dean and Mrs. L., Mr. J. and Miss Williams, W. W. Watson, Mr. and Mrs. W. H. Wiggs, Hon. W. A., Mrs. and Miss Weir, Capt. D. and Mrs. Watson, Lt.-Col. E. F. and Mrs. Wurtele, Mr. F. C., Mr. and Mrs. Wurtele, Mrs. W. D. Waddel, Lt.-Col. W. Wood, Mrs. C. W. and Messrs. Wilson, Mrs. E. E. and Miss Webb, Mr. and Mrs. W. A. Weir, Mr. R. Wickenden, Lt. A. S. Wright, R.C.A., Mrs. J. W. and Misses Wurtele, Miss Whelan, Col. and Mrs. Hanbury Williams, Col. and Mrs. G. R. White, Miss and Mrs. Martin Wolff, Capt. and Mrs. Basil White, Rev. G. Eardley Wilmot, Miss Watson, Mr. and Mrs. L. J. Webster, Mr. F. Wanklyn, Mr. H. S. Wurtele, Gentleman Cadet D. White, Mrs. R. A. Williams, Miss Ward, Miss Williams, Miss Wilgress, Mr. Byron, Mrs. and Miss Walker, Miss Walker, Miss D. O. White, Mr. Rene Wiallard, Lt.-Col. Wadmore, R.C.R., Lt.-Col. Williams, R.C.D., Miss Wells, Sir M. Bromley, Bt. Wilson, Sir Chs. and Lady Rivers Wilson, Hon. J. P., Mrs. and Misses Whitney, Miss Winslow, Miss Watt, Mrs. Frank B. Weston, Mrs. Wurtele, Mrs. C. B. Wood, Mr. George Wolfe, Miss B. White, Mr. and Mrs. Weatherbie, Lt.-Col F. Wedderburn, Mrs. Jas. Wood, Mr. N. F., Miss and Mr. R. C. Wilson, Miss Whateley, Mr. J. C. Watson, Mr. and Mrs. Horace Wallis, Mrs. Wilbur, Mr. W. B. P. and Mr. Miles Weeks, Mr. and Mrs. J. B. Waddell, Major W. D. Weeks, A.D.C., Rev.

ENTRANCE TO CITADEL

Where H.R.H. the Prince of Wales
returned after the Garden Party at
Spencer Wood.

Canon and Mrs. Welch, Mr. Gerald Wood, Mr. and Mrs. E. Waagen, Mrs. F. H. Whitton, Mr. Warren.

Y

Mr. and Mrs. G. B. S. Young, Capt. D. D. Young, A.D.C., Lt.-Col. and Mrs. D. D. Young, Dr. and Mrs. H. B. Yates.

The Prince of Wales had attended the last event given in his honour on shore. From the garden party at Spencerwood he returned to the Citadel where after saying farewell to several people assembled there, he again entered his carriage, this time to once more traverse a familiar route, but for the last time during his present stay. It was the eve of his departure. He now drove to the wharf and left Canadian soil embarking on H.M.S. Indomitable which left again on the morrow to cross the Atlantic eastward bound.

The route from the Citadel to the King's wharf was lined with military guards, behind whom again stood Quebec's populace — this time not to catch a glimpse of the Prince, for he was now a familiar figure in Quebec, but to gaze for the last time at H. R. H., who during his short stay had made himself so popular. Quebecers parted from the Prince with profound regret. Cheers attended the drive preparatory to a homeward journey.

On the Prince's arrival at the King's wharf a new cheer which was given on the Terrace by the many who lined it, traveled downward, where, resumed by the crowd below, it was re-echoed until the Prince had inspected the guard drawn up at the landing, and leaving Canadian soil again embarked on the royal launch which bore him to the mighty Indomitable.

THE GARDEN PARTY

Given by The Lieutenant-Governor and Lady Jetté at Spencer Wood. The Prince may be seen walking up The Path. Drawn by The London Sphere's Special Artist, Signor F. Matania.

The fleet welcomed their returning Admiral in a manner not soon forgotten. Every deck was lined by the sailors on board, while the ships were all decorated. As the ten thousand men stood lined up, the guns of the ships bellowed their salutes. The river was soon covered with a thick mist from which in an unearthly manner were heard the reverberations of the twenty-one shots that were fired. This sound had no sooner ceased than the bands of each ship began to play the national anthem, started by one band and continued by the next until from the distance and over the now quieted waves came the same strains from the French flagship. All was now still on the waters when from H.M.S. Exmouth was fired a single gun and a moment later the waves were again disturbed by the echo of a cheer for the Prince of Wales given by ten thousand voices. It was the last grand cheer for the Prince in Canada. In the morning he had left Quebec.

The last official function in connection with the visit of the Prince was the dinner given by His Royal Highness in the evening to about seventy guests on board H.M.S. Exmouth, flagship of the Atlantic fleet present at Quebec during the celebrations.

The quarter-deck was divided into two apartments by a wall of flags. One side was used as a reception-room, while beyond were the dining-tables splendidly decorated with ward-room plate and flowers. The toasts were few and speeches short. Those present were :—

Capt. E. W. Goodenough, R.N. ; Col. Geo. Denison, Mr. Mackenzie, Capt. A. D. Ricardo, R.N. ; Sir Thos. Shaughnessy, Capt. Winslow, U.S.N. ; Capt. W. O. Boothby, R.N. ; Commissioner Perry, Hon. Sir Jas. Whitney, Lord Annaly, Lt.-Gen. Sir Reg. Pole-Carew, K.C.B., C.V.O. ; Rear-Admiral Cowles, U.S.N. ; Hon. Rodolphe Lemieux, Hon. W. S. Fielding, Right Rev. the Bishop of Quebec; His Honor Sir Louis Jette, K.C.M.G. ; Vice-President Fairbanks, H.R.H. Prince of Wales, His Excellency the Governor-General, G.C.V.O. ; the Earl of Ranfurly, Sir Wilfrid Laurier, Rev. G. H. Williams, Lord Strathcona, Major-General P. H. U. Lake, C.B., C.M.G. ; Brig.-Gen. A. Murray, U.S.N. ; Capt. A. W. Ewart, U.S. N. ; Sir George Drummond, Capitaine De Vaisseau Clemen, C.M.G. ; His Worship Sir George Garneau. Sir H. Montagu Allan, Col. Sir J. Hanbury-Williams, K.C.V.O., C.M.G. ; Mr. Byron Walker, C.V.O. ; Engineer Captain J. E. Chase, R.N. ; Capitaine de Vaisseau Habert, Lt.-Col. the Hon. J. S. Hendrie, Sir Francis Hopwood, Hon. Sir Lomer Gouin, Rear-Admiral Sir J. R. Jellicoe, Major-Gen. Wilson, Brig.-Gen. W. D. Otter, C.B., C.V.O. ; Hon. R. Dandurand, Hon. G. P. Graham, Hon. Frank Oliver, Field Marshal Earl Roberts, V.C., K.G., etc. ; His Honor James Dunsmuir, Vice-Admiral Jaureguiberry, G.C.

V.O. ; Vice-Admiral the Hon. Sir A. G. Curzon-Howe, the Earl of Dudley, G.C.V.O. ; His Hon. G. H. V. Bulyea, Rev. Dr. Duval, Hon. L. P. Brodeur, His Grace the Duke of Norfolk, K.G. ; Sir Chas. Fitzpatrick, Rear-Admiral Kingsmill, Hon. R. F. Sutherland, Commodore King-Hall, Hon. M. Turgeon, C. V.O. ; Lt.-Col. Sir Arthur Bigge, Hon. L. A. Taschereau, Capt. Cuthbert Chapman, Mr. Joseph Pope, C.V.O. ; Capt. R. Huddleston, R.N. ; Lt.-Col. Sherwood, Captain A. J. Hennaker-Hugham, Captain Newton, A.D.C. ; Captain Fawcett, Lt.-Col. Shore.

Historical Ball

The last of the many balls which took place at the Parliament buildings during the celebrations was the historical ball in the evening.

It was a pageant ball. There danced the old courtiers of Henry IV and the ladies of the court of his predecessor Francis I. With them in common step were also peasant women and ladies of the ancien regime whose toggery if not as gorgeous was evidence of the desire of the colonists to imitate the social life of old France. Historical characters also flirted among the dancers. Ages mingled but it mattered not. With Helen Boule, the girl-wife of Quebec's founder could be seen Madeleine de Vercheres, Madame de la Peltrie, and others who lived several decades after. The soldiers of Montcalm danced the same set with an officer of the Carignan-Sallieres regiment. A warrior of Chateauguay waltzed with a lady who had seen Jacques-Cartier. Thus in unsullied glee the ages of the past danced on. It was not the courtly pavane nor the Iroquois war-dance. The dances were of to-day. Everything else was of to-day but the spirit was that of history—the history of the times and peoples that made the Dominion—the history which one is pleased to think of—the history whose thoughts are studied and the garb of whose period is worn. In a thankful manner the spirit of the age was imbued and its garb donned.

The spirit of pageantry and history filled Quebec and even in their enjoyments Quebecers learned, for the ball was a lesson and a pleasant one.

The ball, which was in every respect a most decided success, was organized by the following efficient :—

HISTORICAL BALL COMMITTEE

President—John Burstall.
Vice-President—Hon. P. A. Choquette.
Treasurer—Neuville Belleau.
Secretary—Robert Campbell.
Committee—Major J. D. Brousseau, W. D. Baillarge, Wm. Dobell, Major de L. Panet, Major A. Fages, Harcourt Smith.

Following is a list of those who were present :—

SPECIALLY INVITED GUESTS.

Officers of English ships.
"   "   Leon Gambetta.
"   "   Admiral Aube.
"   "   New Hampshire, Governor-General, Sir John Hanbury Williams, Major General Lake, the Hon F., Mrs. and Miss Oliver, Sir George and Lady Drummond, Mr. Wm. Price, Lieut.-Col. Turner, the Officers of Royal Canadian Garrison Artillery, Hon. Mr., Mrs. and Miss Dandurand, the Officers of the Royal Canadian Regiment, Sir Chas. Lady and Miss Fitzpatrick, Mr. Louis Horbette, Mrs. A. Joseph, Mrs. Williams, Mrs. Millar

GALLERY GUESTS.

A

Miss Maud Audet, Miss M. Ashe.

B

Mrs. W. D. Baillarge, Mr. D. Breakey, Mrs. C. C. Breakey, Mrs. D. Breakey, Miss Bethune, Mr. St. George Baldwin, Mr. Thos. H. Bullock, Mr. J. K. Boswell, Mrs. John Breakey, Mrs. Thos. H. Bullock; Miss Louisa Boswell.

C

Mrs. R. Campbell, Mrs. Campbell, Miss F. Choquette, Miss J. Choquette, Miss K. Campbell, Miss B. Campbell, Mr. O. Boothe Callaghan, Mr. W. S. W. Cook, Mrs. D. P. Conroy, Mrs. Jas. Cosgrove, Mrs. S. W. Cook.

D

Mrs. Dobie, Mr. C. S. Dunn, Mrs. C. W. S. Dunn, Mr. C. N. S. Drunn, Mr. E. J. Duggan, Mr. A. E. Doucet, Mrs. Doucet.

F

Miss Fowler.

G

Miss S. Gibert, Mrs. Jas. Gibson, Mrs. Grosvenor, Mrs. T. N de la Grandville, Miss Gibert.

H

Mrs. Hicker.

K

Mrs. Frances King.

L

The Misses Lawson, (4); Mrs. LeMoyne.

M

Miss N. Molson, Miss E. Molson, Miss M. Molson, Mr. W. Marcott, Mr. Muir, Miss Mitchell, Miss M. Mitchell, Miss Machin, the Misses Meiklejohn (2); the Misses Moshers (2); Mrs. Muir, Mrs. Archibald Miller, Mrs. J. M. McCarthy, Miss McGie, Mr. D. McGie.

N

Miss C. N. Norris.

O

Mrs. Ormbie, Mrs. D. D. O'Meara.

P

Miss Petry, Miss Philips, Mr. H. B. Patton, Mr. W. W. Power, Mrs. Piddington, Mrs. Power, Miss Potter.

R

Mrs. W. H. Rowley, Miss May Riley.

S

Mrs. E. M. Stires, Dr. E. M. Stires, Miss M. Slade, Miss M. Sewell, Mrs. H. H. Sharples, Miss Shchyu.

T

Mrs. Taschereau, Mrs. Tudor, Miss Turcotte, Miss Taschereau, Mrs. R. Turner.

W

Mr. Welch, Miss Wilson, Miss Watt.

GUESTS IN COSTUMES.

A

Miss Atwater, Frontenac Scene; Miss Aime, Court Lady; Miss G. M. Atkinson, Francis I; Mr. Kenneth Angus, Gentleman, Francis I; Miss Andrews, Court Henry IV scene; Miss Violet Atkinson, Scene Henry IV; Miss Aylmer, Lady in Frontenac Scene; Mr. F. H. Andrews, Highlander; Mr. W. F. B. Atkinson, Duke de Mayenne

B

Mrs. Bovey, Lady, 1837; Miss Alice Breakey, Henry IV Court; Mr de Gaspe Beaubien, Cardinal Richelieu; Miss E. Brodie, Henry IV scene; Miss A. B. Brodie, Henry IV scene; Miss E. Burstall, Court Lady; Miss M. Butler, Laval scene; Miss B. Binet, Lady Francis I; Miss A. Binet, Francis I Court; Miss C. Bote, Francis I Court; Miss Bell, Court Francis I; Miss Bell, Court Francis I; Mr. Geo. Belleau, Courtier, Henry IV scene; Mr. C. E. A. Boswell, Gentleman Court Francis I; Miss Bovey, Henry IV; Mrs. J. F. Burstall, Court Lady; Miss E. Billingsley, Lady Henry IV; Mrs. R. M. Beckett, Lady Court Frontenac; Mr. J. A. Brody, Courtier Henry IV scene; Miss B. Beaudry, Henry IV; Miss Boulanger, Henry IV; Miss Benson, Henry IV; Miss H. E. Burstall, Mr. Breakey, Indian Chief, 1700; Miss Breakey, Henry IV; Miss R. Beaudry, Henry IV; Miss Bremer, Lady Leicester; Miss Bate, Court Henry IV; Mr. Joseph Belleau, Don de Dieu Officer; Mr. K. M. Beckett, Gentleman of Court of Frontenac; Mr. G. Barclay, Wolfe's Army.

C

Judge A F. Carrier, General Murray, Miss Comb, Pavane; Mrs. George Carrier, Francis I Court; Miss Jessie Cassils, Frontenac Court; Miss Susie Cassils, Frontenac Court; Miss Chadwick, Henry IV Court; Miss Crombie, Henry IV Court; Miss Cook, Henry IV Scene; Miss D. Cook, Henry IV Scene; Miss M. Cassils, Henry IV; Miss M. Cook, Henry IV; Mr. W. S. Champion, Pavane; Mr. W. H. S. Cote, Wolfe's Army; Mr. Frank Carrel, Commander R.M.A. Wolfe's Army; Mr. G. Carrier, Gentleman Court Francis I; Mrs. H. B. Campbell, Court Francis I; Miss M. Campbell, Frontenac Scene; Master Carrier, Page Henri IV Scene; Master Carrier Page Henri IV; Miss C. Cook, Court of Henry IV; Miss E. Cook, Miss O. Clint, Court of Henry IV; Miss Crosby, Madame de Polignac; Miss J Campbell, Francis I; Master McK. Cloutier, Page, Henry IV Scene; Mr. Kenneth G. Cavan, Henry IV Scene; Miss Chadwick, Henry IV Court; Mrs. Cannon, Lady Henry IV Court; Mrs. L. L. A. Carrier, Lady Court Henry IV; Mrs. J. C. Cloutier, Lady Henry IV; Mr. A. Champman, Courtier Court of Henry IV; Mr. Frank Clark, Courtier in Court Laval; Mr. W. Cote, Officer, Don de Dieu; Mr Ant Couillard, Court Henry IV; Chs. Chartre, Scene Frontenac.

D

Mr. Digby, George III; Miss Duggan, Flora McIvoe, (time of 1650); Miss A. Daly, Laval Tracy Scene; Mr. Guy Drummond, Grenadier Guard; Mr. W. M. Dobell, Francis I; Miss Digby, Frontenac Scene; Mrs. Wm. Dobell, Henry IV Scene; Miss Mary Dobil, Henry IV scene; Miss E. Dobil, Henry IV scene; Major Alfred Dobell, Wolfe's Army.

F

Miss Em. Fiset, Francis I Scene; Mr. Raoul Fiset, Francis I scene; Miss M. L. Van Felson, Princess de la Roche-sur-Yonf; Miss Fairfax, Francis I Court; Mrs. Foley, Lady Court Henry

IV; Miss Foley, Lady Henry IV Court; Miss Leonie Fiset, Francis I Court.

G

Mrs. L. Nap. Gauvin, Frontenac Court; Miss G. Gibson, Henry IV Court; Miss J. Garneau, Henry IV Court; Miss V. Gregory, Francis I Court; Miss Green, Francis I Court; Miss Blanche Genest, Henry IV Court; Miss Therese Genest, Henry IV Court; Miss Gibsone, Lady of Francis I Court; Mr. A. de le Grandville, Don de Dieu; Mrs. G. Gregory, Lady Francis I; Mr. L. Nap. Gauvin, Frontenac Court; Mr. R. D. Greig, Gentleman Court Francis I; Mr. D. A. Greig, Gentleman Court Francis I; Mr. Leon Garneau, Court Henry IV; Mr. Georges Garneau, Court Henry IV, Miss E. Greg, Lady of Court Henry IV; Miss G. Greg, Lady of Court Henry IV; Major Gibson, Wolfe's Army; Mr. L. F. Gibson, Gentleman, Henry IV; Mr. J. Gauvreau, Frontenac; Mr. Dudley Gilmore, Courtier, Henry IV Scene; Mrs. K. F. Gilmour, Pavane Henry IV.

H

Miss Vera Hamilton, Frontenac Court; Miss Jessie Hamilton, Frontenac Court; Mrs. J. K. Hill, Laval Scene; Miss Hary, Francis I Scene; Miss Juliette Hamel, Francis I Scene; Miss Jean Howey, Francis IV Court; Miss Henry, George III Court; Miss Gladys How, Frontenac Court; Mr. W. C. L. Harvey, Court Francis I; Mr. K. Holloway, Frontenac Court; Miss M. Hamel, Court Francis I; Mr. J. W. Hamilton, Lt. Wolfe's Army; Miss V. Hale, Lady Henry IV Court; Miss G. Hale, Court Lady Frontenac; Miss C. Hale, Peasant Frontenac; Mrs. James Hamilton, Lady of Frontenac Court; Mr. Phil. Holliday, Courtier Henry IV Scene; Mr. J. Holliday, Wolfe's Army; Miss B. Hall, Lady Henry IV.

J

Miss C. Jones, Court Lady, 1897; Miss Joseph, Henry IV Court; Miss Jones, Henry IV; Miss S. Jones, Francis I Court; Miss M. E. Joseph, Pavane, Scene Henry IV; Mr. E. C. Joseph, Noble, Frontenac; Miss Judge, Henry IV scene; Miss S. Joseph, Peasant Frontenac Scene; Miss M. Joseph, Court Lady, 16th century; Miss Johnson, Francis I Court; Mrs. Horace Joseph, Lady of Quebec, 16th century; Mr. Leonard Jones, Lieut. Nairn; Miss L. Johnston, The Pavane.

K

Miss Kennedy, Henry IV Scene; Miss Kavanagh, Angelique de Melouse; Mr. R. J. Killan, Henry IV Pavane.

L

Miss Lemoine, Court Lady; Miss Lavery, Henry IV; Miss P. Lemesurier, Henry IV Court; Miss J. Lemesurier, Henry IV Court; Miss Laroche, Francis I Court; Mr. L. E. Labrecque, Gentleman Henry IV; Mr. T. W. Lemesurier, Gentleman Henry IV; Mr. Alexander Lafrance, Gentleman Henry IV; Mr. Geo. Lamothe, Courtier, Henry IV Scene; Mr. W. P. Lindsay, Fraser Highlander; Mr. O. Larue, Suite de Champ; Mrs. W. B. Lindsay, Marie de Bourbon; Miss E. Laird, Peasant, Frontenac Scene; Miss de Lery, Madame Champlain; Mrs. Leonard, Lady Frontenac Scene; Mr. John Laird, Frontenac Court; Mr. Paul Larue, Gentleman Henry IV; Mr. S. A. Lemesurier, Gentleman Henry IV; Mr. Jacques Lantier, Courtier in Court Tracy.

M

Mr. A. O. Meredith, Wolfe's Army; Miss Dorothy Mott, Pavane; Miss M. Milne, Court Lady; Miss Lilian Milne, Court Lady; Miss M. Monaghan, Henry IV Court; Miss B. Meredith, Frontenac Court; Miss A. S. Morewood, Henry IV; Mr. W. F. E. Morewood, Henry IV Scene; Mr. W. F. E. Morewood, Henry IV Scene; Mr. J. B. H. Mongenais, Officer Don de Dieu; Dr. Myrand, Surgeon on Don de Dieu; Mr. C. M. Mowat, Gentleman Henry IV Scene; Mr. J. E. Mahy, Francis I Court; Master Percy Murphy, Page, Court of Henry IV; Miss I. Morewood, Frontenac Scene; Miss E. Meredith, Pavane; Mr K. Molson, Gentleman Wolfe's Army; Mr. A. D. Munro, Court Henry IV; Miss Macpherson, Henry IV Court; Mr. J. McCarthy, Capt. Royal Navy; Mr. B. McLennan, Francis I; Miss D. McNaughton, Lady Henry IV;

Mrs. J. C. McLimont, Court Lady Francis in train of Marie de Medici; Miss Amy McLimont, Frontenac period.

N

Mr. C. V. Norris, Courtier, Henry IV Scene.

O

Miss Mabel Odell, Francis I Court; Miss M. Oliver, Court Lady in Henry IV Scene; Mr. A. E. Ogilvie, Courtier Francis I; Mr. Guy Ogilvie, Francis I; Mr. A. G. Oliver, Gentleman Court Henry IV; Mr. J. S. O'Meara, Officer Royal American Regiment; Mrs. J. S. O'Meara, Mary Queen of Scots; Miss Eileen O'Meara, Court of Napoleon I; Miss Oliver, Henry IV Court.

P

Mr. C. Porteous, Henry IV Court; Mr. H. J. Pinsonneault, Courtier in Henry IV Scene; Mr. H. D. Powell, citizen; Miss Blanche Parent, Pavane, Henry IV Court; Mrs. Pigot, Henry IV Court; Mr. G. Power, Wolfe's Army; Mrs. T. A. Poston, Laval's Time; Mrs. G. Power, Francis I Court; Mr. F. de L. Passy, Maj.-Gen. Wolfe's Army; Mr. A. J. Price, Court Francis I; Miss T. Price, Court of Frontenac; Miss Ethel Perley, Francis I; Court; Mrs E. Pourtier, Louise de Savoie, Mother Queen; Mrs. Pelton, Peasant; Miss Pelton, Citizen Frontenac Court; Miss Lola Powell, Court Henry IV; Mrs. W. Price, Frontenac Court; Mrs. H B. Powell, Frontenac Court; Miss A. Porteous, Lady of Frontenac Court.

R

Mr. W. A. Rodgers, Sir Walter Raleigh; Mr. C. Rhodes, Scene Frontenac; Mr. S. C. Rondeau, Court Francis I; Mrs. Wm. Reed, Court Lady Henry IV; Mrs. J. T. Ross, Court Lady; Mr. G B. Rattray, Wolfe's Army; Mrs. J. Ross, Lady Court Henry IV; Miss D. Ross, Court Lady Henry IV; Miss Mildred Russell, Court Francis I; Mr. W. E. Reed, Court Gentleman Henry IV; Miss Rita Roche, Mdc. Ginchereau de St. Denis, Laval-Tracy Court; Miss Ritchie, Henry IV; Mrs. A. Rhodes, Scene Frontenac; Miss D. Rhodes, Scene Frontenac.

S

Mr. G. Bryant Schwartz, citizen Frontenac Scene; Miss Mary Stewart, time of Louis XIV; Mrs. Slade, Court Henry IV; Miss Hope Sewell, Lady Henry IV; Mr. R. G. Sare, Court of Henry IV, Pavane; Mr. A. M. Strang, Gentleman Francis I; Mr. Norman Strang, Gentleman Wolfe's Army; Miss C. W. Sewell, Henry IV; Miss Olga Schwartz, Peasant Frontenac Scene; Mr. J. R. Strange, Wolfe's Army; Mrs. Spry, Lady of Frontenac Court; Miss Spry, Lady of Frontenac Court; Miss S. G. Stewart, Peasant in Frontenac Scene; Miss M. Scott, Frontenac Scene, Mr. H. H. Scott, Frontenac Scene; Mr. W. B. Scott, Henry IV Scene; Mr. M. S. Stevenson, Officer Wolfes' Army; Miss M. Stain, Peasant Frontenac Scene; Miss Stain, Lady in Frontenac Court; Mrs E. L. Sewell, Duchess in Henry IV Court; Mrs. G. C. Scott, Pavare, Henry IV Court.

T

Miss Maud Thompson, Frontenac Scene; Mr. J. R. Thompson, Wolfe's Army; Mr. Kenneth Thompson, Wolfe's Army; Mr. C. N. Torrens, Wolfe's Army; Miss Townsend, Princess Poca Hontas; Mr. F. Turcotte, Gentleman Henry IV.

V

Mrs. Chas Vezina, Lady Henry IV Court; Mr. Chas. Vezina, Gentleman Henry IV; Mrs. Vanderwerken, Jean Dundonneau, Laval Court; Miss C. Vorelle, Francis I Scene

W

Mr. W. A. A. Walcot, Court Francis I; Mr. John Wiley, Don de Dieu Officer; Miss O. Wright, Peasant; Miss Webster, Court Henry IV Scene; Miss Winslow, Henry IV; Mrs. A. C. Woodward, Henry IV; Mrs. Weston, Lady French Court 1670; Miss Margery Webb, Francis I Court; Miss Dorothy White, Henry IV Court; Mr. B. S. Woodley, Gentleman Henry IV; Mr. W. Wood, 1812 Col ; Mr. H. P. Weiglet, Soldier; Miss Hope Wurtele, Lady Court Henry IV; Miss Wolff, Henry IV Court; Miss Williams, Frontenac Scene; Mr. J. W. Williams, Frontenac.

Y

Miss Yorke, Lady Francis I Court.

Eleventh Day, Wednesday, July Twenty-Ninth

British Fleet Leaves the Harbour

T an early hour in the morning when from the east came the sun's rays sundering the streaks of grey dawn covering the river, the British war-vessels with H.R.H. the Prince of Wales on board the Indomitable, noise-lessly stole out of the harbour and started on their course across the Atlantic.

Quebec was yet asleep. There was no booming of cannon, no echoing of wild cheers, no hand-clapping. All was quiet and from the rocky city nought was heard. Nothing peered from its embattlements but its guns silently pointing in sphinx-like silence on the water beneath. All official farewells and cannonading were over. There was nothing to disturb the sleeping city.

Through the channel of the river wended slowly the solemn and quiet procession of ships. Turning her prow with the tide, H.M.S. Exmouth, the flag-ship of the fleet soon disappeared behind the curve of St. Joseph de Levis closely followed by H.M.S Albemarle. In a long line came the Arrogant, the Venus, the Duncan and the Russel, their grey hulks appearing through the mist as huge phantoms gliding along gracefully and swiftly. H.M.S. Indomitable, on which rested the Prince of Wales after his busy visit came next, at first hardly appearing to move, but in a few minutes passing beyond the gaze of the few who at that early morning hour were watching the fleet's departure from the Terrace. H.M.S. Minotaur followed, bringing up the rear to a naval procession, the glory and the terror of a people.

The ships all flew signal flags—farewell messages to Quebec, and within fifteen minutes of having bestirred themselves left no trace of their presence in the broad river, flowing before Quebec.

An hour later, a farewell salute from U.S.S. New Hampshire and responses from the Citadel and the French warships still in port announced the departure of the United States cruiser.

Thus early in the day began the exodus of the elements that gave to the celebrations their dignified aspect. The Prince of Wales who had come from across the seas to join in the rejoicing of Canadians had departed leaving behind him but many pleasant memories, To His Excellency the Governor-General he wrote:—

H.R.H. Letter to Lord Grey

Citadel, Quebec, 28th July, 1908.

DEAR LORD GREY:

On the eve of my departure, I wish to express in the strongest terms the intense pleasure and satisfaction which I have derived from my stay in Quebec.

THE INDIANS IN CAMP

One of the Telegraph's Prize Pictures taken by J. M. Ritchie.

I have been deeply touched by the enthusiastic and affectionate welcome accorded to me on all occasions, and by all classes, not only from the people of Quebec, but from the vast numbers assembled within her limits from all parts of the Dominion.

From the moment of landing I have received nothing but the greatest kindness, and have been most hospitably entertained by Your Excellencies, by the Lieutenant-Governor of the Province of Quebec, by its Premier and Executive Council, and by the Mayor and Municipality, as also by the University of Laval.

I shall return home with a lasting sense of satisfaction that it was possible to avail myself of the kind invitation of the Canadian Government to take part in the memorable events of the past week, and that I was thus able to help you and the people of Quebec, in giving effect to the great conception you had formed for doing worthy honor to the Tercentenary of Quebec, and to the joint memories of Wolfe and Montcalm. It is my earnest hope that this movement may be still further supported, and that no efforts will be relaxed to ensure the consummation of the work which has been so happily inaugurated.

Upon the interesting and impressive pageant I have already dwelt in a letter addressed to the Mayor, but I desire to express, through your Excellency, to the National Battlefields Commission, and to Mr. Lascelles, the Master of the Pageantry, my sincerest congratulations upon the marvellous results achieved by their historical research, artistic feeling, and untiring energy. Similarly do I congratulate all the authorities, official and honorary, upon the unqualified success which has characterized every incident and detail of the celebrations.

The manner in which the other Provinces . joined with Quebec, and gave both moral and material support to the idea of the Tercentenary celebrations, must do much to strengthen those ties of common feeling and mutual trust so essential to the unity and strength of the Dominion.

It was with the greatest pleasure that I reviewed the Canadian troops, and the seamen and mariners of the French, American and British fleets on Friday last. The presence of sailors on such an occasion is always highly popular, and I feel sure Your Excellency and the people of Canada appreciate the kindness of the French and American admirals in landing their smart detachments to take part in the march past. All I saw, and especially all

CHAMPLAIN laying out plan of the City.

I hear from so high an authority as Field Marshal Lord Roberts, convinces me that the work in the Canadian militia is progressing satisfactorily.

My stay in the Citadel has, indeed, been a most happy one, and I desire to record the expression of my warmest gratitude to you and Lady Grey for your very generous hospitality, and for all the care and trouble which you have so kindly given to every detail which could conduce to my comfort. I also wish to thank the members of your staff for their most efficient and ever-ready services.

It is with heartfelt regret that I bid farewell to Canada. That God may ever watch over and bless its people, inspire their ideals, prosper their work, and guide their destinies, will ever be my earnest prayer.

Believe me, my dear Lord Grey,

Very sincerely yours,

(Signed)   GEORGE P.

✻ ✻ ✻

To Sir J. G. Garneau, Mayor of the city where he had been entertained, H.R.H. wrote :—

𝔥.𝔯.𝔥. 𝔏etter to 𝔐ayor 𝔊arneau

Citadel, Quebec, 28th July, 1908

DEAR MR. MAYOR,

Before leaving Quebec, the Prince of Wales is anxious to convey to you and the citizens of Quebec the expresion of his deep appreciation of the splendid reception accorded to him, and to thank you and the municipality for all the admirable arrangements made in connection with his visit.

He noticed with satisfaction that the police duties were carefully discharged, and he is glad to learn that very few accidents occurred during the week.

His Royal Highness was particularly pleased with the effective and tasteful manner in which the city was decorated, also with the illuminations, the splendor of which was so much enhanced by the beauty of the natural surroundings.

In the pageant itself, the Prince was greatly interested, and, indeed, impressed, by the magnificent scenes illustrative of many of the memorable and stirring events in the history of Quebec. His Royal Highness knows that the hard work involved has been a labour of love to all concerned, but he sincerely congratulates all the men, women and children who played a part, and the organizers, whose efforts have been crowned with such conspicuous success.

To you, Mr. Mayor, personally, and to the municipality, His Royal Highness desires to express his sincerest thanks for your kindness and consideration.

The Prince has very much pleasure in forwarding

to you for the relief of the poor, the sum of one hundred pounds.

In bidding you farewell, His Royal Highness fervently trusts that, under the blessing of Providence, Quebec may, for all time, enjoy the fullest measure of prosperity and happiness.

Believe me,

Dear Mr. Mayor,

Yours very truly,

(Signed) ARTHUR BIGGE.

by were large cauldrons which hung suspended over the fire. All around the tables sat the Indians clothed as in days of yore—the body covered with deerskin broidered with quills and wampum, the head protected with the lofty plumage of eagle feathers.

The banquet which was given by Mr. Lascelles was served in the old Indian fashion. The old men sat down first while the younger members waited on them.

Speeches were made in the Iroquois language by the chiefs while the English reply of Mr. Lascelles was translated into the more romantic language of the primeval savage.

GROUP OF INDIANS WHO TOOK PART IN THE PAGEANTS
Messrs Lascelles and Denis, in their Indian Costumes are standing in the centre.

Iroquois Instal Chief

At the close of the pageant performance in the evening an event of importance took place on the battlefield grounds. Mr. Frank Lascelles was honored by the Iroquois Indians who took part in the pageants by being named an Iroquois chief with the title of Tehonikonraka, which denotes "a man of resources."

Among the tents of the Indians was again enacted a scene as of old when the savage was yet master of the lands now possessed by the white man. The tepees were painted with the various totems of the eagle, beaver, tortoise, moose and the reindeer. Close

After dinner came the actual ceremony. On the pageant grounds a fire was lighted, while around were gathered in a group, the Indians. A chief, began to drum which elicited from another chief, American Horse, a question in Iroquois as to the cause of the drumming. The reply in the language of the tribe was that a great white man was to be enlisted in the ranks of the tribe, whereupon another chief vouching for the stranger said that he was worthy of not merely being made a member but a chief.

The initiation immediately followed. Chief Sozay gave to the white Iroquois a necklace of wampum as a sign that he had treated his brethren well and that he would be similarly esteemed. A feather, the symbol of honour and friendship was also presented to Mr. Lascelles, while a gorgeous head-dress of eagle feathers was placed on his head and the name of Tehonikonraka given to the new chief. The five Iroquois chiefs placing their hands on their new confrere broke into song proclaiming his worthiness. Then came a dance—and Tehonikonraka was a chief of the Iroquois.

With similar ceremony three minor chiefs were made out of white men, Mr. Dennis, who had assisted Mr. Lascelles in arranging the pageants became Sakokonnicensta, "the true friend;" Mr. R. J. Blaney, "Ranenrenhaive," the leader, while Mr. W. Price was designated "Sakokirenteta" the path finder.

* * *

The Last of the Dinners

The last of the dinners given by His Excellency Earl Grey at the Citadel during the celebrations took place in the evening. Many prominent Canadians were present at the function which was given in honour of the representatives of the United States and of France.

The list of invited guests was :—

His Honour Mr. J. Dunsmuir and Mrs. and Miss Dunsmuir, Mrs. R. Dunsmuir, His Honour Sir Louis Jette, Rt. Hon. Sir Wilfrid and Lady Laurier, Hon. W. S. and Mrs. and Miss Fielding, Hon. F. and Mrs. and Miss Oliver, Mrs. A. B. Aylesworth, Hon. R. and Mrs. Lemieux, Hon. R. and Mrs. and Miss Dandurand, Rt. Hon. Sir Charles and Lady Fitzpatrick, Sir Francois and Lady Langelier, Brig.-Gen. Otter, Hon. Sir Lomer Gouin, His Worship Sir George and Lady Garneau, Lt. Col. Hon. J. S., Mrs and Miss Hendrie, Hon. L. A. and Mrs. Taschereau, Lt.-Col G., Mrs. and Miss Denison, Mr. Byron, Mrs. and Miss Walker, Sir Thomas and Lady Shaughnessy, Sir Montagu and Lady Allan, Mr. and Mrs. Joseph Pope, Capt. Hon. A. Hore Ruthven, V.C.; Mr. Walter Callan, Maj.-Gen. and Mrs. Wilson, Mr. and Mrs. Courtney, Marchioness of Donegal, Mrs. and Miss Pickering Hon. A. and Mrs. Turgeon, Lt.-Col. Offley Shore, Mr. and Mrs. W. M. Macpherson, Lady Augusta Fane, Commissioner Perry, Vice-Admiral Jaureguiberry, Mrs. Cowles, M. Herbette, Mr., Mrs. and Miss de Loynes, Earl of Ranfurly, Mr. Wolfe, Capt. Mr. D. Carleton, Capt. Mr. A. Murray, The Mayor of Brouages.

His Excellency the Governor-General, Her Excellency the Countess of Grey, the Duke of Norfolk, Earl Roberts, V.C., Lady Aileen Roberts, Earl of Dudley, Lord Lovat, Lord Bruce, Sir Reginald and Lady Beatrice Pole-Carew, Capt. Hon. Hugh and Lady Susan Dawnay, Hon. Angus Macdonell, Lady Sybil Grey, Lady Mary Parker, Lady Violet Elliot,

Mr. Leveson Gower, Sir John and Lady Hanbury-Williams and Miss Hanbury Williams, Mr. and Mrs. Sladen, Capt. Newton, A.D.C.; Capt. Pickering, A.D.C.; Viscount Lascelles, A.D.C.

* * *

Civic Reception

The last official reception took place in the evening. It was the civic reception given in the City Hall.

Throughout the celebrations the civic home had been one of the city's features. Its exterior was marked by many decorations. It was covered by bunting of every shade, while as if to shed lustre on the already gay colours, were streamers of electric lights in every nook of the building. Hung above it were suspended rows of lights between various towers.

The interior of the hall did not lack decorations. The spacious halls were covered with tapestry while the walls were hung with ensigns and shields interspersed with folds of bunting. The ceilings were ornamented with ribbons of elb lights. The Council chamber where the reception and dance were held was also tastefully decorated. The Mayor's throne was replaced by a dais above which was suspended a cluster of electric lights and streamers of red, white and blue bunting while a crown illuminated with lights covered the whole.

The guests were received by the Mayor, Sir J. G. Garneau, Pro-Mayor Picard, Mrs. Cannon, Mrs. Baillarge, Mrs. Fiset, and Aldermen Fiset, Galipeault and Pouliot. Hundreds of citizens paid their respects to the Mayor. Among those present were Admiral Jaureguiberry, the Duke of Norfolk, Sir Wilfrid and Lady Laurier, Sir Louis and Lady Jette, Lady Sybil Grey, Lady Evelyn Grey, Hon. W. S. and Miss Fielding and Mrs. Aylesworth.

The reception was the final official one of the celebrations. Those present, aware of it, consequently took opportunity of the occasion and it was not until the shades of night had begun to depart that the guests gave thought to the morrow and its cares.

* * *

During the celebrations many messages of congratulations were received from all parts of the world. Now as the Tercentenary was drawing to a close, the following cablegram was received from Lord Crewe, Secretary of State for the Colonies :—

Lord Crewe to Lord Grey,

"Now that the Quebec celebrations are at an end, I wish to congratulate Canada and the Governor-General upon the singular success which has attended them. The British Empire as a whole, is much to be congratulated upon the evidence which has been given of loyalty and hearty co-operation within its borders, and is a happy omen for the future."

GEN. RICHARD MONTGOMERY

Twelfth Day, Thursday, July Thirtieth

French Flagship Departs

THE celebrations were now drawing to a close. His Royal Highness the Prince of Wales and the British warships had departed. Most of the official guests had also gone and but few visitors remained in the city, for the last fortnight a scene of brilliancy and splendour.

In the afternoon the harbour was once more the scene of action. The French flagship, the Leon Gambetta at five o'clock lifted her anchor, fired a farewell salute and headed for the turn at the east end of the city whence leads the course opening into the Atlantic ocean.

This departure was unlike that of the English ships. Instead of the quietness which marked the latter, the leaving of the Leon Gambetta occasioned much stir. Pinnaces and launches were seen hurrying to and from the large vessel. Several thousand people watched the preparations which ceased with the mighty farewell by the French cannons.

✸ ✸ ✸

Last of the Illuminations

In the evening were exploded the last rockets that were left with the officials caring for the spectacular displays of the celebrations. The fireworks of the previous week had been successful and were now repeated on as lavish a scale and with as much effect. The scene alone was changed. The fireworks were now given from Victoria Park.

A VIEW OF THE TENTED CITY

It seemed as if the whole city and what remained of its guests had been transferred to the beautiful park. The night was a dark one, causing the scintillations of the descending explosives to be more sparkling than ever. Out of the darkness, the bright colours were more striking. Throughout the whole city and in the country districts for miles around the glare could be distinguished. It was the last of the Tercentenary's spectacular events.

THE FRASER HIGHLANDERS
Of Wolfe's Army lined up in front of the
Drill Hall.

Thirteenth Day, Friday, July Thirty=First

Last Performance of the Pageants

FRIDAY, the last day of the celebrations, was marked by no very memorable event. The harbour was now deserted of its battleships and launches. Even the little Don de Dieu had been moved from the berth where she had stood, lost as it were in an age not her own. The streets were deserted of the tourists who had gathered in Quebec. The Terrace was also minus the crowded promenaders who had admired from it so wondrous a scene.

Of all the prominent characters of the celebrations, the pageant performers, in their varied costumes, alone remained. But for their appearance on the streets, and for the decorations and illuminations, the city had about resumed its normal appearance. The pageanters and their gorgeous costumes no longer attracted attention. Ancient Quebec seemed to regard its old costumes as natural.

Before a large number of spectators the last performance of the pageants took place late in the afternoon. Each scene was enacted with realism and despatch. Especially effective was the final scene in which the English and French regiments join in a living picture—a picture of fraternity and unity.

There stood the regiments of Wolfe and Montcalm in the contemplation of those who were witnesses of the last pageant. Before them stood the fauns of the court of Henry IV. It was a picture of harmony and peace. From above, whence he directed the scenes, came down Mr. Lascelles, the master of the pageants. A faun presented him with a bouquet. Cheers were given. The soldiers marched off and the last pageant was over.

But there is yet an incident to be recorded before the history of these celebrations is brought to a close.

✳ ✳ ✳

Close of the Celebration

After the pageant the French and English grenadiers marched together to the City Hall. There Capt. Wm. Price of the British Grenadiers entertained the members of the French Grenadier corps. Compliments were exchanged and speeches emphasizing the entente cordiale were made. When they parted there was a closer understanding between the representatives of the two nationalities inhabiting the city of Quebec, who had participated so fraternally in the celebration of the birth and development of their common country.

THE ROYAL ARTILLERY REGIMENT
Of Wolfe's Army.

Great Scenes of the Historical Pageants

First Pageant---Scene 1

THE LANDING OF JACQUES-CARTIER AT STADACONA. OCTOBER 19, 1535.

The Pageant ground is clear and all is still. Nothing can be seen on it save the totemed tepees of the Indians situated near the cliff. To the north is a thicket of bushes; to the west, the forest; in the south is seen calmly gliding the broad river bare of all craft and bordered on each side by high cliffs.

The scene is simple and beautiful. From the wig-

THE INDIANS GREET JACQUES CARTIER
And his Crew as they Land.

wams comes an Indian, his body clothed in deerskin, his head covered with a crown of eagle feathers. He places himself before the river and with hand shading his eyes gazes below as if contemplating the past and blindly staring into the future. Of a sudden he beholds on the river three sails and on board are strange beings—white faced people. What means this curious apparition? The astonished Indian utters a cry, and in a moment he is surrounded by his kinsmen, young and old, who come flocking from their primeval dwellings. All look with fear upon the pale strangers and their gigantic craft. They seem excited but are silenced by wonder and hesitation.

From the shore the white men come up to where

stand the timid savages. Jacques-Cartier, followed by his sailors, who sing the old French ballad

Ali, alo, pour mâcher
Ali, ali, alo!
Il mange la viande
Et nous donne les os;
Ali, ali, alo!
Ali, ali, alo!

approaches the now calm redmen who dance about the new arrivals, feeling their faces, stroking their beards and touching their clothes, all the time crying "Agouzac". It is their welcome to the white men.

The French captain orders bread and wine to be distributed among his hosts who squat on the ground around him. For Jacques-Cartier and his followers mats are brought and while they are seated, a chief makes a harangue in the Indian tongue. Agouhana, the lord and king of the new land, too feeble to stand and too aged to talk, is brought on a skin and placed before the white chief whose healing touch is implored. The captain rubs the old chief's limbs.

Another throng of men, women and children, maimed and infirm are placed before Cartier to be touched by him. Arising, he places himself before the large wooden cross which the sailors had in the meanwhile erected and which bore the inscription "Franciscus Primus Dei gratia Francorum rex regnat" imposed on a shield of France, and with eyes uplifted heavenward prays, "Eclairez-les, Seigneur, car ils me prennent pour un dieu"!

A vos apôtres seuls et à vos saints il appartient d'exercer des miracles. Je ne suis pas digne, Seigneur, d'être l'instrument de votre puissance et le ministre de vos miséricordes. Dieu éternel et tout puissant, Esprit Saint, auteur et dispensateur des Sept Dons, renouvelez en faveur de ces âmes et de ces corps malades le prodige du Cénacle. Et de même que vos apôtres parlaient des langues qu'ils n'avaient pas apprises, de même ces infidèles comprendront la langue inconnue que je parlerai en lisant l'Evangile leur apprenant, avec votre nom, l'origine de la Lumière que vous avez créée et de la vérité dont vous êtes le Verbe."

Jacques-Cartier then read to the suppliant savages a portion of the gospel of St. John :

"In principio erat verbum, et verbum erat apud deum, et deus erat verbum."

Turning to the cross Cartier spoke :—

"Croix de Clovis, de Charlemagne et de saint Louis, garde jusqu'à mon retour cette peuplade et ce royaume.
Éclaire de tes rayons les ombres de la mort où Stadaconé est assise.
Fais sentinelle, au nom du Christianisme et de la France, sur cette frontière de la Barbarie jusqu'à l'arrivée des missionnaires de l'Église et de la Civilisation !

Comme un phare sur l'infini de la mer, brille sur l'immensité de cette terre enténébrée de paganisme, en attendant l'aurore puis le jour de l'Évangile qui se lèvera demain sur le Canada tout entier.—O crux, Ave !"

The Indians in silence and with respect listen to this unknown tongue from the voice of the mysterious stranger.

Presents are again scattered among the redmen. Knives, hatchets, images, bells, combs and rosaries are eagerly grasped by them from the hands of the white sailors. To the chief Cartier presents a cloak of Paris red, set with yellow and white buttons of tin and ornamented with small bells.

In return Cartier is presented by the Indians with a small girl—a sign of alliance which arouses from the multitude cries of joy. The visitors taking with them the chief of the tribe and three of his subjects descend toward the river, and escorted by several bark canoes for some distance, start on their voyage back to old France to place before their king the men of a new world.

Organizer—Mr. Geo. C. Scott.

Jacques-Cartier—Mr. J. M. A. Raymond; Guillaume Le Breton Bastille, Captain and Pilot of "L'Emerillon"—J. E. Gourdeau; Thomas Fourmont, Master—J. B. Routhier; Jacques Maingard, Master of "L'Emerillon"—J. Elz. Poulin; Guillaume le Marie, Master of the "Petite Hermine"—Paul Dupre; Francois Guitault—J. B. Peters; Priest—Father O'Leary; Marc Jalobert, Captain and Pilot of the "Petite Hermine"—Jules Lelievre.

Sailors:—N. Soucy, F. Julien, Emile Desrochers, Jacques Simon, Arthur Roy, C. Bergeron, Gustave Beaubien, E. Gourdeau, Eug. Michaud, J. C. Bourassa, Pierre Giguere, R. R Langlois, H. Maheux, Albert Laprise, Paul Dupre, E. Frenette, D. Roberge, R. Laroche, A. A. Chamberland, A. Giroux, W. Birard, Ed. Gingras, Philippe Paquet, Geo. Parent, Octave Begin, H. St. Hilaire, O. Grenier, H. Fisher, G. Blais, G. Bouthillette, F. Renaud, Adolphe Asselin, Adjutor Fortin, A. Parent, J. A. Faber, Alex. Faber, Jos Dompierre, J. Fitzback, Adelard

Noel, Albert Matte, E. Marcotte, A. Noel, J. B. Bergeron, M. Malouin, A. Roth, Alp. St. Hilaire, H. Noel, Art. Jobin, La. Allard, Pierre Jobin, Geo. Aird, Eug. Germaine, J. H. Bourassa, J. Ansalone, H. Quironet, E. Cloutier, G. S. Belleau, S. St. Hilaire, Wilfrid Martel, E. Laflamme, Jos. Patry, J. L. Santerre, N. Gingras, Elz. Lapointe, Elz. Genest, J. Houde, W. Bigaouette, E L'Heureux, J. Parney, Jules Noel, W. Simpson, H. Picard, L. Lapelant, Ad. Jobin, Onesime Parent, Ad. Cantin, J. E. Drouin, Albert Fortier, A. Faucher, D. St. Hilaire, H. Soucy, E. Desrosiers, L. Beaubien, Jos. Chamberland, Raoul Emond, Jos. Houde, M. Gourdeau, J. B. Routhier, J. A. Poulin, Jules Schien, J. B. Peters, D. Bolger, Auguste Sirois, Emile Vallerand, J. B. Bergeron, R. Barbeau, Geo. St. Hilaire, H. Boisseau, Paul Dupre, Albert Dansereau, H. Labonte, A. Letourneau, A. Roberge, L. Laverdiere, Jos. Vermette, A. Vaillancourt, Oscar Arel, Oliva Pelletier, Jos. Chamberland, Phileas, A. Fortier, Ernest Mailloux, Louis Breton, C. A. Beaudette.

MR. MOISE RAYMOND

As Jacques Cartier.

THE COURTIERS OF FRANCIS I

In the Pageants.

First Pageant---Scene 11

JACQUES-CARTIER REPORTS TO KING FRANCIS I. AT THE COURT OF FONTAINEBLEAU.

The pageant ground is once more vacant. The soft light of the late afternoon casts its reflection on the shrubbery, here and there tinged with a tuft of roses. From various parts of the ground leap joyously into the air narrow streams of water issuing from fountains encased in huge vases of white marble. Scents of many flowers fill the atmosphere. Before us we have the gardens at Fontainebleau.

From a distance of several hundred yards dotted with thick foliage something is seen as if moving in the direction of the gardens. As the sound becomes more distinct the clatter of hoofs is heard. Nearer and nearer the body moves until there comes in view a cavalcade of courtiers. Trumpets sound in the forests whence come the nobles riding steeds as richly caparisoned as their masters. Nothing is lacking in the brilliancy of the costumes. The courtiers of the sixteenth century are clad in velvet and in satins which glitter no less than do the arms which hang from them.

The long and brilliant procession slowly proceeds and halts, but, when at the merry fountains, groups of ladies and attendants of the courts station themselves. The noble ladies add to the scene their own charm and the glitter of jewelled costumes.

Then come the King and his Queen. They ride under a canopy borne by four attendants. The vestments of Francis I. and of his consort are embroidered with gold and jewels which are even dimmed by the sheeny covering of the steeds which bear them. Golden dishes of fruit and bowls of wine are placed before their majesties while for the pleasure of the King a troop of fauns with bodies covered by leopard skins and a set of satyrs, head girt with floral

crowns and bodies in long white flowing robes, danced through the gardens.

At the king's coming the merry laughter of the court dames and the jests of the gentile hommes cease. The King gives a command to Philippe de Chabot, grand amiral de France, and a few seconds later stand before the King the hardy Breton explorer Jacques-Cartier, Donnacona, the American King, two Indian interpreters and a young Indian girl.

In response to the King's enquiries as to his discoveries, Jacques Cartier says :—

"J'ai découvert trois royaumes : celui de Saguenay, celui de Canada, et celui d'Hochelaga. Leurs territoires réunis dépassent en superficie l'étendue de notre France. Je me suis même laissé dire que l'Europe y tiendrait!"

Surprise seized all and with astonishment every eye is directed toward the captain and his dusky companions.

MR. J. E. BOILY

As King Francis I.

Donnacona is presented to the King of France,
The savage with pride and majesty, greets his fellow-
King and by means of an interpreter recounts the
vastness and extent of the new world. With interest,
Francis I. and his gay court listened and wondered.
The King turns to Francois Bohier, bishop of St.
Malo and expresses the desire—

"Que ces Canadiens soient enfants de Dieu avant d'être
Français! Que la lumière de la Vérité les éclaire au lieu
de les aveugler. Apprenez-leur qu'il existe dans une
autre vie et dans un autre monde, encore plus ancien et
plus durable que celui-ci, un royaume plus beau que le
mien; qu'auprès de lui le faste de ma Cour et l'éclat de
mon diadème ne sont que des pâleurs d'aube comparées
au soleil. Qu'ils ne passent point des ténèbres du Paganisme à l'éblouissement du siècle, et que l'orgueuil légitime de mon trône ne soit pas pour eux une cause de
scandale ou de perdition. Qu'ils sachent enfin, par vous,
que le Christ seul est le roi, l'"agouhanna" véritable, et

B. McLennan, Irenee Gagnon, G. A .Vandry, J. E. Mahy,
Edgar Clement, George Carrier, Dr. J. D. Duchene, Uld.
Gauvin, F. X. Morency, A. E. Marois, Ed. Tanguay, George
A. Malouin, C. Sewell, M. Giroux, W. Sharpe, C. L. Hervey,
A. Morgan, Jos. O'Donnell, A. G. Piddington, M. S. Ray,
Geo. P. Weir, A. Walcot, Henri D. Barry, Edgar Lamon-
tagne, Oscar Roy, E. Dorion, J. A. Plamondon, Dr. C. O.
Samson, R. D. Greig, D. A. Greig, Ls. S. Vien, Henri
Robitaille, Jos. Tessier, Chs. Chartre, R. Turcotte, H. E.
Lavigueur, Geo. St. Amant, W. Davis, Capt. F. Blouin,
Stanislas Hamel, Louis Boivin, Ernest Ross, M. Montma-
gny, jr., Master St. Amant, Dr. Robert LaRue, A. A. Clou-
tier, J. Art. Vermette, J. F. Dumas, A. Murison, Henri
Lavigueur, jr., Alb. Laforet, Capt. L. LeDuc, Alf. Robitaille.

Gentlemen of the Court on Foot:—S. J. Myrand, Jos. W. Rous-
seau, J. Et. Samson, A. A. Roy, Jean Lanctot, A. Benyon,
Ernest Vandry, Phil. Boucher, Raoul Guay, Ed. Corriveau,
Moise Letourneau, R. Fiset, D. J. Griffin, Eugene Amyot, J.
S. Strang, L. S. Gagne, J. O. Fontaine, A. A. Love, G. B.
S. Young, L. E. Gaudry, J. M. Gaudry, Jules Giroux, J. A.
Bisson, Albert Rouillard, Jules Rouillard, A. Berrigan, Jules
Bernier, Henri Arsenault, S. Guenette, S. R. Woodley,
Demers, J. C. Michaud,
Alf. Mazmette, G. Lam-
bert, Odilon Rondeau
Antono Thibault.

Guards of the Court:—
Stanislas Grenier, Jules
Galarneau, N. Joseph S
Rondeau, Alfred Thibault,
J. H. Turgeon, Chas
Phil. Lefebvre, D. Du
fresne, Omer Robert, Elz
Belanger, Z. Michaud,
Ph. Grenier, Alb. Bou
let, Elie Noel, Jos. Cha-
lifour, Hector Grenier,
Nap. Boucher, H. Dorion
Jos. Chas. Giroux, Jos.
Rainville, Apolin Grenier
Alf. Giroux, Leo Blouin
A. Morin, G. McClish, A.
Laliberte, Gaudiose Le-
clerc, G. Carignan, E.
Fronette, Lucien Beau-
lieu, Henri Chartrain, J.
A. Blouin, Joseph Gagne,
Joseph Michon.

**Ladies of the Court on
Horseback:**—Mrs. S. T.
Green, Miss Webb, Miss
Bate, Miss Perley, Miss
B. Leonard, Miss L

DONNACONA ADDRESSES KING FRANCIS I.

que les princes de la terre, même les plus magnifiques,
n'en sont que les représentants indignes et les humbles
vassaux.

C'est là, Monsieur de Saint-Malo, ce que je voulais vous
dire et ce que vous ferez."

With the prelate, Cartier and the Indians retire.
The court assumes its former aspect. The King is
again gay, surrounded by an entourage of smiling
ladies and laughing men while the satyrs and fauns
humour the master of France. The mounted courtiers
followed by the ladies and intendants withdraw into
the forest. The procession winds its way stately and
slowly until it is soon out of sight and the gardens of
Fontainebleau are no longer disturbed save by the
leap of the cooling fountains.

Organizer:—Jos. Savard.

Gentlemen of the Court on Horseback:—J. Savard, J. E. Boily,
A. J. Price, W. M. Dobell, A. E. Ogilvie, Guy Ogilvie, Capt.

Amyot, Miss Breakey, Miss Atkinson, Miss R. Green, Miss
A. Burstall, Miss Gibson, Miss Weir, Miss J. Murphy, Mrs.
Gust, Simard, Mrs. H. D. Barry, Miss Brosnan, Miss Law-
rence, Miss Duchesnay, Miss Pouliot, Miss Power, Miss Petry,
Miss McNaughton, Miss Duggan, Mrs. Lacasse, the Misses
Ellis (2), the Misses Poston (2), Miss Price, Miss Lesage,
Miss Dessane, Miss Blair, Miss Brown, Miss Bell, Mrs. Bell,
the Misses Wiggs (2), Miss Parent, Miss Bush, Miss L. Mille,
Mrs. Geo. Carrier, the Misses Russell (2), Miss E. Dunlop,
the Misses Parkin (2), the Misses Flood (2), Miss M. Glass,
Miss Avery, Miss G. Sewell, Miss M. L. Van Felson, Miss
Wyse, Mrs. A. Taschereau, Mrs. Whitehead, Miss Lennon,
Miss Angers, Miss Turcot, the Misses Vandry (2), the Misses
Ross (2), Miss Lucea, Miss Muir, Miss Gallagher, Miss Du
chene, Miss Laberge, the Misses Baillairge (3), Miss Bate,
Miss Hughson, Miss Joseph, Miss Ramsay, Miss Laliberte,
Miss Blais, Miss Gourdeau, Miss Daly, Miss Normand, Miss
Vocelle, Miss Gagnon, Miss Breton, the Misses Robitaille (2),
Miss C. Deronne, Miss Fiset, Miss Verrault, Miss M. Kerr,
Miss Labrecque, Mrs. C. A. McCord, Miss Lefebvre, Miss
Fremont, Mrs. L. A. Hudon, Mrs. Morse, Miss Edith Le-
Moyne, Miss Johnston, Miss LaRoche, the Misses M. Guay

KING FRANCIS I.

And his Queen under the canopy

(2), Miss S. Casault, Miss E. Simard, Miss E. Boursi, Miss Tierny, Miss McCarthy, Mrs. Marechal, Mrs. Renaud, Mrs. Duggan, Mrs. Grenon, Mrs. L. L'Herault, Mrs. Pourtier, Mrs. Fontaine, Miss Arsenault, Miss Lasniers, Miss Dube, the Misses Frederic (3), Miss Lavoie, Miss Caouette, Miss Hamel, Miss Burns, Miss Binet, Miss Bosquet, Mrs. Lindsay, the Misses Cloutier (2), Mrs. Oscar Hudon, Miss Pineault, Miss Giguere, Miss Ethel Wolff, Miss Mary Jane St. Amant, Mrs. Harold Campbell, Mrs. O. Drouin, Mrs. Gregory, Miss Gregory, Miss Molson, Miss Bosworth, Mrs. Stanislas Hamel, Miss E. Boivin, Mrs. P. R. Plamondon.

Ladies of the Court on Foot:—Miss Weir, the Misses Benson (2), Miss Borden, Miss Ray, the Misses Anctil (2), Miss Parkin, Miss Wiggs, Miss Taylor, Miss Pinsonnault, Miss Davis, Miss De Martigny, the Misses Muir, Miss Yorke, Mrs. Levasseur, Miss de Vere, the Misses Couture (2), Miss Soulard, Miss J. A. Morin, Miss Normand, Miss Tremblay, Miss M. Drolet, Miss Fiset, Mrs. Reinhart, Miss Reinhart, Miss Belanger, Mrs. DesRochers, Mrs. Fontaine, Mrs. Dupuis, the Misses Arsolone (3), Miss E. Cantin, Miss Stella Roberge, Miss Belanger, Miss Falardeau, Miss Magnan, Miss Chesnel, Miss Legare, Miss Grondin, Miss Labrecque, Miss Binet, the Misses Julien (2), the Misses Hamel (2), Miss B. Pelletier, the Misses White (2), Miss Dorion, Miss Darveau, Miss L. Green.

Charles Duc D'Orleans, King's son—Ernest Vandry; Jean de Lorraine, Cardinal's page—George Vandry; Diane de Poitier, Dame de la Cour—Miss Alfreda Vandry; Marie d'Albre, Dame de la Cour—Miss Irene Vandry; Antoine de Bourcy, Chevalier de France—G. A. Vandry.

Second Pageant---Scene 1

CHAMPLAIN RECEIVES FROM HENRY IV A COMMISSION TO SET OUT FOR NEW FRANCE.

A period of seventy years elapses before the next scene takes place. Henry of Navarre is now on the throne of France—a rugged soldier seated there "meting" out unequal laws unto a savage race, that feed and sleep and horde and know not me." His old activity had not declined but lay rusting with his courage amid a phlegmatic court disturbed but by the factions of his mistresses. He consequently took no little interest when De Monts proposed an expedition to Canada and hastily gave that commission to Champlain, so eagerly desired by the chivalrous man of action.

The scene is in the palace of the Louvre where the King and his court were in sixteen hundred and eight. The walls of the palace are of a deep blue colour dotted at regular intervals with golden fleur-de-lys. The ground is covered with a large blue car-

THE DANCE OF THE SATYRS

In the Francis I pageant.

pet. In the palace is set up a throne on a raised dais decked with a canopy.

The palace is beautiful and grand even in its solitude. The entry of the Halbardiers and Royal Guards announces the approach of the King. The soldiers place themselves on either side of the throne while a few moments later into the defile thus made comes lightly a throng of courtiers and court ladies. The former are decked with ruffles, while farthingales of brilliant colour and beset with sparkling stones mark the latter.

Gaiety is everywhere and the palace resounds with the merry laughter of the moving and garrulous nobility. The sound of a trumpet is heard from the distance and through the court entrance troop in officials and pages of the court followed by the bearded King and his Italian Queen. The gentlemen of honour and maids-in-waiting form the rear of the stately procession which as it wends its way through the bowing crowd leaves behind it silence and reverence.

The King and Queen are now seated on the throne. All are quiet but the court jester who in demoniacal garb dances and leaps before the solemn ruler. Monsieur de Monts, who has received from His Majesty letters-patent to make a voyage of exploration to America, approaches the King and demands the royal sanction to his choice of Champlain as his lieutenant on the expedition. The King replies:

Approchez, M. de Champlain. Votre personne et vos mérites nous sont connus. Déjà le Commandeur Aymar de Chastes m'avait fait cet éloge que M. de Monts répète aujourd'hui et que cinq années de nouveaux et inestimables services justifient davantage. La France vous doit sa bonne renommée en Amérique.

Votre constance à suivre une entreprise, votre fermeté dans les plus grands périls, votre sagacité toujours en éveil et toujours prompte à saisir un parti dans les affaires les plus épineuses, la droiture de vos vues, l'honneur et la probité de votre conduite, tout cela Monsieur, me confirme dans la résolution que j'ai présentement de vous faire reprendre et poursuivre l'héroïque expédition de Jacques Cartier! Je vous crois digne de lui succéder, d'exercer comme lui un sacerdoce politique, de lire comme lui l'Évangile en guise de proclamations royales, et d'arborer les armes de France sur la croix du Christ, aussi loin que vous pourrez marcher à l'Ouest du Nouveau Monde. Dites-moi, Mr. de Champlain, acceptez-vous?

Champlain.—Vous ne songez, Sire, à étendre votre domination dans les pays infidèles que pour y faire régner Jésus-Christ, et vous estimez, comme nos rois, vos prédécesseurs, que le salut d'une âme vaut mieux, lui seul, que la conquête d'un grand empire!

Que Dieu vous entende, Sire, et qu'il fasse prospérer cette entreprise à son honneur et à sa gloire.

Sire, j'accepte!

A murmur of approval echoes through the court, and the modest Champlain withdraws from before the King. The court again resumes its former aspect

MADAME AUGUSTE CARRIER
As the Queen of Henri IV.

MR. ANT. COUILLARD
As King Henri IV.

KING HENRY IV. GIVES A COMMISSION TO CHAMPLAIN
To sail to Canada.

SCENE IN THE HENRY IV. PAGEANT

THE PAVANE DANCE IN PROGRESS

ANOTHER VIEW OF THE PAVANE DANCE

A GROUP OF COURT LADIES

Of the Henri IV scene

and in the palace once more is heard the babblings of the attendants and the laughter of the velvet clothed merry-maker.

The lutes, violins and high-toned oboes now peal forth the strains of d'Arbeau's "Pavane" dance. About forty couples leave the throng of courtiers and go through the graceful measures of the dance. The hoop-skirted dames move lightly over the sky-coloured carpet, while their partners, with swords uplifted, accompany the steps of the high-heeled shoes of the dainty court ladies.

The dance is over and the King and Queen retire from the flower bedecked palace while the court sings :

Vive Henri quatre!
Vive ce roi vaillant!
Ce diable à quatre
A le triple talent de boire et de battre,
Et d'être un vert galant.

The attendants follow and the ruffled courtiers leading the richly attired ladies leave the palace, still beautiful, but dreary, with its throne and rich tapestry.

Organizer—Honore J. Pinsonnault.

Personages:—Henri IV—Ant. Couillard; Sieur de Monts—George Belleau; Champlain—Alfred J. Pinsonnault; Henri II, Duc de Montmorency—Honore J. Pinsonnault; Marquis de Mirabeau—N. Lajeunesse; Aubigne, Marechal de France—Jos. Pouliot; Philippe du Plessis, Mornay—F. X. Guerad; Charles de Cosse, Brissae—Leon Dugal; Brulart de Sillery—A. A. Gaumond; Jean-

THE INDIANS CARRYING THE BLUE CARPET

For the Henri IV scene,

nin, Ministre—J. A. Royer; Duc de Guise—Theodore Fontaine; Prince de Joinville—Alf. Forgues; Duc de Mayenne—Adj. Turcotte; Marquis de Montpesat—Alm. Lacasse; Duc de Epernon—Geo. Paquet; Comte de Auverne—Emile Fontaine; Duc de Lesdiguieres—Emile Labrecque; De Villeroy—J. F. Lemieux; Duc de Vendome—Eug. Lemieux; Roger de Bellegarde—Emile Dorion; Comte de Moret—E. V. Norris; Chancellier Charles Faulet—J. A. Chabot; Conseiller d'Etat Lenet—Elz. Carmichael; Du Teuil—Raymond Gauvin; Jean Rosny—L. A. Reinhardt; Marquis de Liancourt—Charles Vezina; Duc de Montbazon—Aurelien Beaubien; Marquis de la Force—Art. Martineau; M. de la Noue—Ernest LaRochelle; Lt. Gen. Roquelaure—Walter J. Ray; Marechal de Lavardin—A Jolicoeur; M. de Crillon—Elz. Halle; Jean D'Albret—Odilon Devarennes; M. de Villegontlain—J. A. Galibois; Concino-Concini, Marechal d'Ancre—Geo. Mitchell; La Reine, Marie de Medecis—Mrs. L. Auguste Carrier; Fils du Roi, Dauphin Gaston d'Orleans—Mr. George Garneau; Fille du Roi, Elizabeth—Miss Geraldine Hamel; Fille du Roi, Christine—Miss Berthe Garneau; Fille du Roi, Henriette—Miss Pauline Lanctot.

Followers of the Queen—Eleonore, Marquise d'Ancre—Mrs. Jules Garneau; Princesse de Conde—Miss Jeanne Garneau; Mademoiselle d'Annale—Miss Leda Burroughs; Duchesse de Mayenne—Miss Arline Burroughs; Jacqueline de Bueil—Miss Olivier; Carlotte des Essarts—Miss Turgeon; Marquise d'Elboeuf—Miss Simard.

Pages:—Mr. Paul Carrier, Mr. Pierre Murphy, Mr. Lucien Fontaine, Mr. J. A. Lacasse, Mr. A. Blagdon, Mr. E. Fecteau, Mr. Charles Carrier, Mr. Charles Parke, Mr. Leon Fontaine, Mr. E. Lacasse, Mr. J. M. Blagdon, Mr. Jules Garneau, Mr. Edgar Wiggs, Mr. Paul Fontaine, Mr. Andre Turcotte, Mr. A. Fecteau.

Halberdiers:—C. J. Bergeron, Simeon Boiteau, F. X. Breton, Alfred Duperre, Eloi Duperre, M. Duchene, Wm. Desbiens, Eug. Guilmette, Avila Garant, J. Henry, L. Harvey, P. Labrie, Arthur Lortie, Art. Lachance, Geo. Letourneau, P. L'Heureux, J S. Matte, Edouard Morin, Victor Noel, Eugene Pouliot, John Paquet, Joseph Paquette, Henri Roy, Aime Roy, J. L. Rosa, F Rainville, Jos. Savard, W. Thivierge.

HALBERDIERS, HENRY IV SCENE

Guards:—D. L. Auge, Elzear Audet, Willam Beaulieu, J. L. Bedard, Rossaire Brulotte, J. J. Blondeau, Art. Blondeau, Syl. Beaulieu, L. A. Cantin, Ernest Dube, Thomas Dugal, Jos. Dompierre, Edm. Drolet, Jos. Dery, Jos Fontaine, Arthur Godbour, Jos. Gagnon, J. B. Jobin, Alb. Lapointe, J. A. Lavoie, A Laroche, J. O. Marier, Norman McCaley, Jos. Moisan, Ernest Marier, Gaudiose Poitras, J. L. Royer, Pierre Tremblay, Odina Villeneuve, Victor Vezina.

Noblemen:—Eugene Amyot, Atkinson Stuart, D. Atkinson, J. P. Bernier, D. Bruneau, J. E. Bergeron, Edmond Boutet, Louis Boissonnault, Joseph Binet, Emile Bilodeau, J. E. Brousseau, Ernest Brousseau, Arthur Bernier, R. E. Boisseau, A. Bilodeau, U. W. Benson, Georges Cote, Alphonse Cantin, A. G. Chapman, A Cantin, Hector Colomb, A. A. Dube, J. A. Drapeau, E. Dufour, Raphael Dery, Leon Desrosiers, J. P. Doherty, G. E. Dion, J. A. Dery, W. A. Dall, Hon. W. A. Edwards, J. F. Forgues, Leon Fontaine, Edm. Forgues, Lucien Fontaine, Leon Fontaine, E. R.

STAGE AND SETTING OF KING HENRY IV. SCENE

KING HENRY AND HIS QUEEN

Fafard, J. A. Ferland, L. J. Guay, Simeon Guerard, Armand Garneau, J. E. Ganyin, J. A. C. Gignac, R. W. Gavey, Philippe Holliday, J. Hill, G. H. Judge,D. Jacson, Joseph Kenneth, Eug. Lauziers, J. C. Lacroix, B. E. Leclerc, os. Leclerc, Alex, Lafrance, E. Lefebvre, Alb. Legare, Geo. Lamothe, J. B. Lebrun, J. A. Langlois, R, Lapointe, Emile Marineau, J. Moffett, C. A. Mailly. W. Mercer, H. C. Matt, E. Montreuil, O. Masson, Jacques Malouin, F. Oliver, S. E. Plante, J. Paquin, J. A. Roy, Geo. Pichette, G. G. Stuart, A. N. Santoire, A. Simard, Ernest Turgeon, Alb. Toussaint, Pierre Trudel, W. T. Wilson, Jos. Wright, C. Neil, Reg. W. C. Patton, A. Pereire, Robt. H. Reid, W. E. Reed, Rolfe, R. G. Sare, F. M. Stanton, Hope Scott, C. S Smith, W. Teller, Percy Turcotte, S. B. Woxdley, Eust. C. Wurtele, I. Breakey, W. S. Champion, C. L. Fare, K. E. Gilmour, D. F. Gilmour, J. F. Gibsone, I. R. Gibsone, E. C. Gooday, J. A. Johnson, E. W Killam, L. A. Lemesurier, G. W. Lemesurier, Paul Larue. A. D. Munroe, E. M. Mowat, H. McGreevy.

Court of Henri IV.—Ladies:—Miss Blanche Alarie, Miss Ashe, Miss Andrews, the Misses Burroughs, Miss Brown, Miss Aline Breakey, Miss Albertine Bergeron, Miss Beaudry, Miss Yvonne

COURTIERS BOW BEFORE KING HENRY IV.

Belanger, Miss Billingsley, Miss Constance Bowey, Miss Aug. Carrier, Miss Carruthers, Mrs. Craig, Mrs. Camden, Mrs. Carr. the Misses Chommard (2), Miss J. Choquette, Mrs. J. Carrier, Mrs. Cloutier and sister, Miss Clark, Miss Clint, the Misses Dunlop, the Misses J. S. Dunbar, the Misses Drouin (2), Miss Alice Dube, the Misses Douglass, the Misses Dufault, the Misses Wm. Dobell, the Misses Fraser, Mrs. Frothingham, Mrs. Foley, he Misses Flool (4), Miss Ines Fortier, Miss Alice Gagne, the Misses Gignac (2), Miss Genest, Mrs. Kenneth Gilmour, Mrs. Holliday, Miss Gladys Hood, Miss Alice Houde, Miss Hartley, Miss Wm. A Home, Miss E. Holland, Miss Herot, the Misses Jolicoeur (4), Mrs. E. Jones, Miss Jackson, Mrs. Thomas Lehlane, Miss Eva Lefrancois, the Misses Laroque (3), Miss Ju liette Langelier, Miss

A. Langelier, Miss Milne, the Misses Marsh, Miss Mailly, Miss Neilson, the Misses Olliver, Mrs. E. D. Paquin, Miss E. Patton, Mrs. Parrock, Mrs. W. Reid, Miss Rathburn, Miss Russell, the Misses Rickaby, Miss C. Reid, Miss Wenda Robson, Mrs. Reginald Ross, the Misses Rouillard, Mrs. Slade, Mrs. E. L. Sewell, Miss W. Scott, Miss C. Swell and Cousin, the Misses Samson (2). Mrs. J. J. Sharples, Mrs. Allan Sutherland, the Misses Thomp

SCENE IN THE HENRY IV. PAGEANT

son, the Misses Turcotte (2), Mrs. W. Turgeon and Miss Simard, Mrs. Chs. Vezina, Mrs. Lennox Williams, Miss Welch, Miss Watson, Miss Wright, Mrs. Woods, Mrs. Walker, Miss Winslow, Mrs. Geo. Blouin, Miss Balfour, Mrs. Bell, Miss Hazen Benson, Miss Annie Breakey, Mrs. Barrington the Misses Beaudry (2), Miss Molly Cook, Miss N. Coombe, Miss Chambers, the Misses Cook, Miss Callaghan, Mrs. Church, Miss E. Cote, Miss M. Dugal, Miss Dobie, Miss Dombille, Miss I. Dutean, Miss Dossaint, Miss Dunnston, Miss Duteau, Mrs. W. C. Edwards, Miss F. Emond, Miss W. A. Emond, Miss M. Fry, Miss Yvonne Furois, Miss Fortier, Miss Grant, Miss D. Gibsone, Mrs. Jules Gauvreau, Miss Hope Glass, Miss Imilda Gannoche, Miss Gilbault. Mrs. Mrs. Gregg (2), the Misses Gravelle (2), Miss L. Hall, Miss B. Hall, Mrs. Harries, Mrs. Hughson, Miss Hale, Miss Hoare, Miss L. Johnston, Miss W. Judge, Mrs. Judge, Miss Muriel Joseph, Miss Irene Joseph, Miss Jinchereau, Miss Cecile Joncas, Miss

Second Pageant---Scene 11

CHAMPLAIN AND HIS WIFE ARRIVE AT QUEBEC IN 1620.

The court scenes have now ended and the pageant ground is again clear. Suddenly from all sides come trooping men, women and children. It is the population of Quebec which comes to the shore to welcome Champlain returning after a two year's absence in France and his girl-wife who has come to share with her husband the cares of a new country.

The total white population of New France numbers

THE CREW OF THE DON DE DIEU

Larue, Mrs. Norman Leslie, Miss Mariette Lavoie, Miss Corine Landry, Miss E. Meredith, Miss Mills, Miss Mary Monaghan, Miss Matthews, Miss Mackay, Miss D. Note, Mrs. Victor Noel, Mrs. Geo. Parke, Mrs. Pigot, Miss Parent, Miss Robitaille, Mrs. W. Ray, Mrs. and Miss Ross, the Misses Remillard, Miss Ritchie and friend, Miss Robitaille, Mrs. James Scott, Mrs. George Scott, Miss Maud Shaw, Miss H. Sewell, Mrs. G. G. Stuart, Miss Claire Souci, Miss Vary, Miss Charlotte St. Victor, Miss H. Wurtele, Miss Wilson, Miss Witley, Mrs. Douglass Young, Mrs. Young, Miss Young.

Swiss Guards:—Hector Cote, Alex. Venne, Alfred Senechal, Jos. Senechal, Victor Blanchet, Raoul Blanchet, Emeric Blanchet, E. Gilbert, J. Gilbert, Alb. Bedard, F. C. Lessard, W. Guay, J. Villeneuve, Geo. Leclerc, Eug. Blais, Geo. Matte, R. Matte, Jos. Paquin, R. Plante, L. Depeyre, J. B. Langlois, E. Thivierge.

eighty, all of whom are clothed in their best to greet the new settler. The men are dressed in garments imitating those of the French nobility at court. The women are also clothed in robes which though not as gorgeous, effectively mimicked those of the Versailles pattern. The whole shows a population whose experiences are hardy, but who are possessed of a strong yearning for the life of the country which bore them. In the group are a number of Indians clad in deerskin and presenting a strange contrast to their white friends.

The cannons of the Abitation fire a feeble salute and

CHAMPLAIN AND HIS WIFE
Drawn by Quebecers to church on a cart
from which the ox had been unharnessed

the bells of the little church softly fill the air of the silent forest beyond, as Champlain and his wife debark and step on the shore of New France. The Frenchmen greet their governor with shouts which proclaim an earnest welcome. The Indians stand quietly by gazing at the beautiful young woman who has come to live among them.

As a sign of peace and goodwill the Indians present to the new arrivals the calumet—the pipe of peace. The French viceroy and his wife are seated on skins in the place of honour, while the Indian chiefs gather around and smoke the pipe of peace. Champlain relates to them how he first visited their country to see its beauties and help them in their wars against their enemies. To ensure their white neighbour of their friendship they perform a dance while the pipe is being passed round.

On a mat which is placed on a piece of ground surrounded by branches and young trees, is laid the manitou of the tribe, and beside it the calumet and trophies of war. The members of the tribe seated upon foliage sing the refrain

"Heia Heia Yonken honone,
Heia Heia Yonken honone"

as the dance goes on. The first
dancer, a chief, gesticulates with
the calumet, while he throws himself into various positions as if
about to leap on something. Another Indian joins him. He is fully
armed and menaces an attack which
can only be opposed by the pipe of
peace.

The dance continues until several chiefs have joined. The calumet
is passed from one to the other. It
is then handed to Champlain, who
shows it to his wife. The chief stores it away and
the dance is over.

CALUMET DANCE
In the Champlain scene.

Sieur duGas reads a commission, giving to Cham-
plain the power to establish himself as Viceroy of
French America in Quebec. The new official replies
and recalls the love which he bears to La Nouvelle
France while the redmen stand still. A cask of wine is
brought forth and drunk amid shouts of "Vive le Roi,"
"Vive Champlain" and "Bienvenue." To these the
Viceroy replies "Vive la Nouvelle France" and "Vive
Quebec."

A cart drawn by an ox is brought on the scene.
Champlain and his wife ascend it. The exultant men
unharness the animal and themselves drawing the cart
bring the visitors to the Abitation, while the women
follow singing

"C'était une frégate
Mon joli coeur de rose,
Dans la mer a touché
Joli coeur d'un rosier."

SCENE CHAMPLAIN.

Champlain—Hon. Chas. Langelier; Eustache Boule—P.
Hamel; Duc de Montmorency— W. R. Larue; Marquis de
Laroche—Lieut.-Col. L. T. Bacon; Marquis de la Gamache—
Capt. A. Gamache; Sieur de Caen—O. Larue; Sieur de Caen, fils
—G. Routhier; Sieur de Poutrincourt—O. Gagnon; Sieur Grave—
Aime Talbot; Claude Desmarais—Paul Belleau; Pierre Chauvin—
G N. Blais; Pierre Dugas—E. Laliberte, E. Gauvreau, J. A.
Gagne, J. V. Leclere, L. Letellier, A. Leclere.

A FEW OF THE PERFORMERS
In the Henri VI pageant.

HON. CHAS. LANGELIER, SHERIFF, AND MISS DE LERY

As Champlain and Madame de Champlain.

Bourgeois—Louis Hebert; G. Couillard—J. A. Mercier; Louis Couillard—A. Mercier; Abraham Martin—Henri Bernier; Nicolas Pivert—V. Charland; Pierre Desportes—Lucien Canon; G.

Huboust C. Power; Marsolen—A. Girard, John Roy, A. Bolduc.

Organizer—Mrs. A. Turgeon; Madame de Champlain—Miss Y. DeLery.

Followers—Miss T. DeLery, Miss G. Samson, Miss Samson.

Citizenesse—Miss Lessard, Miss L. Turgeon, Miss W. Bender, Miss J. Lantier, Miss M. Gauvreau, Miss de la Grave, Miss B. Frechette, Miss J. Grenier.

Citizens, Girls and Boys—Miss L. Lantier, Miss M. Dunn, Miss H. G. Hardy, Miss J. Hardy, Miss C. Stafford, Miss M. Brunet, Miss O'Connell, Mr. C. O'Donnell, Mr. P. DeGuise, Mr. M. Samson, Mr. P. Falardeau.

Revd. Sister St. Theodore in charge—Peasants, girls, boys, recruited from among the orphans under supervision of the Sisters of Charity.

Champlain—Hon. Chs. Langelier; Sieur de Pont Grave—T. Donohue; Sieur de Monts—Geo. Belleau.

CREW OF THE DON DE DIEU.

Officers on Board—Henri Couillard—Ed. Laliberte; Etienne Brule—E. Taschereau; Chir. Bonnerme—Dr. R. Myrand; Ant. Natal—Neuville Belleau; Sieur de la Taille—Vicomte de la Granville; Nicolas Marion—L. H. Gaudry; Sieur de Morel—Felix Turcotte; Sieur de Routhier—Aime Talbot Sieur le Testu—Gust. Simard; Pierre Canane—Geo. Parent, M.P., J. H. B. Mongenais, O. Larue, Jos. Belleau, Emile Mariot, Dr. Devarennes, Ernest Taschereau, A. Vallieres, W. Carkner, Ches. Donohue, H. O'Sullivan, Donat Gendron, J. H. Bossvert, John Wiley, A. Dery, Ste. Foye Belleau, G. N. Blais, Mr. Colston, J. Reid, M. A. Lemieux, J. A. Feeteau, J. A. Fortier.

Most of the above-mentioned members of the crew of Champlain's ship, realizing the signal honour which would be borne by those selected to man, during the Tercentenary, the vessel on which the founder of Quebec crossed the Atlantic, volunteered their services several weeks in advance of the fetes, to the local Executive, by which they were gladly accepted.

THE FAIRIES AND SATYRS

In the Henri IV scene.

THE HOSPITALIERES AND URSULINES
Arrive in Quebec

Third Pageant

MERE MARIE DE L'INCARNATION REACHES QUEBEC WITH THE URSULINES AND JESUITS, AUG. 1, 1639.

Three generations have passed since the foundation of Quebec. The settlers now number two hundred and fifty. The Abitation has become a well-fortified post and is daily guarded by soldiers. There are signs of prosperity among the little group.

It is now well on into the summer. The scene is a quiet one with the simplicity characteristic of a new colony. Soon the spot is transformed. From every direction seem to come, men, women and children, rushing hither and thither, apparently in expectation of something important about to happen. It is the coming of the Ursulines and the Hospitalieres.

The colonials are orderly and neatly dressed. Among them now arrives the Governor, Hualt de Montmagny, attended by a military escort. The soldiers are uniformed in brilliant colours and present a gay picture al ngside the simple white-clad colonists.

All the officialdom of the little colony has been brought together. The missionaries already in the colony stand nearby with long black robes and broad hats.

Cannon booming from the small fort announce the arrival of the welcome ship. The men and women

MR. A. J. MONAGHAN AND FAMILY
Showing the enthusiasm with which Quebecers took part in the pageant,

look expectantly toward the river while the children run to the cliff the better to see the approaching craft bearing their new teachers. While waiting, the assemblage remains silent, until a clamour of joy bursts forth

MISS G. LEFAIVRE

As Marie de l'Incarnation.

as Mere Marie de l'Incarnation is seen coming in the distance followed by three Hospitalieres, and Madame de la Peltrie and her three Ursulines with three Jesuit priests.

The new arrivals fall prostrate on the ground and kiss the soil, filled with joy at their safe arrival. They are welcomed by the people among whom they are to labour. Madame de la Peltrie embraces all the Indian children whom she sees, while mother Marie de l'Incarnation gathers about her all the little children of the white settlers and embraces them.

The first act of the nuns and priests is to wend their way to the small church in the lower town to offer thanks for their safe arrival after a trying voyage of twelve weeks across a rough ocean. They are preceded by the Governor and his soldiers, and march along slowly, followed by the little children singing the old French carol, "D'ou viens-tu-bergere?"

Organizer:—Mr. J. H. Larochelle.

Ursulines:—Mme de la Peltrie—Miss Grondin; Mere M. de l'Incarnation—Miss G. Lefaivre; Mere Ste. Croix—Miss Marie L. LeMoine; Mere St. Joseph—Miss F. Duquet; Mlle Barri—Miss Frechtte (dame de compagnie de Mme de la Peltrie.)

Hospitalieres:—Mere M. Guenet de St. Ignace—Miss M. Sirois; Mere Anne le Cointre de St. Bernard—Mrs. Vallerand; Mere M. Forestier de St. Bonaventure—Miss B. Beaudry.

Ladies:—Mrs. Bellerive, Mrs. M. Carrier, Mrs. C. J. Laberge, Miss B. Mercier, Miss Delisle, Miss Derome, Miss Jacques, Miss L. Dube, Miss J. Gingras, Miss Adj. Gosselin, Miss B. Lemay, Miss B. Kirouac, Miss E. Kirouac, Miss G. Kirouac, Miss Aug. Roy, Miss Aug. Lemoine, Miss Bertrand, Miss M. Louise Lemoine, Miss J. Pelletier.

Children:—Miss Marguerite Neilson, Miss Annette Neilson, Miss M. Plamondon, Miss J. Beaupre, Miss B. Dussault, Miss A. Dussault, Miss Page, Miss Page, Miss Bertrand, Miss Devore, Miss Rouillard, Miss Kirouac, Miss Kirouac, Miss J. Dussault, Miss E. Lessard, Miss J. Lafrance, the Misses Gaumont (3).

Boys:—Mr. H. Neilson, Mr. Vallerand, Mr. Vallerand, Mr. Bertrand, Mr. Plamondon, Mr. Page, Mr. P. Beaupre, Mr. C. Craig, Mr. H. D. Baril, Mr. Baril, Mr. W. Brunet, Mr. G. Beaudry, Mr. Gosselin, Mr. Kirouac, Mr. M. Carrier, Mr. L. P. Couture, Mr. Alb. Larochelle.

J. E. H. Larochelle—Governor De Montmagny.

Courtiers of the Governor.

J. E. Nolin—Chevalier de Repentigny; L. C. Jacques—Martial Piraube as Secretary of Governor; L. Gingras—Mr. de la Pomeraye; E. Larochelle—Mr. de Chavigny; A. Boisjoli—Francois de Re; P. Vallerand—Jean Juchereau de More; S. Bedard—Ant. de Chateau Fort; A. Lachance—Noel Juchereau; R. Petitclerc—Andre de Malapart; P. L. Jobin—Jean Bourdon; G. Ardouin—Simon Guyon; J. A. Raymond—Martin Grouvel.

A GROUP OF COURT LADIES

In the Pageants

INDIANS AND COLONISTS
Awaiting the arrival of Champlain
and his Wife.

Fourth Pageant

THE IROQUOIS ATTACK THE FORT OCCUPIED BY DOL-LARD DES ORMEAUX AND HIS COMPANIONS.

The pageant ground is once more clear save for a small wooden fort which is situated amid the bushes by the cliff. The entrenchment is defended chiefly by stakes showing signs of much use. On the ground in front is a fire around which sit in three groups the allies who have combined to hold the fort against the Iroquois.

In one group are Dollard des Ormeaux, a young man of twenty-five, and sixteen other French boys. They have left Montreal determined to rid New France of its dread—the savage Iroquois who are planning the extermination of the colonies at Montreal, Three Rivers and at Quebec. Propped up by courage and the resolution with which they parted from their friends in Montreal where they made their wills, confessed and received the final sacraments, the seventeen men, imbued with the spirit

AN INDIAN
At the Pageants.

of the hardy colonist blended with that of the early crusader, sit around awaiting the arrival of the enemy. They meditate, pray and sing "Veni Creator." Forty Hurons under Anohotalia form another group, while Chief Mitiwemeg with five Algonquins compose the third element of the allies.

As they pray around the fires over which are slung their kettles a shot is heard among the bushes. The Indians doing duty as sentries appear and announce the arrival of Iroquois canoes. From afar, penetrating through the woods is heard the fearful echo of the enemy's war-cry. The Hurons and Algonquins leave their fires and kettles and enter the fort. Dollard cries to his companions : Aux armes! aux armes! Voici l'heure du sacrifice et du martyre! Haut les cœurs! Haut les courages!

His companions :—Adieu frère! Adieu parent! Amis, adieu!
Dollard :—Rappelez-vous le serment! Pas de merci, pas de quartier! Pas de prisonniers!
His companions :—Rien à l'ennemi, que nos cadavres!
Dollard :—Mon âme à Dieu, mon sang à la Patrie!
Dollard and his companions :—Canada ! Canada! ceux qui vont mourir te saluent !

AN INDIAN CHIEF
At the Pageants.

AMERICAN HORSE
An Iroquois chief at the Pageants.

The Iroquois have now emerged from the thick bushes and immediately attack the palisade but are easily repulsed. They open a parley. One of them goes up to the fort and is met by a Frenchman. Terms cannot be agreed upon, and a moment later the Iroquois are grouped a short distance from the fort anxious to repeat their assault.

Before so doing a war-dance is held. The dusky chief blackens his face, shoulders and breast, sings a song recounting his own exploits and those of his ancestors and offers a sacrifice to the god of war whose assistance he invokes! he! The other warriors fully armed reply with ho! ho! The chief then raises a war-song and while striking a vessel with his club

steal out of the fort and desert to the incensed enemy to whom they explain the plan of the fort.

The Iroquois make a third attack. Again they are driven back by the heavy fire which issues from every loophole. Some are discouraged and would abandon the evidently impossible scheme. The chief rallies them decides on a new plan of attack and instils courage into his men.

The chief places sticks in the ground at equal spaces from each other. These are to indicate the position of each leader whence he is to attack. Crouchingly, cautiously and in a squirming manner they advance to the fort. From a low position where they escape the fire of the white men's muskets they shoot their

IROQUOIS INDIANS

Carrying the Scalps in the
Dollard des Ormeaux Scene

begins to dance. The body is kept close to the ground and in this crouching position the savages dance on while at intervals the song of the chief is disturbed by the doleful dirge he! he! from the others.

The dance over, the besiegers again march on the little fort and with their bows throw light arrows into the rough but weak palisade. The allies keep up a steady fire and again the enemy are forced to fall back. Of their number, several have fallen. The Hurons in the fort rush out and scalp them, exposing their trophies on the high stakes fencing the palisade. At this the frenzied Iroquois howl with rage. The Hurons among them shout to their tribesmen in the fort. Some remain faithful to their allies. Others

arrows. They approach nearer and nearer until almost within reach of the fusilade.

Dollard feels his plight. His position is a desperate one. He is outnumbered and but poorly defended. He fills a large musketoon with powder, lights it and as the enemy are about to scale the walls of the entrenchment directs it to them. In its course it strikes a branch and rebounds into the fort where it explodes and causes havoc among the allies. To add to the confusion the Iroquois charge the fort, and fire through the loopholes. The distance is still good, but a breach is made and in a moment the enemy is inside. Flames are seen to arise, a savage yell is heard and—all is over.

THE IROQUOIS CARRYING OFF THEIR DEAD
After the assault on the fort occupied by Dollard des Ormeaux.

The seventeen Frenchmen and their faithful allies have sacrificed their lives in a brilliant defence. They have been subdued and slaughtered but their heroic struggle has alarmed the Iroquois, and the colonies of La Nouvelle France escape the fate that was being prepared for them. Black smoke still issues from the spot where the heroes were massacred. The victors cry "Koay" to celebrate their victory. The scene is one of carnage and yet amidst the black smoke, with forms of the dying men around the fort, there breathes a spirit of grandeur and heroism. The defence has rightly been called the Marathon of the new world. The Iroquois pick up their dead, and place the heads of their enemies on tall pikes. They sing a mournful funeral dirge and march off slowly, their trophies upright, their own dead heroes respected, while of the fort, nought but a few blazing embers remain.

Organizer—F. de B. Gourdeau.

Adam Dollard Sieur des Ormeaux—F. de B. Gourdeau.

List of Sixteen Braves:—C. de Lery, Jacques Lantier, W. E. Bender, Henri Roy, Robert Roy, Charles Gauvreau, Valere Desjardins, Philippe Desjardins, Henri Brochu, R. Brochu, Gaston Beaupre, Henri Trudelle, Paul Lanctot, Charles Fontaine, N. Larrivee, Albert Roy.

American Horse and about one hundred Indians.

Fifth Pageant

MGR. DE LAVAL, BISHOP OF QUEBEC RECEIVES MARQUIS DE TRACY, LIEUTENANT-GENERAL OF NEW FRANCE, IN JUNE, 1665.

The rude fort of the French heroes has now disappeared from sight. The victorious savages have retreated bearing their dead and the scalps of the white men. The warlike scene is over and nothing now mars the pageant ground but clusters of bushes which guard the river below.

From among them one suddenly beholds the coming of men, women and children. It is the French colony at Quebec, now more than half a century old, gather-

MRS. W. H. WIGGS AND FAMILY
In the Pageants.

ing to greet the Marquis de Tracy on his arrival from France. The men are richly attired. The women are in neat white clothes.

The strains of military music are heard and from the distance is seen to come the regiment of Carignan-Sallieres. The native Quebecers unused to the well-drilled French Militia gaze at them astonishingly as with bright uniform and plumed hats the soldiers march to take up their position.

There is bustle and excitement among the old colonists. The New Governor is about to arrive, and there are many surmises as to his character, his appearance, his qualities, etc. But again all is still on the scene. The ecclesiastical procession is slowly advancing and preceded by a priest carrying a crucifix, on either side of whom is another priest carrying a lighted taper, while surrounded by acolytes perfuming the air with fragrant censers, comes the saintly Bishop Laval, the first Canadian church dignitary who has come to welcome the temporal master of French Canada. The representative of Louis XIV, clothed in a brilliant red suit gorgeously decorated with gold, has already arrived from the landing place, and surrounded by his nobles awaits the Bishop. An address of welcome is read from the Sovereign Council to which a clear and short reply is given.

The Bishop of Petralla has now approached. De Tracy kneels and kisses his hand and the crucifix. The welcome of the church is extended by the ecclesiastic. The new Governor replies briefly. The spiritual and temporal heads of the community then leave the scene and following the Governor's guards proceed to the church where special thanks are offered by the governor after his lengthy journey.

Church bells are heard to ring. The Te Deum is sung. The Indians pay homage to the new Governor, while the white men follow their newly-arrived friends from old France.

L'ABBE VACHON
As Mgr de Laval.

Organizer:—Mr. J. C. Lockwell.

Mgr. Laval—M. l'abbe Vachon.

Rev. Father J. Ths. Nadeau, representing Carney de Fuzon, Grand Vicar.

Revds. Messrs. Maxime Fortin, Arthur Gauthier, Fortin Edmond Coran, Philippe Mathieu, Cleophas Leclerc, Oscar Bergeron, Eugene morisset, Hercule Nicole, Valerien Pelletier, Janvier Lachance, Adelard Picher, Cyrille Labrecque, Frs. Xavier Lefebvre, Arthur Premont, Jos. Larochelle, Philippe Nadeau, Alphonse Coriveau, Alfred Cote, Alphonse Morel, Victor Lemieux, Zephyr Marois, Celestin Fillion, Pierre Crepault, Gedeon Jobin, Mr. Frechette, Leonidas Verrault, Jos. Dumas, Moise Fradette.

Marquis de Tracy—Mr. C. E. Rouleau; Secretary—Mr. W. Laberge.

Nobles—Raoul Leclerc, Mederic Cleroux, Frederic Fiset, Alfred Hamel, Louis Dupuis, Antonio Rouleau, Z. Dion, A. Plamondon, J. A. Lagace, J. E. A. Pinault, X. Dion, G. Richard, J. E. Desrosiers, J. E. Deslongchamps.

Officers:—L. Lefevre, C. Vezina, Alp. Berard, F. X. Dumontier, P. A. Bourget, J. A. Hamel.

Laquais:—W. Villeneuve, J. O. St. Antoine, J. P. Matte, Z. Berube, A. Dumas, J. Fontaine.

Pages:—N. Cote, E. Donati, B. Richard, J. Laveau.

Sovereign Council:—Mr. J. E. A. Pin.

Members of the Council:—Messrs. J. N. Bruneau, T. Boucher, H Chouinard, P. Croteau, P. Cote, H. Croteau, J. Drolet, A. Demers, A. Gagnon, O. Gilbert, F. Laroche, D. Laforce, J. J. Menard, S. Poulin, Ed. Pepin, J. Ratte, L. Shink, J. C. Sioui, L. Villeneuve.

Carignan Regiment,—F. X. J. Dorion, A. Gauthier, O. Villeneuve, E. Colomb, J. E. Boijoli, E J. H. Gingras, N. Lafrance, J. Landry, E. Noreau, J. Robitaille, A. G. Robitaille, J. Bouchard, A. Gaumond, T. Dionne, G. E. Richard, Alex. Hardy, G. E. Richard, E. Richard, A. Emond, C. A. Rouleau, J. A. Desroches, A. Grenier T. Leclerc R. Noreau, L. Bouchard, S. Lefebvre, S. St. Pierre, A. Bouchard, A. Tremblay, A. Tremblay, J. Rigali, Henri Paquet, A. Noreau, V. Menard, J. Germain, L. Lamothe, E. Julien, J. O. Chalifour, N. Drolet, A. Gagnon, O Fortier, G. St. Pierre L. Giroux, F. Gauvin, P C. Cote, A. Donati, G. Julien, P. Langlais, L. P. Laliberte, E. Lemieux P. Dolbee, E. Rioux, A. Demers, J. A. Caron, L P. Poitras J. Roberge

BISHOP LAVAL AND HIS ATTENDANTS
In the Laval-Tracy scene.

A LADY OF THE OLD REGIME

MARQUIS DE TRACY

P. Fournier, E. Laverdiere, W. Noreau, G. Gagne, A. Lefevre, E. St. Pierre, L. C. Lamonette, J. Thibault, N. S. Benoit, A. Lizotte, J. E. T. Morency, J. G. Dubois, H. Noel, W. Barbeau, J. A. Lepire, A. Godin, D. Dube, J. A. Berube, H. Fortier, F. Normand, C. Billaudeau, T. Godbout, L. Verrault, G. Landry, A. Blais, E. Poitras, J. Verrault, A. Lebel, J. E. Dion, A. Darveau, E. Dore, H. Nansot, A. Laverdiere, V. Lavigueur, W. Noreau, C. Gosselin, E. Lemieux, A. Santerre, J. Demeules, Alb. Noreau, Nap, Belleau, P. D'Auteuil, J. St. Pierre.

Citizens:—Joseph Renaud, Ph. Grenier, J. C. Gauvin, A. Carmichael, W. Gauvin, R. Simard, A. Lafrance, J. Cauchon, R. Dionne, A. Gignac, A. Lapointe, H. Bouchard, J. Havard, A. Bussiere, G. Godbout, E. Tremblay, E. Taschereau, G. Gunner, A. Marineau, S. Parent, J. Rioux, J. Goldberg, L. Alain, L. Andy, A. Audy, L. Bourbon, J. Poulin, A. Laporte, A. Grenier, J. Angers, T. Gagne, P. Dubois, A. Bedard, J. Lapointe, O. Lessard, E. Chartrain, A. Falardeau, P. Laprise, H. Fortier, H. Jobin, H. Dionne, O. Lamontagne, E. Drolet, A. Belleville, Edg. Gignore, C. Plamondon, A. Parent, D. Laforce, P. Cote, S. Poulin, A. Gagnon, H. Chouinard, J. C. A. Sioui, H. Proteau, P. Grenier, G. T. Gerret, Perry Gerret.

Civic Guard:—B. Barrette, A. Bazin, D. Tremblay, Ed. Begin,

Swiss Guard:—H. Cote, Alf. Senechal, Alp. Senechal, Jos. Senechal, V. Blanchet, R. Blanchet, E. Blanchet, Alb. Bedard, F. C. Lessard, J. Villeneuve, G. Leclerc, E. Blais, G. Matte, R. Matte, Jos. Paquin, R. Plante, Ls. Depeyre, E. Thivierge.

Children of the chorus:—Maurice Vezina, Edgar Vezina, Jos Dery, Alb. Laberge, Maurice Lemieux, Art. Lepinay, Jos. Cote, Rodolphe Jalbert, F. X. Dussault, Henri Lacasse, Alex. Bedard, Gaud. Fiset, Adel. Jobin, L. Letarte, Eug. Gervais, Ern. Pelletier, Art. Villeneuve, Leon Faguy, Aurele Mercier, Emile Charrier, Mr. Latulippe, Honore Cote, Raoul Tardif, Noel Clavet, Henri Poulin, Chs. E. Guimont, Laurent Malonin, Joseph Moisan, J. Er. Poulin, Antonio Fortier, Emile Rouleau, Louis L. Rouleau, Lucien Watters, M. Lamontagne, Joseph Julien, Alfred St. Hilaire, L. Bussieres, Alex. Donati, Raoul Dery.

Merchants' wives:—Miss A. McBain, Miss Stella Kerwin, Miss Wynn, Miss H. Burke, the Misses O'Sullivan, the Misses Brady, Miss Nellie Burton, Miss D. Julian, Miss Marie Waite, Miss Blanche Roy, Miss Alice Gauvreau, Miss L. Gauvreau, the Misses Silk, Miss Savard, Miss Gauthier, Miss Boldue, Miss Demers, Miss C. Coss, Miss Leeda Morin, Miss Alice Rondeau, Miss Lea Rochette, Miss Susie Silverman, the Misses Duggan,

THE ENORMOUS CROWD ON THE GRAND STAND
viewing the pageant performance. One of the Telegraph's prize pictures taken by J. M. Ritchie.

E. B. Blumhart, C. Bleau, A. Boutet, J. B. Boucher, J. N. Despatis, E. Demers, D. Delisle, J. Genest, L. Clavet, Alex. Dery, E. Darveau, G. Grenier, A. Donati, P. D'Aigle, J. C. Dallaire, A. P. Dallaire, N. Drolet, O. Fournier, R. Dionne, H. Faguy, N. Fournel, H. Godbout, O. Gervais, J Gauvin, O. Lemieux, J. Goly, H. Donaldson, J. Savard, Frs. Lacasse, O. Lagueux, L. Labrecques, J. E. Larochelle, D. Lagueux, J. La roche, E. Bidegare, A. Martin, E. Morency, N. Richard, G. Marceau, E. Marceau, N. Pageau, F. Pruneau, M. Patoine, P. Poliquin, N. Pare, J. Poitras, A. Roberge, A. Robitaille, Eug. Rochette, Jos. Rochette, Jos Tremblay, Elz. Vezina, E. Dery, A Mercier, J. A. Mercier, P. A. Lagueux, L. A. Lagueux, J. O. Lagueux, J. C. Langlois, Nap. Trepanier, J. W. Tremblay, A. Leclerc, M. Villeneuve, Lax Meyer, E. R. Lepine, J. Renaud, P. Grenier, J. E. Langlois, J. W. Gauvin, R. Delisle, A. Tur geon, J. Turgeon, A. D'Auteuil, P. Dery, V. St. Pierre, N. Vezina, X. Loiselle, G. Loiselle, O. Gagnon, J. Garneau, O. Dube, A. Monier, E. Gregoire, Jos. Drolet, O. Drolet, G. Lagueux, J. L. Morency, J. A. Drolet, Jos. Laverdiere, L. Be langer, L. Robitaille, J. H. Vincent, E. Julien, V. Gamache, O. Dallaire, J. O. Binet, R. Grenon, L. Julien, L. C. Trudel, E. Gagnon, R. Hebert, J. Guay, W. Mercier, P. Rochon, N. Richard.

Miss M. Wintle, Miss Wright, Miss Yvonne Cote, Miss Nora Bresnahan, Miss B. Golberg, Miss Eva Nolet, Miss Leulu McCleary.

Peasants:—Miss Blossom Steeth, the Misses Julian, Mrs. Willie Buchanan, Miss Jessie Buchanan, Miss May MacFarlane, Miss Annie MacFarlane, Miss Rose McMillan, Miss Muriel Mc Millan, Miss Eileen Brown, the Misses Piton (3), Miss Corinne Lawlor, Miss H. B. Knight, Miss Paquet, Miss Muriel Mc Beach, the Misses Nolet, Miss Mary Johnson, Miss Mabel Jack son, Miss Louisa Talbot, Miss Ethel Hogan, Miss Gertie Thomas, Miss Kathleen Dooley, Miss Grace Fanning, Miss A. Burns, Miss Irene Dempsey, Miss Cora Boulet, Miss Albertine Boulet, Miss Albertine Cote, Miss D. Hearly, Mrs. Jules Tessier, Mrs. Fabre, Miss Marguerite Duchesnay, Miss Webster, Miss Bridie, Miss Wright, Miss Gignore, Mrs. Hill, Miss Buttler, Miss Powell, Mrs. Adkin, the Misses Gignac, Miss Gibaux, the Misses Morin, Miss Noel, Mrs. G. E. Dery, Miss Dery, Miss N. Lamontagne, Miss Y. Lamontagne, Mrs. Van Derwerken, Mrs. A. Scott, Miss MsNaughton, Miss Martineau, Mrs. Jolivet, Miss Blanche Mar tineau, Mrs. de Lotbiniere-Panet, Miss Black, Miss Yvonne Costin, Miss Gabrielle Martineau, Miss Mildred Moore, Miss Muriel Moore, Miss Alma Boldue, Miss Yvonne Boldue.

MR. FRANK LASCELLES
Director of the Pageants.

Sixth Pageant

DAUMONT DE SAINT-LUSSON TAKES POSSESSION OF THE WESTERN DISTRICTS FOR THE KING OF FRANCE, JUNE 14, 1671.

On the pageant ground comes from a distance a small band of Frenchmen. Among the roughly-clad fur-traders and colonists are four dark-gowned Jesuits who have come from the settlement on Lake Huron to share with their brethren the hardships and dangers to which the desire for new wealth had exposed them. With these is Simon Francois Daumont de Saint-Lusson, the chief of the party and the trusted envoy of Talon. He has come to take possession of the western country for the King of France and incidentally to search for copper mines on Lake Superior.

The Indians have heard of the white men's visit and are prepared to meet them. The feathered repre-

sentatives of fourteen tribes are gathered and greet their guests with every sign of welcome. ,

With hospitality is blended curiosity. The red men hover about the priests and gaze on their strangely simple vestments. The solemn ceremony now commences and even the savages gaze with veneration at the wooden cross which is raised by the Frenchmen, who bareheaded sing in unison after a priest has pronounced his blessing over the religious symbol implanted on pagan soil. A Frenchman places a wooden post beside the cross and overlays it with a metal plate charged with the Royal arms while another priest offers prayers for the King. The French chief raises heavenward one hand clasping a drawn sword and with the other lifts a clod of earth. Volleys are fired and "Vive le Roi" is cried. This ends the official ceremony and the western regions have become French.

Father Allouez makes a harangue in the Indian tongue and relates the might of the Lord for whom has been erected the cross and the grandeur of the King whose royal arms have been placed alongside. His powers are no mean ones for "he is the captain of the greatest captains, and has not his equal in the world." The leader of the French expedition eloquently eulogizes the great King and is thankful that he has acquired new subjects across the sea. The Te Deum is sung and the Frenchmen depart—their task over. The Indians follow—new subjects of France.

Daumont de Saint-Lusson—Dr. J. E. Belanger; Nicolas Perrot—Interpreter of the King—Emile Theberge; Jolliet—Edouard Fafard.

PROFESSOR F. H. NORMAN
Maitre de Ballet and assistant to Mr. Lascelles.

Fur Traders and Colonists:—Jacques Mogras—T. Morin; Pierre Moreau—B. Nolin; Denis Masse—T. Burnside; Francois de Chavigny—J. Guerin; Jacques Lagillier—R. Drapeau; Jean Maysere—L. J. Bourget; Nicolas Dupuis—P. Houde; Francois Bibaud—Geo. Murphy; Jacques Joviel—Jos. Laperriere; Pierre Porteret—J. O. Richard; Robert Duprat—J. B. Duclos; Vital Driol—Aug. Laperriere; Guillaume Bonhomme—S. Burnside.

Sailors of the Daument de Saint-Lusson:—Alf. Godbout, H. Langlois, J. Guilbault; P. Marcoux.

MR. H. D'ARTOIS

As Frontenac.

Seventh Pageant

FRONTENAC'S RECEPTION OF PHIPS' ENVOY AT QUEBEC, OCTOBER 16, 1690.

The pageant ground is once more the scene of considerable activity. It is covered with hundreds of men, women and children who are dressed in the neat garb of the old Canadian settler. The assembly seems uneasy and gazes now and then toward the river as if expecting some ominous sign. Nor does it have long to wait, for soon, coming up the stream, are seen several ships with guns pointed landward. It is the English fleet under Sir William Phips, which has come to take Quebec, on whose summit now stand its early colonists.

The congregation of rugged settlers, traders and Indians is not alone awaiting the enemy. The old governor, Frontenac, is also there. He has fought hard battles in Italy and in Canada and is prepared to do so again. His age does not fetter his activities, but like a true hero of the old regime he is determined to fight, and, if necessary, to die for the King, and he will not yield or give way to the demands of the English aggressor. He is surrounded by his sovereign councillors, who appear in solemn black dress and large hats of the same colour. Nearby stand the governor's guards, for Frontenac yet loves a display of grandeur and might. Nobles of New France mix freely with the armed musketeers who are on the field.

The enemy has now come and the French are anxiously waiting to see what will happen. Suddenly there is a stir among the crowding and jostling inhabitants of Quebec. An English officer has come on shore to demand the surrender of the town. Blindfolded, he is led by two sergeants through the noisy crowd, which sings : "Voila! Monsieur Colin-Maillard qui vient nous faire visite," until he comes before the sturdy old governor.

All are now quiet and listen to the following conversation between the English parliamentary and sturdy Frontenac :—

THE PARLIAMENTARY.—May I speak to Count Frontenac.....

FRONTENAC (*briskly interrupting him*)—C'est moi, Monsieur !

THE PARLIAMENTARY (continuing where he left off)— lieutenant-general and governor for the French King at Canada......

FRONTENAC (*interrupting*)—C'est moi, Monsieur !

THE PARLIAMENTARY (*continuing*)—Or, in his absence, to his deputy or him or them in chief command at Quebec?

FRONTENAC.—C'est moi, Monsieur !

VALRENNE: (*captain of Frontenac's guards*).—Nommez-vous d'abord.

THE PARLIAMENTARY.—What?

BIENVILLE (*the interpreter*).—Your name, Sir?

THE PARLIAMENTARY.—Captain-Lieutenant Thomas Savage.

BIENVILLE.—In what capacity?

THE PARLIAMENTARY.—As bearer of a summons from Sir William Phips, Knight, General and Commander in and over their Majesties' forces of New England, by sea and land, to Count Frontenac.

FRONTENAC.—Très bien, Monsieur, je vous écoute.

THE PARLIAMENTARY.—The war between the two crowns of England and France doth not only sufficiently warrant, but the destruction made by the French and Indians, under your command and encouragement, upon the persons and estates of their Majesties' subjects of New England, without provocation on their part, hath put them to the necessity of this expedition for their own security and satisfaction.

FRONTENAC (*interrupting*).—Je n'ai jamais été familier avec l'Anglais, aussi, M. de Bienville, vous seriez fort amiable de me traduire ce document.

BIENVILLE (*to the parliamentary*)—That paper, please.

The interpreter reads Phips' summons for surrender in the French language. Frontenac is asked to reply within one hour. The contents of the document create great discontent among those assembled, who utter remarks of disapprobation and contempt. At the end of the reading the

THE COURT OF FRANCIS I

Retiring from the Scene

more violent of the French inhabitants show signs of animosity and are about to attack the envoy, but are calmed by the officers. The envoy and Frontenac alone remain silent and evidently undisturbed.

The Parliamentary pulls out his watch and insolently puts it before the governor's visage, saying:—"It is ten o'clock, Sir, and by eleven, I must have an answer!" This infuriates even the officers present and Valrennes furiously exclaims:—"A la potence! bandit! A la potence! Traitons cet insolent comme l'envoyé d'un corsaire. Phips, son digne maitre, n'a-t-il pas violé la capitulation de Port-Royal? retenu Menneval prisonnier, et contre sa parole et contre le droit des gens? Retour de politesse, alors. Hé! *Rattier! Rattier!* sus à la vermine! Apporte ton échelle et tes cordes!

"En vérité, monsieur, vous en causez à votre aise du droit des gens! et l'appliquez à merveille! Pendre un parlementaire! Le procédé serait bien français! Seulement, rappelez-vous ce qu'il vous en a coûté, l'an dernier, d'avoir envoyé aux galères les ambassadeurs iroquois! Auriez vous oublié déjà le massacre de La Chine? Franchement, le bourreau n'a pas besoin de venir ici: le premier d'entre vous me fera bien mon nœud de cravate (à Valrennes) *M. du Chanvre*, je suis à vos ordres!" Continuing, the envoy insists upon an answer from Frontenac, who replies:—

"Ma réponse positive? la voici:

Dites à votre général que je ne connais point le roi Guillaume et que le prince d'Orange est un usurpateur qui a violé les droits les plus sacrés du sang en voulant détrôner son beau-père: et que je ne sais, en Angleterre, d'autre souverain que le roi Jacques; que votre général n'a point dû

être surpris des hostilités qu'il dit avoir été faites par les Français dans la colonie du Massachusetts, puisqu'il a dû s'attendre que le Roi, mon maitre, ayant reçu sous sa protection le roi d'Angleterre, étant près de le replacer sur son trône par la force de ses armes, comme j'en ai nouvelles, m'ordonnerait de porter la guerre en ces contrées chez les peuples qui se seraient révolté contre leur prince légitime.

Vous avez entendu, Monsieur le parlementaire, les murmures d'indignation soulevés autour de moi par votre arrogante sommation. Eh bien! sachez que ce sentiment est commun à tous nos gentilshommes et à tous nos paysans, aux premiers comme aux derniers d'entre eux!

Votre général croit-il, quand il m'offrirait des conditions plus douces, et que je fusse d'humeur à les accepter, que tant de braves gens, que voici, voulussent y consentir, et qu'ils me conseillassent de me fier à la parole d'un homme qui n'a pas gardé la capitulation qu'il avait faite avec le gouverneur de Port-Royal, et d'un rebelle qui a manqué à la fidélité qu'il devait à son légitime Roi, en oubliant tous les bienfaits qu'il en avait reçu, pour suivre le parti d'un prince qui, en essayant de persuader qu'il veut être le libérateur de l'Angleterre et le défenseur de la Foi, y détruit les lois et les privilèges du royaume, renversant la religion catholique. C'est ce que la justice divine, que votre général réclame dans sa lettre, ne manquera jamais de punir quelque jour sévèrement."

THE PARLIAMENTARY.—Monsieur le Gouverneur voudra bien me donner cette réponse par écrit.

FRONTENAC.—Et que faites-vous de ma parole? Par écrit? Non, jamais! Je vais répondre à votre maitre par la bouche de mes canons! M. de Valrennes, ramenez le parlementaire à son canot. Courons, messieurs, à l'ennemi! Vive le Roi!

The envoy is again blindfolded and led back to the shore amid the hooting and yelling of the Frenchmen, who make all the noise possible in order to confuse the envoy and deceive him as to their number. He is kicked and pinched as he is led back, while the mob sings :

Messieurs les Anglais de Boston
Va, va, va, p'tit bonnet, tout rond,
Se sont fâchés pour tout de bon,
P'tit bonnet, grand bonnet, p'tit bonnet tout rond
Et va, va, va, p'tit bonnet, grand bonnet,
Et va, va, va, p'tit bonnet tout rond.

nier, J. Burstall, J. A. Boisjoly, J. M. Blanchet, V. E. Beauvais, Jos. Boldue, J. L. Bertrand, R. M. Beckett, L. H. Begin, J. Brady, Eug. Brochu, F. X. Blouin, Frank Dronin, Wilfrid Duclos, J. E. Dussault, Chs. F. Darveau, Philippe Duclos, S. P. Dugal, Dr. J. T. Dussault, Harold Kennedy, U. Genereux, M. F. Griffin, C. J. Griffin, Geo. Guenet, Jules Gauvin, Alphonse Germain, Dr. J. L. Gilbert, Roger Godin, C. E. Gauthier, Dr. Alphonse Laroque, Ephrem L'Heureux, J. Aim. Richard, Jules Rouillard, Chs. Rhodes, Wilbrod Richard, E. C. Joseph, Alph. Huard, N.P., J. Arthur Morin, W. Mulrooney, Hubert Moisan, Louis Morency, H. C. Foy, J. A. Marier, Emile Morissette, Jos. Paquet, St. Denis Provost, Paul Plamondon, A. O. Pruneau, E. Sauveville, Harcourt Smith, Arthur Smith, J. A. Soulard, H. Thivierge, J. E. Tanguay, Adrien Falardeau, Alf. T. Tanguay, Jos. D. Thibeault, Oct. Talbot, Dr. Jos. Vaillancourt, Ths. LeBlanc, Alex. Morency, John Laird, A. E. Dery, F. W. Williams, A. E. Tremblay, T. H. Morewood, Frank Dronin, John Burstall, Ulric Moisan, T. Maranda, Eug. Montreuil.

SIR WILFRID LAURIER, SIR LOUIS JETTE AND LORD STRATHCONA
At the Pageants.

Spokesmen.

Frontenac..H. D'Artois.
Bienville..J. E. Talbot.
Lt. Thos. Savage..Oscar Morin.
Varennes..Art. Larue.

Halberdiers:—W. R. Peacock, A. L. Gamache, Omer Paquet, L. N. Gauvin, M. Frechette, J. P. Bertrand, W. J. Guillot, P. A. Allain, Z. Delisle, A. Gosselin.

Sovereign Council:—Napoleon Dorion, Leader; A. G. Auger, J. A. Chaunette, J. E. Chapleau, Jos. Cote, Dr. C. H. Beaupre, L. N. Dorion, Intendant; Albert Demers, Jos. Delaney, J. A. Dumontier, J. A. Dery, Geo. Racine, Eug. Furois, J. A. Renaud, Jos. A. Paquet, Dr. Albert Jobin, R. Plamondon, Dr. Jos. Guerard, Dr. E. A. Lebel, J. B. Gosselin, L. H. Peters, M. Monaghan.

Nobles:—R. Anctil, J. Anctil, J. O. Auger, C. Cantin, J. A. Chicoine, J. N. Cloutier, L. E. Fortier, P. E. Fugere, J. T. Four-

Citizens:—Louis Anctil, J. E. Audibert, A. Amyot, Aime Anctil, R. Anctil, J. E. Chartre, Alexandre Dumas, Geo. Begin, A. J. Boucher, Arthur Beaubien, Donat Bousquet, S. Belanger, Chas. Boutet, G. B. Schwartz, Leo. Dugal, Geo. H. Duquet, Jos. Delage, C. Dubuc, Jos. Falardeau, Henri Forgues, Armand Falardeau, H. H. Hudon, V. Garant, Jules Gauvreau, jr., Ernest Lepinay, Onesime Goulet, Alphonse Cote, jr., E. W. Larue, Aderic Leclerc, H. Laroche, Odilon Lechasseur, Gregoire Richard, K. B. Thomson, J. A. Menard, J. A. Trudel, Hubert Moisan, jr., C. H. Moisan, H. Moisan, J. Morency, J. P. Plamondon, Albert Thibaudeau, J. O. N. Tanguay, Arthur Vaillancourt, E. Greenwood, Alex. Becain, Albert Delisle, Jos. Thivierge, Chs. Gagnon, Jos. Darveau, Leo Falardeau, Emile Boutet, Joseph Boutet, Adolard Boutet.

Citizens forming the choir:—Adolard Arteau, Alidor Boulet, E. Buteau, Ls. Bilodeau, Ernest Bussiere, Alfred Begin, J. A. Blais, Cyr. Bruneau, Jos. Delisle, D. Dallaire, A. Dallaire, Alexandre David, J. D. Dionne, E. H. Falardeau, Lucien Frigon, Alb. J. Gagnon, Ernest Garneau, J. B. Gingras, A.

Gingras, Alb. Gagnon, E. Hilpert, Henri Raymond, Nap. Jacques, Raoul Kirouac, J. A. Kirouac, H. Lamontagne, A. Lizotte, J. B. Lamontagne, J. B. Lemieux, T. C. Morissette, Alb. Morissette, J. L. Montreuil, Elz. Poitras, Pierre Pouliot, T. Poitras, Etienne Poitras, J. A. Renaud, Sam. Richard, E. Rochette, Alb. Samson, J. A. Simard, G. S. St. Laurent, Eug. Trudelle, jr., F. Vanderbergen, J. A. Savard, A. Tardif, J. H. Raymond, Jules Falardeau, Ovide Levesque, M. T. Renaud.

Musketeer Guards:—J. A. Audet, Art. Charrier, A. Cote, Wilfrid Charest A. C. Faguy, C. N. Falardeau, Lieut, Alf. Fyen, Pierre Blouin, Lucien Borne, P. E. Belanger, Ludger Beauregard, Alf. Dorval, Ed. Demers, A. Duquet, Arthur Dumontier, Lieut. Paul Hebert, Paul Hamel, Ovide Hamel, Guide W. J. Kelly, Chs. Emond, J. I. Gourdeau, Leo, Gauvreau, A. Gaumond, L. A. Gaumond, Lucien Gauvreau, Alex. Laliberte, J. E. Larochelle, M. Landry, J. L. Leclerc, J. L. Lamonde, Jos. M. Rochon, Achille Roy, Laurest C. Roy, J. S. Royer, J. A. Mercier, Jos. L. Mercier, J. B. Mercier, J. A. Morin, Alph. Noel, J. C. Giguere, J. A. Pettigrew, J. D. Piche, J. O. Parent, J. B. Poirier, Jos. Plante, P. Petit, Dr. E. St. Hilaire, F. Simard, H. Simard, George Trudel, A. E. Tremblay, C. E. Tremblay, J. N. Tremblay, L. A. Trepanier, L. P. Turgeon, L. Turgeon.

Sergt.-Trumpeter Robert, R.C.A., and four trumpeters.

Captain Geo. Van Felson, Capt. Michael LeNeuf, Sieur de Valliere et de Beaubassin.

CALLIERES REGIMENT.

Officers:—Capt. A. Morency, J. T. St. Pierre, J. O. Parent, Art. Parent, F. Maranda, F. X. Gobeil, P. Emond.

Fife and Drum Corps:—M. Lafrance, J. E. Bellemare, A. Ouimet, E. Bernier, A. Blais, S. Picard, C. Loiselle, R. Samson, W. Beland, A. L'Heureux, J. O. Leclerc, A. Rinfret, H. Bernard, M. Martineau, A. Chasse, L. Rippe, O. Pelletier, E. Allard, Adj. Laliberte.

Drum Corps:—J. Cantin, A. Vaillancourt, R. Lafrance, J. Taillon, J. B. Lalonde, J. L'Heureux, P. Royer, A. Cantin, E. Armand, J. Lizotte, E. Paquet, E. Duchesne, Elz. Bacon, R. Nadeau, Em. Clavet, Alb. Laliberte, Alph. Proteau.

Regiment:—Ad. Mercier, H. Gravel, A. Faucher, J. Joannette, A. Fortin, F. Laferriere, O. Drolet, J. Nolin, A. Tremblay, U. Saindon, N. Turcotte, R. Gobeil, A. Letourneau, H. Lamontagne, C. Brousseau, A. Jacques, H. Larochelle, E. Dussault, H. Langevin, A. Noreau, L. Dugal, N. Armand, A. Leblanc, O. Renaud, N. Vaillancourt, J. Ferland, E. Jalbert, Louis Desrochers A. Pouliot, J. Delauniere, L. P. Filion, P. Nolin, P. Vezina, L. J. Nadeau, A. Paradis, O. Taillon, N. Blais, L. Marier, Etienne Bacon, O. Metayer, H. Marcoux, O. Kirouac, A. Gingras, Alb. Gingras, N. Cote, J. Metivier, J. Lessard, Jos. Hudon, P. E. Julien, Eu. St. Cyr, L. Derosier, Ed. Lepine, Jos. Grenier, O. Nolin, R. Huot, Jos. Poulin, A. Bilodeau, O. Cyr, Ed. Tremblay, Achille Latulippe, Geo. Bouchard.

COURT LADIES, TOWN LADIES AND CHILDREN.

Mrs. Harold Kennedy, Mrs. A. Rhodes, Mrs. W. Price, Mrs. H. B. Powel, Mrs. A. Price, Mrs. James Hamilton, Mrs. C. Whitehead, Mrs. R. Beckett, Mrs. H. Foye, Mrs. J. F. Burstall, Mrs. H. Burstall, Mrs. A. Smith, Mrs. Orchard, Mrs. Napier and baby, Mrs. Nolet.

Miss D. Rhodes, Miss Nancy Horewood, Miss Mary Williams, Miss G. Williams, Miss T. Price, Miss B. Meredith, Miss E. Burstall, Miss Caffin, Miss M. Stuart, Miss Wolfe, Miss D. Bishop, Miss M. Evans, Miss Billingsley, Miss Penney, Miss H. Campbell, Miss Stein, Miss O. Wright, Miss R. Webb, Miss M. Thomson, Miss D. Digby, Miss M. Scott, Miss E. Laird, Miss O. Schwartz, Miss Fitzgibbon, Miss Sophia Joseph, Miss R. Joseph, Miss S. Joseph, Miss K. Hall, Miss A. Sharples, Miss B. Powel, Miss M. Hunt.

The Misses Carter(2), the Misses Boswell (3), the Misses Hamil

MARQUIS DE LEVIS
And l'amiral Chadot.

ton (2), the Misses S. and J. Cassils, the Misses Porteous (4), the Misses Hall (3), the Misses Simpson (2), the Misses Pelton (2), the Misses Craig (2), the Misses Hamilton (2), the Misses Avery (2), the Misses Home (3).

Master Elton Scott, Master Lex Smith, Master H. Laird, Master Hale, Master H. Powel, Master Hugh Joseph, Master Walcot, Master C. Parke, Masters Burstall (2), Masters Price (3).

Madame Gauvin, Madame Hamelin, Miss Dumoulin, Miss Michaud.

Mrs. J. B. Lemieux, Mrs. J. E. Talbot, Mrs. P. Blouin, Mrs. C. F. Falardeau, Mrs. J. Pacaud, Mrs. D. Artois, Mrs. A. E. Lebel, Mrs. J. A. Morin.

Miss Guay, Miss Furois, Miss H. St. Cyr, Miss A. Hamel, Miss G. Belanger, Miss J. Soucy, Miss Cannon, Miss Walsh, Miss Genereux, the Misses McManamy, the Misses Jolicoeur, the Misses Donati, the Misses Drolet, Miss Beatrice Hamel.

Children:—Miss Elizabeth Gauvin, Miss Mariette Hamelin, the Misses Dubuc, Master Albert Gagnon, Master Joseph Dubuc, Master Delaney, Master Philippe Genest, Master Henri Roy, Master C. Ed. Roy, Master P. A. Dumontier.

Drummers:—J. A. Miller, J. Fortin, G. Lasante.

Standard Bearers:—J. A. Gosselin, J. W. Tardif, A. Vallerand.

Guards:—E. Picard, A. Jinchereau, J. A. Baronet, J. L. Ferland, C. Legare, J. N. Parent, E. Fortin, T. Cantin, F. Drouin, N. Picard, T. Gravel, J. Tremblay, G. C. A. Picard, J. A. Berube, L. Pouliot, J. B. R. Dion, L. Fecteau, L. Vidal, G. Caouette, J. B. Caouette, C. Deslauriers, E. Lamothe.

Mousquetaires:—L. Trudel, D. Tremblay, E. Laforte, J. Gagne, E. Bedard, A. Grenier, W. Pouliot.

Soldiers:—A. Clavet, J. Rousseau, F. Raymond, J. Ferland, G. Pageot, A. Lessard, L. N. Jacques, L. Falardeau, J. A. Pageot, R. Guimont, J. Tardivel, A. Jobin, J. Bourbeau, F. T. Pouliot, P. Langlais, E. Ferland, H. Maheux, A. Hawey, O. Gauvin, C. Darveau, R. Roy, J. W. Deslaurier, A. Caouette, J. Legare, R. Lefebvre, F. Fleury, J. A. Ratte, H. Lapierre, J. M. Charrier, A. Grenier.

Officers:—Capt. J. P. Robert; Lieutenants, Arsene Morency, Nap. Therrien; Sergeants: Ernest Giroux, Jos. Tindland, Albert Laprise, Rosario Laroche; Buglers: Ernest Gauvin, Mandoza Malouin.

Volunteers:—R. Richard, Emile Garant, Edouard Gingras, W. Bouchard, Phydime Bilodeau, Edouard Hunt, R. Langlois, Pierre Giguere, A. Parent, Lucien Blackburn, R. Zanettin, Frank McArdle, Onesime Parent, Narcisse Bergeron, Paul Leclerc, Jos. Joinette, Jos. Berube, Pierre Jobin.

IN MONTCALM'S ARMY

Eighth Pageant

The dramatic Frontenac scene ends the pageants proper. The history of Canada has been revealed in picturesque fashion. The sufferings and toils of the early settlers have been represented by three thousand people, who have turned back the hands of time and shown again the events of past years. There is, however, a nobler scene yet. It is the grand finale,—the pageant of pageants—and in it we see the object lesson of the Tercentenary.

The picture now before us includes two armies—those of Wolfe and Montcalm. Both in turn have been victors and now pass together before the eyes of the Canadian people. Old strife has been forgotten. Concord alone marks the picture. Under the fleur-de-lys and the Union Jack march the armies of the two great nations. They are now united and together they stand on common soil moistened by the blood of both.

Montcalm, Wolfe, Levis and Murray are in the front rank. Their standards, different in colour, point faintly to an era now happily past. These are now linked and have each lent their share in producing the Canadian national ensign.

Behind the leaders stand the regiments which fought on the ground now the scene of pleasant reunion. To the back of these is seen from the distance and through the mist of falling night, Jacques Cartier and his cross, Champlain and his sailors, the Ursulines and Hospitalieres, Dollard and his companions, St. Lusson and Frontenac. They gaze upon the land and its institutions—the result of their combined efforts.

Beyond, a deep blue sky already tinged with spots of red, hangs over the blue-coloured waters of the St. Lawrence river, which peacefully glides along, while from the shores across are heard the pealing of church bells, whose echo grows faint amid the singing of the national anthem by the members of the two bodies of soldiers.

The armies salute, and the pageants are at an end.

ROYAL AMERICANS.

Officers:—Lt.-Col. Wm. Wood, Capt. J. S. O'Meara, Lt. F. S. Coolican, Lt. F. W. Marsh, Capt. Parmelee and Lt. Johnston.
Regiment:—Daniel Doyle, W. Redmond, Wm. Gunn, Jno. Delaney, M. Murphy, E. Wyse, A. J. McCusker, Wm. McGeo,

LIGHT INFANTRY REGIMENT
Of Wolfe's Army.

Patk. Henchey, Wm. Davidson, G. Sutcliff, Ths. Dillon, Jno. Murray, Geo. Myers, T. Fleming, D. Power, R. B. Whyte, Hy. Young, J. Hennessy, M. Quinn, R. Burston, J. Kenney, J. Walsh, J. Livingston, J. Byrne, A. Bonenfant, J. Fitzgerald, A. Bergeron, W. Kelly, T. Prendergast, C. N. Dawson, C. Cathcart, P. Gore, A. S. Buckle, D. Neilson, J. Scallen, G. Love, J. Allan, H. Trumble, Jno. Gair, B. McKay, M. Burns, N. Fletcher, T. H. Craig, F. Hale, J. D. Laurie, H. Greenwood, E. Greenwood.

LIGHT INFANTRY.

Officers:—Major G. Gibson, Capt. E. H. Woodside, Capt. H. Price, E. F. Wurtele and H. J. Webb.
Regiment:—F. Wells, C. W. Cary, S. P. Ross, A. Burns, M. H. Murphy, G. A. Melville, C. G. Green, Robt. Carswell, J. C. Thompson, W. Lane, F. A. Fanning, S. Murphy, A. Cope-

A. Reynar, J. Powers, W. C. Jacques, F. W. Russel, A. V. Nicholson, R. S. Mayes, W. W. Staveley, C. McMillan, A. M. Valleau, A. De Bonlay, H. K. Baird, I. Lizotte, H. Brown, Alf, Jacques, W. P. Osborne, P. Caine, T. Fortnum, J. T. Mace, R. Eselby, J. Read, F. R. Thorn, W. Sharpe, J. A. Smith, A. Love, C. P. Knight, J. A. Kerrigan, C. J. Fletcher, J. Duncan, M. Frenette, Percy Wilkinson.

HIGHLANDERS.

Officers:—D. Watson, Capt. Lindsay, H. B. Bignell, F. Home, A. W. Hay, R. J. Davidson, J. Bignell.
Regiment:—J. Tobin, W. Redmond, F. H. Andrews, A. Forrest, A. Russel, F. C. Wurtele, J. Staton, R. Somerville, H. Kennedy, A. Cooper, H. C. Jones, W. H. Ellis, G. E. Little, H. Aird, J. D. Sutherland, J. Hill, J. McD. Wilson, W. Stevenson, R. Mellin, J. G. Goudie, A. Fraser, A. G. Duncan, S.

THE HIGHLANDERS OF WOLFE'S ARMY

man, J. Roe, J. Marshbell, L. Lemelin, W. Creighton, E. Johnston, L. Denis, J. Angus, H. Copeman, J. S. Bursford, P. Jordan, J. Carter, G. Copeman, J. Kelly, J. Scott, J. Shirley, Jas. Berrigan, A. Turpin, W. Hansen, E. Donohue, G. Shepherdson, H. G. Deguise, P. Sunderland, J. H. Broomfield, E. Martel, Alf. Plumb, L. Roach, C. Diefenthal, W. Macfarlane, John Cox, Wm. Fanning, Allan Copeman, P. Falardeau, W. A. Fellow, J. Lemieux.

GRENADIERS.

Officers:—W. Price, E. C. Temple, G. W. F. Evans, H. S. Wright, C. E. Sword, G. W. Torrens, J. R. Strang.
Regiment:—H. L. Lee, C. J. Fletcher, C. J. Strachan, C. Diefenthal, M. Labbe, T. E. Andrews, J. R. Carrington, G. Quartz, P. Watt, O. Fortin, S. Elliott, T. Light, A. Roussin, C. J. Creedon, P. Wolff, R. H. Powell, E. Fleming, A. Little,

G. Newton, E. Young, T. M. Ross, L. B. Ramsay, M. Slater, W. Aird, N. D. J. Alexander, F. W. Porter, W. Tobin, F. W. Marsh, C. Fossey, W. A. Ross, B. McKay, E. D. Jenks, W. Jewell, W. R. Murray, E. Armstrong, J. S. Bridgeford, T. M. Houghton, H. B. Poston, H. Higgins, C. Bignell, Jas. Morrison, C. Thorn, D. Keogh.

WOLFE'S BUGLE BAND ACCOMPANYING ROYAL AMERICANS.

R. Wilkinson, J. Wyser, J. McDonald, F. Huxley, W. A. Dall, R. Jacques, J. Halligan, W. M. Grannary, J. Philips, H. Grannary, J. Shanahan, D. H. St. Claire, D. M. Courtney, J. Walsh, E. G. Fry, C. W. Burford, Thos. A. Bridgeford, Jas. McDonald, John Young, Jeff Malone, C. Diefenthal, J. Applin, C. Wilkinson, H. Wilkinson.

THE ROYAL NAVY IN WOLFE'S ARMY

LINE REGIMENT.

Officers:—J. A. Scott, H. B. Polinka, J. Power, R. Anderson, A. C. Dobell, E. Rattray, P. H. Wade.

Regiment:—J. Jewell, E. Ivers, Jos. Morton, A. Bisset, A. D. Scott, J. B. O'Regan, J. Gibault, O. A. Paquet, R. D. Adams, G. Atkinson, F. Bowden, L. C. Moore, F. Power, R. Gore, J. Barbeau, W. Learmonth, F. P. Bisset, P. Quinn, O. E. Scott, H. Hartley, J. Laliberte, C. Elliot, L. H. Peters, A. H. Anderson, W. J. Moore, W. Mylett, J. A. Audet, A. Lacasse, P. Demers, S. B. O'Connell, H. Scott, A. S. Bigaouette, J. N. Barbeau, D. Wilson, J. Blanchet, A. R. Fanning, N. A. Alcombrach, A. C. Dobell, W. McEwen, J. Fellows, Jos. Giltman, Jas. Brown, J. Carrigan, S. M. Richardson, A. Ashmead, R. Corbett, P. C. Lumberland.

ROYAL ARTILLERY AND NAVY.

Officers:—Frank Carrel, Dr. F. M. Wells, A. R. Henry.

Regiment:—E. W. Willard, W. Langton, E. Lobry, R. L. Dyte, F. Fiske, A. Treasurer, J. A. Timmony, C. F. B. Rowe, Richard Shaw, J. O'Brien, John Sim, H. Harding, W. Baillarge, F. Berrigan.

Navy:—Admiral C. E. A. Carr, Capt. D. Lesperance, Capt. J. McCarthy, Lt. J. E. Woodley, Lt. G. S. F. Robitaille, Lt. A. Chambers, Lt. Rev. C. R. E. Wilmot, H. G. Leech, (Standard Bearer.)

Guards:—W. M. Andrews, H. H. Oliver, J. R. Thomson, H. Hull.

Petty Officers:—H. Woodley, H. Doddridge, H. Quartz, R. Cressman, Jno. Walsh, F. Salter, H. Beauchamp, J. H. Russel.

Sailors:—T. Jewell, J. A. Johnston, H. Meredith, B. Byrne, F. Lawrence, J. Stoyles, F. Sutherland, T. Tierney, O. Hannan, T. L. Morritt, A. D. Laurie, J. O'Sullivan, F. Power, L. P. Pelchat, C. Power, E. Leonard, T. Ross, E. Langton, G. Burns, W. Reade, B. W. Gavey, W. Hallesy, E. S. Burford, E. Poulter, Jas. Davis, W. Deronin, J. Fitzpatrick, G. Joynt, M. Getz, L. Byrne, Geo. Beach, J. Montambault, J. Byrne, J. Feiezewicz, T. Medley, J. Joynt, W. Ryan, F. Berrigan, A. H. Baker, C. J. Bignell, M. Lawlor, C. Angers, F. O'Brien, E. Ready, W. Paul, E. Burke, W. Wolff, C. Montminy, G. Gourdeau, E. C. Lariviere, V. Mathieu, L. P. Morin, R. Wallace, J. Goodman.

Marine Artillery:—J. B. Taylor, Alf. Marois, E. Jackson, A. Boucher, F. Sheehan, J. Quinn, Jos. Poitras, H. Martin, R. Hunter, J. Barbeau,, J. Lomas, Jules Gingras, F. Gingras, C. Doherty, W. H. Hyde, S. R. Smith, H. Cowling.

Rangers:—J. O'Rourke, J. W. Coleman, J. Burke, J. Fogarty, J. Power, A. Labbe, E. Read, H. C. Davis, T. Dionne, Wm. Findlay, L. McGinniss, J. O'Reilly, M. Driscoll, Eug. Moussette, M. Dunsford, G. M. Kelly, P. Jewell, J. Stenhouse, W. Taylor, J. Middleton, E. Patry, W. Batterston, Oscar Bedard, Jas. Cantin, J. Read, Maj. Petry, Capt. A. C. Joseph.

Fusiliers:—Capt. J. Kahring, Standard Bearer H. Gale, Bugler H. Andrews, Drummer C. W. Wiggs.

Regiment:—Jos. Jackson, Jno. Gair, C. Wellsmore, N. Smith, E. Dion, J. Turcotte, G. Lamontagne, W. Jewell, J. Murray, M. Cross, S. J. Lower, L. A. Russel, A. S. Bignell, J. Marcotte, H. Jackson, W. Dempsey, W. Taylor, B. Shelter, E. T. Rogers, F. Davis, E. Reynolds, D. Harris.

Priests and Monks:—J. W. Arel, Louis Anctil, J. E. Audibert, M. Beaudry, Omilien Beaubien, Onesime Brulotte, A. M. Dechene, Ed. Delisle, Alexandre Dumas, E. H. Falardeau, Simeon Harpe, Euclide Houde, Jos. Guay, Andre Gagnon, Elzear Gregoire, Onesime Goulet, Alfred Garant, Harold Greenirood, L. Gagne, Jos. Levesque, Louis Lagueux, Wilfrid Laberge, Joseph Lozier, J. A. Richard, Lucien Rondeau, Noel Rondeau, Arthur Savard, H. St. Hilaire, O. Marceau, Ulric Moisan, J. Octave Matte, M. Matte, C. H. Moisan, Geo. Marechal, G. Parent, H. Taugnay, Alp. Tardif, Ant. Thibault, Ferdinand Vandry, Elz. Poitras, Jos. Thivierge, W. Boisseau.

ROYAL ARTILLERY.

Officers:—Capt. J. W. Gagnon, Lieut. J. A. Cantin, Sergt. Gunner, Geo. W. Scott, Sergt. Gunner Lynden.

Regiment:—Gaudiose Tremblay, Henri P. Hamel, Elz. Gregoire, Jules Lepine, Louis Demers, Henri Morin, Geo. Vincent, Jos. Byrne, J. N. Dionne, Honore St. Hilaire, A. Lesage, Chs. Rondeau, Geo. Mackay, C. D. Bonhomme, J. A. Tardif, J. A. Bilodeau, D. R. Guay, J. C. Rondeau.

Mr. D. Watson

Capt. of the Highlanders in Wolfe's Army.

MR. J. E. SAMSON

As Admiral Philippe de
Chadot.

MR. T. P. ROSS

As a color-bearer of
the 78th Highlanders
of Wolfe's Army.

MONTCALM'S ARMY.

General Marquis de Montcalm—Capt. Thomas A. Vien, B.A.,
A.D.C. M. de Bougainville—Capt. J. A. Foeteau.
General Chevalier de Levis—Major Emile Gully.
A.D.C. Marquis de Bourlamaque—Mr. Armand Lavergne,
M.P.P.
Standard-Bearer—Capt. Henri Arsenault.

FRENCH GRENADIERS

Officers:—Col. L. G. Chabot, Capt. R. Trudelle, Capt. P. E.
Trudelle, Lieut. A. H. Grenier, Lieut. J. A. Beaubien, Lieut. Art.
Thiboutot, Lieut. A. Beaubien, Serg. F. E. Moisan, Serg. Alph.
Papillon, Serg. Alph. Bilodeau, Serg. J. P. A. Patoine, Serg. H.
Dussault, Serg. S. Don Carlos, Serg. Jos. Lamarche, Serg. Geo.
Matte, Buglers J. G. Savary, L. Richard, Drummers Emile Cote,
L. H. Vallee.

Regiment—Amedee Saucier, Adolphe Petit, Jos. Morel,
Albert Bergeron, Nap. Garneau, Chs. Chabot, E. Gobeil, Aug.
Dubuc, Gedeon Soucy, Pierre Tremblay, L. Dolbec, Leon Soucy.

Grenadiers:—Joseph Gaudet, Philippe Gailloux, Philippe
Cote, Jos. Bigaouette, M. J. Tremblay, Edgar Legare, A. Drolet,
Joseph Angers, Geo. Clement, Jos. Tremblay, Albert Soucy, Real
Cote, Leonidas Dionne, O. Matte, U. Drolet, Joseph Huppe,
Phileas Martel, Gaud. · Paquet, Omer Cote, L. Faguy, Jos.
Bedard, A. A. Tremblay, Edm. Savard, Arth. Magnan.

LINE-REGIMENT

Officers:—Capt. Nap. L'Heureux, Capt. J. Vallee, Capt. M.
L. E. Jacques, Lieuts. R. Watters, F. X. Couture, Leon Gagnon,
W. A. Boucher, Sergt. Frs. Trepanier, A. L'Heureux, Alp Be-
rube G. Letarte, W. Drolet, Emile Cote, Art. Cote, E. Curodeau,
Buglers, G. Fortier, Jules Marcoux, Drummers, Alf. Matte, Adj.
Letarte,

Regiment:—Eug. Cote, A. Robitaille, Rene Trempe, J.
Trempe, C. Duggan, J. Letarte, A. Letarte, Eug. O'Dowd, P.
Gourdeau, A. Matte, J. A. Turgeon, W. Gagnon, Art. Fournier,
J. Kirouac, J. Drolet, L. Cote, E. Rochon, Art. Jacques, Jos.
Noel, N. Bussiere, Jos. Dore, A. Poitras, G. Boily, Alp. Lebrun,
L. Miville, J. Jacques, A. Darveau, R. Savary, A. Girard, F.
Moisan, L. Guilmet, J. O. Bertrand, H. Voyer Alf. Morin,
Emile Morin.

LE ROYAL ROUSSILLON

Officers:—Major J. E. P. Bergeron, Lieuts. Jos. Levesque,
Jos. Dorval, Nap. Leger, Geo. Wells, Jos. Drapeau.

Regiment:—Jos. Arteau, Art. Bourget, H. Bissonnette, E.
Belanger, J. Boucher, J. Bernier, Ls. Bernard, R. Bourget, J.
Brulotte, J. Bonneau, T. Carbonneau, H. Dion, J. Dumont, Jos.
Guay, Art. Guay, Phil. Guay, Jr., H. Garneau, F. X. Gosselin,
Ph. Guay, Sr., Phi. Guay, Alb. Goupil, Gau. Houde, Jos. La-
montagne, Alex. Lavery, F. X. Latulippe, M. Larivee, Jos. Lam-

bert, O. Martineau, Ed. Moore, H. Martin, W. McKibbin, D. Nolin, F. X. Nolin, Ed. Noel, Leo Picard, Jean Picard, Alb. Poirier, A. Richard, A. Robitaille, Jos. Royer, Dos. Rancourt, L. P. Samson, Ad. Samson, R. Samson, P. Trepanier, L. P. Simard, Art. Voyer, A. Vachon.

MARINE ARTILLERY

Officers:—Lieut. E. Boissinot, P. Guay, F. X. Robitaille.

Regiment:—Mr. Lesage, Mr. Lesage, Mr. Lacasse, Mr. Michaud, Mr. Rheaume, Mr. Perrault, Mr. Bolduc, Mr. A. Guay, Mr. E. Bernier, Mr. Nadeau, Mr. Rattee, Mr. Lamontagne, Mr. Thibault, Mr. Mignault, Mr. Collet, Mr. Despres, Mr. Bourassa, Mr. Poliquin, Mr. Lavoie, Mr. Corriveau, Mr. Dion.

BAND

Bugle Major—Eudore Dion.

Buglers:—Henri Ruel, Romeo Bourassa, Henri Corriveau, Henri Verret, Rosario Samson, Louis Giguere, Philippe Samson, Rodolphe Bourget, Henri Carrier, Joseph Paradis.

Drummers:—Real Despres, Jos. Despres, Antoine Despres, Lucien Myrand, Evariste Boulet, Arthur Guay, Arthur Bourassa, A. Courcy, Charles Lavoie.

SALABERRY GROUP

Salaberry—Mr. Rousseau.

Voltigeurs de Salaberry

Officers:—Capt. T. Trudel, Lieut. O. S. Riverin, J. B. Martel, Sergt. A. E. Simard, E. Girard, W. Lafrance, Eug. Grenon, Drummers, R. Houle, S. Tardif, Buglers, J. Demeule, L. Dubuc.

Regiment:—A. Lacombe, O. Fiset, N. Barrette, A. Dubuc, E. Ouellette, A. Langevin, E. Gingras, Jos. Metivier, A. Bertrand, L. Gaboury, S. Gazelle, P. Gilbert, A. Mercier, V. Latulipe, J. Larocque, A. Trudel, A. Rainville, Jos. Ouellette, L. Racine, W. Vaillancourt, J. Savard, L. Boule, J. Gazelle, O. Charbonneau, A. Bissonnette, J. Harvey, Jos. Menard, L. Frechette, Jules Gauvin, Nap. Robitaille, J. A. Bernier, L. Bourgelas, Art. Menard, A. Fortin, J. Lavoie, L. Lemieux, Jos. Simard, E. Servestre, Jos. Vaillancourt, Ant. Gagnon, Isaie Ouellette, Geo. Parent, P. Bedard.

FOUR REPRESENTATIVES OF WOLFE'S ARMY

Officers:—Col. Nap. L'Heureux, Major Jules Vallee, L. E. Jacques, Capts. A. L'Heureux, Leon Gagnon, W. A. Boucher. Frs. Trepanier, Lt. F. X. Couture, Romeo Watters, Sergeant W. Drolet, E. Curoleau, Art. Cote, Alp. Berube, G. Letarte.

Regiment:—E. Cote, Adj. Letarte, Eug. Cote, A. Robitaille, R. Trempe, C. Duggan, P. Power, J. Letarte, Alb. Letarte, Nap. Bouchard, Hector Voyer, Rene Plamondon, Gus. Fortier, E. O'Dowd, P. Goudreau, E. Morin, J. O. Bertrand, Art. Matte, Alf. Matte, J. A. Turgeon, Art. Fournier, Jos. Drolet, Jules Marcoux, L. Cote, Art. Jacques, Jos. Noel, Julien Trempe, Nap. Bussiere, Jos. Dore, Adelard Poitras, George Boily, Alp. Lebrun, David Chamberland, Jos. Jacques, Alp. Darveau, R. Savary, G. Beaudry, Alf. Girard, Alfred Morin, L. Minville, F. Moisan, L. Guilmet.

GROUP OF HURON INDIANS FROM LORETTE
Who took part in the Pageant.

Editorial Comment on the Tercentenary Celebration

Most people who were not at Quebec are interested in knowing just how the celebration "went off." They want to know the real measure of enthusiasm aroused and what aroused it. And at the risk of—well being dull—I have told the truth about this phase of the Tercentenary.

To sum up the matter, it might be said that the Tercentenary resolved itself into more than one celebration. The fetes and ceremonies in honour of Champlain, who brought the French flag and the Catholic religion to Canada, were successful, because they interested Quebec. Officialdom, militarism and Imperialism, as institutions, were also all glorified successfully. The decorations, which made the city gay and which represented C a n a d a , Britain, France, t h e Catholic church a n d our neighbor, Uncle Sam, all fluttering more or less together, made one ponder on the pettiness of glorifying any faction or institution to the detriment of a universal patriotism. And after all, the Quebec Tercentenary, brilliant as it has been, and successful beyond expectation, will bear its richest fruits in the suggestion that will arise in many minds that some day in the future Canada will have a celebration, which, in point of united sentiment, if not in color, will make the event just closed look as insignificant as the Don-de-Dieu in comparison with the Indomitable.—Toronto, Saturday night.

* * *

Canada has certainly started well in the twentieth century race. While Ireland and Ireland's problems are worrying the statesmen of Great Britain, while the problem of how to manage India is troubling the same group of administrators, and while Australia's federal system stands in danger of falling to pieces, Canada is all peace and harmony. The Provinces have no great differences with the Federal Government, nor has the Federal Government any fault to find with the provincial administrations. The two great races are being drawn closer to each other, and the newer citizens of the country—Ruthenians, Swiss, Swedes, Icelanders or United Statesers—are showing a most commendable and desirable interest in the general affairs of their adopted land. The national unity is undisturbed.

ONE OF THE SOUVENIR PHOTOGRAPHS OF THE TERCENTENARY

Financially and industrially, Canada is also doing well. The world-wide depression of the past twelve months has limited development but has not stopped it. The harvest prospects are the best of any of the twentieth century years and last autumn's disappointments will soon be forgotten. The Quebec Tercentenary and the Prince's visit have served to emphasize the growing world-importance of the new nation of the North. The world's eyes have been turned this way, and the impression created abroad must be favourable to our national reputation.

In this world-demonstration French-Canadians are playing a prominent role. It is true that French-Canadians are still true to the faith, language, tradition, and customs of old France, from whose splendid stock they spring, and it would not be possible for them to enter into the spirit of the national festivity if the victory of Wolfe and the defeat of Montcalm were the prime objects to be commemorated. They realize, however, that these rejoicings, of which ancient Quebec is the scene, and in which all Canada, with many important representative guests from the Colonies and abroad are taking part, are of far wider scope; in a word that we are celebrating the birthday of the great Canadian nation, in which all her people, with equal pride in her past and illimitable confidence in her radiant future, whether those people be French-speaking or English, Catholic or Protestant, can fully participate.

Quebec, the battleground of the new world, a city five times besieged; Quebec, the Gibraltar of North America, whose military glories are unsurpassed, is still the pride and glory of all French-Canadians. They flocked here in tens of thousands from all parts of the province, first, as they will tell you, to celebrate the landing of Samuel de Champlain 300 years ago, and, secondly, to

SIR LOMER GOUIN, K.C.
Premier of the province of Quebec recipient of one of His Majesty's Tercentenary Honors.

greet with loyal affection the Prince of Wales, as representing King Edward—two great objects important in themselves, but both, as French-Canadians affirm, yielding place to the "celebration of the nation's biggest birthday."—*The London Daily Telegraph.*

* * *

"Lord Grey is to be congratulated upon the brilliant success which has attended the celebration of the birthday of Canada. It was not only a birthday, it was also a commemoration of the most stirring scenes in Canadian history. It is seldom that any state has been so fortunate as Canada in being able to celebrate within less than two centuries, with equal enthusiasm, victories that were gained by the two nations that dwell in peace under a common flag. The Prince of Wales was received with immense enthusiasm. The pageant was a great success, and nothing appears to have marred the harmony of an international celebration unique in history."—*Review of Reviews.*

* * *

"The destiny of Canada is bound up with that of the United States in its commercial and industrial relations. We may leave to the unknown and unknowable future the question of political union. And meantime we may join with all Canada in the celebration of the tercentenary of Champlain."—*Boston Post.*

* * *

"It is then not only Canadians, whether of British or of French descent, but Americans also who have been profoundly affected by the issue of the battles on the Plains of Abraham which are now commemorated. Our national fortunes, no less than their's were staked upon those stricken fields."—*New York Sun.*

* * *

"Canada is essentially young, notwithstanding the three centuries Quebec is celebrating. That city is an ancient gateway to a new empire, a picturesque old fortress guarding a river which drains much untested and unused wilderness."—*Cleveland Leader.*

* * *

"The United States was the largest gainer by

England's capture of Quebec by Wolfe in 1759."—*St. Louis Globe-Democrat.*

* * *

"Whether or not Canada and the United States will ever be linked together rests with destiny. There never was a period of more general satisfaction by the Dominion with English rule."—*Baltimore American.*

* * *

"Bearing upon the question which confronts the whole world more urgently than any other, the relations of Canada and the United States afford an impressive illustration of the peaceful neighborliness possible to nations. Europe doubtless recognizes more profoundly than do the people of the Americas the significance of the astounding circumstance that the longest frontier in the world is dotted with no more portentious evidences of international suspicion and jealousy than custom houses."—*Providence Journal.*

* * *

The splendid welcome given to the Prince of Wales when he landed at Quebec and the fact that one of the two first visitors on board the Indomitable when she anchored in the St. Lawrence was the French Admiral, proved the aptness of the Duke of Argyll's remark recently made that Canada is the real Franco-British Exhibition. No part of our great Empire is more devoted in its loyalty to the Throne than Canada, and the harmony that exists between the French and the British races is well illustrated by the possibility of bringing Montcalm and Wolfe into the same historic pageant without arousing any bitterness of memories. It must have been a picturesque scene that the Prince looked upon in the streets of Quebec, for the pageant represented with living figures the history of the country in celebration of the 300th anniversary of the founding of the city by De Champlain, and in the crowds were all kinds of historical costumes, amongst which red Indians were prominent. No doubt St. Malo will to-day remember Jacques Cartier,

SIR J. G. GARNEAU

Mayor of Quebec, recipient of one of His Majesty's Tercentenary Honors.

who in 1534 explored the Gulf of St. Lawrence, and in 1535 sailed up the river to Montreal, for the "Malouin" explorer will be figuring prominently in the pageants on the heights above Quebec."—*Westminster Gazette.*

* * *

"Of all the ceremonies in which the new friendship of France and Great Britain has been given visible shape none have approached for romantic significance that which took place on the soil of Canada. The arrival of the Prince of Wales at Quebec set the seal upon months of earnest preparation for a celebration worthy of the Dominion as the increasing wealth, power and progress of recent years have made her. In New France was fought out that wonderful contest between French and British that ended in the handing over of lake and forest touched by civilization; a contest that was dignified by the heroism of a great leader on each side, and made illustrious by one of the most thrilling episodes in the history of warfare. The dedication of the Plains of Abraham to the memory of the heroes of Quebec, both of the attack and the defence, will be, not only for those who witness it, but for the two nations at large, a striking pledge of the performance of a friendship that has become the corner-stone of our policy."—*London Daily News.*

* * *

"It is right and proper that Canada should celebrate the founding of Canada by a man who is not of British race. For there is no more wonderful characteristic of that race than its assimilative powers. Dane and Norman have been absorbed in the past, and welded into a strong and harmonious whole...... The animosities of the past are buried. That memorable battle before Quebec will long live in song and story. Wolfe is one of the long line of Empire builders whose names form a roll of honor the like of which no other country can show. John Smith, Governor Bradford, Clive, Waren Hastings, Rajah Brooke, the two Lawrences, are all men whose fame will last long as the Empire. Montcalm died in the hour of defeat, but he died nobly after living well, and we can all of us lay our tributes on the shrine of a brave and noble antagonist and a great man.

Of the future of Canada, who shall dare to prophesy, or put limits to its expansion? Already it has become the granary of the world. Great highways have crossed the boundless prairies of the Northwest, and pierced the Rockies to the Pacific slope. Every years sees some new province opened up, and some new possibility of wealth discovered. Canada has her troubles like other countries. She has her periods of depression and her periods of prosperity. But all the while there is steady progress. In the near future she may see passing through her territories the great highway of the Empire from West to East. And when she remembers the little band of trappers and traders who three hundred years ago planted themselves on the spot where Quebec now stands, she may give thanks with pardonable pride for the great things she has accomplished in that time." — *Lloyds Weekly.*

ANCIENT AND MODERN

Sergt. W. J. Sharpe, British Grenadiers and Curp. S. A. Major, 1st York and Lancaster Regt., India.

* * *

At last it is gone, that fever of fair days and gorgeous pagenatry. The mighty fleet and marching hosts have departed, and once more the old city is left to its summer dream. The looming crag, the stately sweep of river, and the sublimity of distant azure hills alone remain.

And what are the lessons to be learned from this historic week? What remains to be said?

Little or nothing, if we regard it all as merely a gigantic circus or theatre, and the city as an old curiosity shop for the superficial sight-seer and the inquisitive globe-trotter.

But, to the thoughtful mind, the grim fortress city and its late pageant mean much. They both stand for something which is not found elsewhere on this continent.

MR. LAWFORD DALE

Designer of "Le Don de Dieu".

Quebec is, without doubt, the true and ideal capital of Norman Canada. Moreover, she is the Mecca of the Norman ideals and dreams of the New World.

Of all the European peoples, France and Britain were the sole rivals in the discovery, conquest and colonization of North America and when one stands on this ancient crag, and, amid the multitude of pilgrims from either hemisphere to commemorate the history of this old city, views the vast river, the blue mountains, and distant Norman villages, and hears the tongue spoken, as much Norman as British, and recognizes the names of the great dead who are venerated on this occasion, it would almost appear that France, equally with Britain, has retained her hold, and perpetuated the genius of her race ideal in the new world.

And why not?

* * *

Had she not much to do with the pioneer history of our vast western territories? Were not her's, the great pathfinders of this continent? Without Cartier, La Salle, Champlain; Marquette and Radisson to blaze the way, would we as a people have her penetrated into the unknown, mysterious interior, with its great rivers, saltless seas and boundless prairies? Perchance we might have. But to them remains the glory of this early achievement.

Then why should there not be a French America as well as a British America? Does not Europe owe much to French civilization? And why should she not have her place as a great people on this continent?

There is room for us all; and it seems as though, some day, the two great historical conquests, that of the American, and that of the British at Quebec, will be annulled, and the original conditions to a certain extent resume their sway. Certainly the French people are happy and prosperous in their ancient occupation of the valley of the St. Lawrence, and

MAJOR ED. LALIBERTE

Commandant of Le Don de Dieu'.

the American people are more British than they were seventy years ago. They have begun to realize that mere political ties or barriers, the result of the struggle of one generation, are after all petty in comparison with the many ties of blood, heredity, tradition and common glory in the past.

"One thousand years of Britain's pride, One hundred of her own,"

cess, pride and haughty spirit would certainly rob us of the fruits of a century's planting.—Canadian Courier.

* * *

"Canada seems well on her way to complete independence. She may never be joined to us politically, but she should not forget that it was American blood and prowess that made her British. We have no jealousies of the rising nation across the border, but

ST. JOSEPH STREET
Showing the elaborate street decorations.

after all, sums up the tradition of the American people; and this is as it should be, and it is but natural that the New France should feel the same filial sentiments toward the Old as the New England experiences. This does not, in either case, entail any lack of loyalty to the flag under which both have achieved their present happy conditions.

* * *

Confident, cool, clear-headed should be Canada's attitude. While everything points to a brilliant suc-

she should not ignore what we have done for her."—*Philadelphia Inquirer.*

* * *

In Europe to-day we see a close and growing cordiality between the British and the French peoples. They recognize a common ancestry in the past; and, in spite of difference of language and race genius, each feels that in the other it finds its complement; and it is but meet that here in America Norman Canada should gradually assume her own place as a

PART OF PAGEANT PASSING THE BASILICA
Opposite the Daily Telegraph Building.

great and important influence in the civilization of our future under the British Crown.

The question may be asked: What has Norman America yet to give, and how is she to make herself felt in the destinies of the continent?

The answer to this may be shown in the strange and mysterious ways in which peoples and communities rise and sink, change and develope; and cling to, or forget, their ideals.

Some peoples are born iconoclasts and natural pioneers. They shine forth pre-eminently when stern individuality is necessary; and so the peoples of New England and their contemporary British pioneers made themselves felt in the first centuries of the New World. They were self-ruling, self-contained, self-absorbed, and fiercely local and democratic, intensely impatient of any central rule or outside check or what they regarded as the divine right of the individual to carve his own road to worldly or celestial destiny.

This continued successfully for a century and more; and no doubt, as a great social and political experiment in the American Community and Commonwealth, it influenced Europe. It affected staid England. It encouraged France to continue in her own democratic destiny. It determined the fortunes of British Canada in many aspects. It even penetrated conservative, old world, Norman Quebec; though her least of all did it affect by its passing influence.

* * *

But such strong passing waves of human ideal

must in time waste themselves. All lands alike to tyrants are a spoil; and to-day the tyranny of mere wealth and money-getting has absorbed the genius of the great American people. Society has also, for many reasons, become more complex, and the great democratic spirit is not as strong and as sincerely community-swaying in its influence as it once was. Life demands a safe anchorage as well as a broad and shining roadway.

Into this vast maelstrom of American modernism, Norman Canada brings the element of conservatism and aristocracy; and that real hope of any race, the true children of the soil, a happy, contended, and prolific peasantry. Two of the gravest problems of modern life are demanding our attention, that of the life of the race and that of the rural community. How to get the people back to the land and how to preserve the family as a social institution is a difficult question, which many thinkers are studying to-day. And yet Norman Canada regarded by modern America as obsolete, and ancient, and out of touch with up-to-date conditions, has, alone, of all the American communities, solved both of these vital problems.

Perchance this old-heroic pathfinder, for the early achievement of our continent, may yet lead us out of the wilderness of our social despairs which at present surround and beset us.

Whether this will be so remains for the future to reveal. Some of our present-day students and idealists seem to think that the French Community will gradually be absorbed in the great English-speaking

PRINCE ARRIVING AT THE CHAMPLAIN MONUMENT
Troops lined up in foreground.

MR. WILLIAM PRICE

Who took a very prominent part in the organization of the celebration.

CAPT. EMILE TRUDEL

Who so successfully handled the police arrangements during the celebration.

democracy about them. But, with each succeeding year, the tendency grows less and less in this direction.

* * *

Meanwhile the ancient c i t y of Champlain stands to-day the western citadel of the most conservative aspect of Christianity as well as of modern democratic, yet monarchial, Britain. S h e represents not only a great and heroic past, but the ideals of a steadfast present. She may be silent and seemingly indifferent to the world about her; but, self-contained in her ancient dream, she can afford to wait. She has a gift in her hand which she knows the world needs, and that to the weary children of this seething modern Babylon her spirit will each succeeding year grow more and more necessary. She can also, to-day, look out, and backward, and read great names and heroic lives; stories of tragedy and of human beauty; historical despairs and eternal hope mingled in the exquisitely colored warp and woof of her haunted past. Acadia, Louisiana, the old Ohio, the Red River vistas, all are linked in the romantic sweetness of her dream. Daulac and La Salle, Brebeuf and Laval, Madeline and Evangeline; these are the names created of life or of genius, which come with the Angelus of vesper bells, and the sobbing of the desolate Gulf in the weir stakes at Les Eboulements, or the sad, far-away, receding tides of the haunted Tantramar.

WILFRED CAMPBELL.

augmented f o r the occasion by a most efficient detachment of eighty men kindly lent to the city for the period of the fetes by the mayor and the police authorities of the city of Toronto, while at C h i e f Trudel's suggestion t h e city detective department under the direction of Chief Detective Tom Walsh was aided by special detectives f r o m t h e leading American and Canadian cities, who were a b l e to identify itinerant "crooks" from their own localities as soon as they reached Quebec. These latter were ordered out of town immediately on arrival here, under penalty of being immediately locked up, and thus petty thefts and other crimes seldom inseparable from the existence of big crowds of people were scarcely heard of in Quebec during the fetes, and the good order and general respect for law everywhere prevailing were matters of universal comment.

Chief Trudel and Police Arrangements

There is only one voice in regard to the police arrangements at the Tercentenary, and that is one of praise for Captain Emile Trudel, the popular Chief of the city of Quebec police force, for the efficiency of the police and detective work accomplished under his orders and direction. The city police force was

THE IONIC ARCH

In Front of Parliament.

PRINCE OF WALES AND LUNCHEON PARTY

At Petit Cap, in St. Joachim.

A Few Specimens of Tercentenary Poetry

Champlain Hears the Call

I.

Long have we, Minstrels, sung vainglorious lays
Of warfare and destructive deeds, and long
Our themes have been of what we are and what
We shall be when our argosies have passed
To every mart, and come, like laden bees
Returning home, with wealth from orient lands.

Enlarge we now our theme and sing of him
Who first made pregnant the waiting womb of fate,
Begetting where his ancient city stands
The lusty Child which patient Time hath made
Parental of a people yet to be
The world's predestined ministers of Peace.

II.

Lo! at the cruel cadence of the years
When all the land was carpeted with snows,
A star shot flaming across the northern skies
Portentous of a passing soul that had
No soilure from the murky crew of men
Who wrought with him. Avid of gain were they,
And thus they lived their futile years and died!
But he, when his life's dayspring dawned within,
Heard on the inward ear, in solemn tune,
The august choir of myriad streams and plains
And woods and winds—the whole, wide mighty land,
And aborigines all chorusing
A single song : "Come unto us," they sang ;
"Long have we been unknown, and are unseen,
Save by the wild beasts searching for their prey
And by those far-off immemorial eyes
That flock the heavens and shepherd us at night,—
Come, Sire, and build a new Hesperia here,—
A city in the West, cast as a seed
On consecrated soil. So shalt thou raise
A patriot people, and spread from sea to sea
The holy power of Christian empery!"

III.

He came whose heart was stauncher than the walls
Of his famed city which he built. And there
He wrought his inextinguishable deeds,
Whose soul was whiter than the Christmas snows
So heard Champlain the call and wrought and passed :
His city is God's acre vast monument!

J. D. Logan.

The Battlefield of Quebec

Shrouded in mist and snowdrift,
But dim in the dawning light
From the Icelandic Sagas,
The "New Lands" spring to sight.

When into a mighty river
Came Viking Chiefs of yore
And sailed under steep and headland
And ran their ships ashore.

Eric, and Leif, and Thornun,
Did they break through the silent floe?
Did they rouse the sleeping monsters?
Did they find them friend or foe?

Did they track racoon and marten
And sleep in the wild dog's lair?
Did they rifle the hoard of the chipmunk
And steal his coat from the bear?
As they sailed up the great St. Lawrence
Did they look to a day once more,
When a handful of dauntless sailors
Should land on that upland shore?
Did they dream of the strife and struggle
A continent lost and gained?
Of a field once green as the Chestnut
Then red as the Maple stained.
When the heart of a far small island
Three thousand miles away
Would thrill at the deeds of valour
That were told of Her sons that day ;

Would glow as She laid Her tribute
The olive branch and the palm,
Alike upon friend and foeman,
On Wolfe and on brave Montcalm.

And how friend and foe would mingle,
Till a world-wide nation grew,
A nation of equal sonship,
Wherever her banner flew.

And those fields once red as the maple
Would be as green as her leaf in May,
When the clash of arms was silent
And Britain's Rule held sway.

And Her Sons from that far small island
As they stand on the Liner's deck
Would be shown a great peace Angel
On the heights above Quebec.

Dorothea Gore Browne.

Canada

AN ODE

Read at the Special Meeting of the Royal Society of Canada, on the Occasion of the Quebec Tercentenary, July 22nd, 1908.

Out of the Clouds on Time's horizon dawneth the
    new Day, spacious and fair;
  White-winged over the world it shineth; wide-
    winged over the land and sea.
Spectres and ghosts, battles and hatred flee at the
    touch of the morning air:
  Throned on the ocean, the new Sun ariseth;
    Darkness is over, we wake, and are free.

Ages of ages guarded and tended mountain and
    waterfall, river and plain,
  Forests, that sighed with the sorrows of God in
    the infinite night when the stars looked down,
Guarded and tended with winter and summer, sword
    of lightning and food of rain,
  This, our Land, where the twin-born peoples,
    youngest of Nations, await their crown.

Now, in the dawn of a Nation's glory, now, in the
    passionate youth of Time,
  Wide-thrown portals, infinite visions, splendours
    of knowledge, dreams from afar,
Seas, that toss in their limitless fury, thunder of
    cataracts, heights sublime,
  Mock us, and dare us, to do and inherit, to mount
    up as eagles and grasp at the star.

Blow on us, Breath of the pitiless passion that pulses
    and throbs in the heart of the sea!
  Smite on us, Wind of the night-hidden Artic!
    breathe on us, Breath of the languorous
    South!
Here, where ye gather to conflict and triumph, men
    shall have manhood, Man shall be free
  Here hath he shattered the yoke of the tyrant;,
    free as the winds are the words of his mouth.

Voice of the infinite solitude, speak to us! Speak to
    us, Voice of the mountain and plain!
  Give us the dreams which the lakes are dreaming
    —lakes with bosoms all white in the dawn;
Give us the thoughts of the deep-browed mountains,
    thoughts that will make us as gods to reign;
  Give us the calm that is pregnant with action—
    calm of the hills when night is withdrawn.

Brothers, who crowd to the golden portals—portals
    which God has opened wide—
  Shake off the dust from your feet as you enter;
    gird up your loins, and pass within:

Cringing to no man, go in as brothers; mount up to
    kingship, side by side:
  Night is behind us, Day is before us, victories
    wait us, heights are to win.

God, then, uplift us! God, then uphold us! Great God,
    throw wider the bounds of Man's thought!
  Gnaws at our heart-strings the hunger for action;
    burns like a desert the thirst in our soul:
Give us the gold of a steadfast endeavour; give us
    the heights which our fathers have sought:
  Though we start last in the race of the Nations,
    give us the power to be first at the goal.

FREDERICK GEORGE SCOTT.

Wolfe and Montcalm

Wolfe and Montcalm! Montcalm and Wolfe!
Two heroes of a kindred soul
To whom a people tribute pays;
In life divided but by death united:
To-day in glory one.
This year we dedicate
The far-famed field of honor,
Where heroes fought and fell,
And of their mighty deeds remembrance set.
Not ours to triumph but to honor heroes,
Where all fought nobly, all were victors;
And none the vanquished:
Wolfe and Montcalm an equal glory share.
With honor crowned to distant ages borne,
Their names shall echo with a just renown,
Teaching Canadians of a common soil
That though distinctive they may yet be one
In loyalty to high ideals, of duty nobly done,
Of life unselfish and of death heroic.

Where fell the mighty dead,
Heirs of their valor and their glory gather
Their memory to honor.
Hushed all contention; healed all division;
Peace reigns where discord dwelt of yore.
Upon this sacred ground join hands as brethren;
High sound the pæans in their honor;
With fitting pageant celebrate,
While all the world their fame acclaims;
Erect the tablets to their worth;
Their deeds in sculptured story trace;
While high over all, with folded wings,
The Angel of Peace shall stand
In benediction on our native land.

JOHN BOYD.

Champlain

"Through the gateway grim
He sailed into St. Lawrence's broadening gulf;
Nor paused until the mighty buttressed peak
Of Mount Ste. Anne, thrust through its rope of green
And dyed with iron hues of Ochrey red,
Flamed in the sunrise. Perce Rock below,
Like some Titanic ruin, lit by the sun
Whose rays streamed through the double arches, lay—
Its huge mass stretched along; its cloudy top
Clamorous with sea-fowl. On he sailed and passed
The coast of Honguedo, dark with pines,
And high above the river flood, which washed
Its craggy shores. Far north the cruel teeth
Of Manicouagan's fateful reef just showed
Through the long line of breakers. Short his stay
At Tadousac. With favouring wind and tide
He stemmed the flowing current, till he reached
The wondrous strait, where close th' opposing hills
To build the stately portal of the West.
There, at the foot of that stupendous rock
Which towers above a basin sheltered round
By mountains slowly stooping from their heights
In terraces of verdure to the deep
And ever tranquil water. In that charmed spot
Of solemn beauty was the cradle placed
Of our Canadian Empire.

And such a site whereon to plant the tree
Of rising Empire! Holds this varied world
No peer to its majestic beauty. Look!
Those solemn hills which close the distance dim
Of the far horizon, how their contours, clothed
With summer foliage, smile as they slope down,
Bathed in the sunlight, to the rippling flood
Which laps their bases; and the azure vault
Mirrors its brightness with the changing hues
Of blue and purple in the dimpling waves.
An amphitheatre, whose circles vast
Rise upward from the central basin, reared
For high assembly of the earlier gods,—
And Zeus' high seat might rest upon the Cape
And dominate the concourse. All the scene
Was clad in summer's livery. Blue in the sky
And water; on the hills a living green
Sheening to yellow in the twinkling birch
And glooming in the pines—all glowing tints
Of the upper rainbow for the summer hues
Of crimson, gold and scarlet were not yet.
Time fails; nor is it now my task to tell
The labours and the anxious toil and want
Which threatened year by year to crush Quebec—
For so, in Indian speech was called the Strait
Where mountains curb St. Lawrence waters in
Before the basin widens; and the name
Was given to the city. Champlain's care

Urges on the work, and his far-seeing eyes
Prepared for every danger. Still he strove
To learn the secrets of that glorious land
Of woods and waters, on whose threshold stood
His infant city."   —S. E. Dawson.

Montcalm and Wolfe

High on the glory-roll of fame,
    With like effulgence glow
Two names that set the soul aflame—
    The soul of friend and foe.

Montcalm and Wolfe! Bayards in all—
    Chaste, courteous, just and bold,
Their blameless, valiant lives recall
    The chivalry of old.

Honor they prized more—aye, far more,
    Than place, pelf—nay, than life—
Generous foes, no hate they bore
    E'en in the heat of strife.

"A foeman worthy of his steel"
    Each recognized in each,
And vied they each with righteous real
    Their rival goals to reach.

Both for the cause they deemed was right
    Fearlessly fought and bled.
The plains of Abraham's fateful fight
    Mourning both 'mongst its dead!

Then, let Montcalm and Wolfe to-day
    Our whole allegiance own—
Types of two gallant nations they,
    Few types more worthy known.

Let Anglo-French and native-born
    With one accord acclaim,
Heroes whose worth and works adorn,
    The hallow'd fane of fame.   A. L. Fraser

The Plains of Abraham

The cynosure of Briton and of Celt,
    These plains again give back the tramp of feet;
    Across dead Hate the same two peoples greet;
They come to-day as men who oft have knelt
In holy fanes and worthy feelings felt,
    Yea who had visions of high emprise,—
    That, East and West, beneath Canadian skies,
To feuds of blood and creed death may be dealt!

They dig the gathered moss from his great name,
    Who blazed the trail three centuries ago;
    They deed to Peace this sacred field of Fame,—
These dizzy heights that make our annals glow:
    From purposes of mere utility
    This place where heroes fell now be free!
                              W. O. Farmer.

Members of the Executive Committee

WM. POWER, M.P.
Vice-Pres. Executive Committee

THOS. McDOUGALL
Hon. Treas. Executive Committee

E. T. D. CHAMBERS
Joint Sec. of Executive Committee

G. A. VANDRY
Pres. Committee on Publicity

P. B. DUMOULIN
Pres. Finance Committee

**JOSEPH POPE, Esq.,
C.M.G., I.S.O.**
Under-Secretary of State

HON. CHS. LANGELIER
Pres. Committee on Enrollment

JOS. VÉZINA
Pres. Committee on Entertainments

ALD. LEMAY
Chairman Committee on Works
and Embellishments

W. H. DUNSFORD
Chairman Committee on Tickets
and Privileges

F. C. COCKBURN
Treas. Ticket and Seating Committee

Members of the Executive Committee

LT.-COL. MACPHERSON
Pres. Naval Entertainments

JULES HONE
Pres. Com. on Hotels and Lodgings

HON. T. CHAPAIS
Pres. Com. on History & Archaeology

COL. WM. WOOD
Vice-Pres. Executive Committee

E. MYRAND
Sec. Com. on History & Archaeology

COL. HANBURY-WILLIAMS,
C.V.O. C.M.G.
Military Secretary to His Excellency

R. E. W. TURNER, V.C.
Pres. Committee on Horses

LT.-COL. RAY
President Sports Committee

MRS. WILLIAMS
Joint Secretary Ladies' Committee

MRS. E. B. GARNEAU
Joint Pres. Ladies' Committee

A. J. PAINCHAUD
Chairman Committee on Costumes

Members of Committees

The following is the list of members of the Executive and General Committees and Chairmen and Members of the various Sub-Committees of the Tercentenary Celebration:

EXECUTIVE COMMITTEE

HIS WORSHIP THE MAYOR, Sir J. G. GARNEAU, Chairman
HON. A. TURGEON.... ....Vice-President.
WM. POWER, M.P.... ....Vice-President.
LT.-COL. W. WOOD, F.R.S.C.... .. Vice-President.
THOS. McDOUGALL.... ....Treasurer.
H. J. J. B. CHOUINARD.... ....General Secretary.
E. T. D. CHAMBERS.... ....Joint Secretary.
DR. A. LESSARD.... ....Joint Secretary.

Members of Committee:—Messrs. P. B. Dumoulin, Hon. Ths. Chapais, R. P. Lemay, Lt.-Col. Ray, Jules Hone, Jr., G. A. Vandry and Jos. Vezina.

The following are members of the General committee, in addition to those on the Executive Committee:

Mgr. Marois, Mgr. Mathieu, Mgr. Gagnon, Hon. A. Chauveau, Hon. A. Robitaille, M.P.P., Dr. Albert Jobin, Mr. Georges Tanguay, Dr. J. Dorion, Mr. Cyr. Duquet, Mr. Georges Belanger, Mr. S. Lesage, Dr. P. H. Bedard, Lieut.-Col. Turnbull, Mr. John Hamilton, Mr. Mont Joseph, Mr. Th. Hethrington, Mr. W. Shaw, Mr. Jos. Ahern, Mr. J. B. Laliberte, Mr. J. H. Holt, Rev. Camille Roy, Hon. Chas. Langelier, General Henry, Mr. Ernest Myrand, Senator Choquette, Mr. Arthur Lachance, M.P., Mr. C. F. Delage, M.P.P., Hon. Ed. Garneau, Dr. Ed. Morin, Mr. L. P. Sirois, N.P., Mr. Ernest Gagnon, Mr. G. E. Amyot, Dr. Dussault, Mr. Joly de Lotbiniere, Mr. Fairchild, Mr. E. E. B. Rattray, Col. Hanbury Williams, Mr. D. Watson, Mr. Frank Glass, Mr. A. J. Painchaud, Mr. Nazaire Fortier, Mr. J. E. Martineau, Dr. Harper, Mr. Cockburn, Mr. Wm. Price, Rev. Amedee Gosselin, Rev. Father O'Leary, Hon. Sir F. Langelier, Hon. R. Roy, Mr. Auguste Carrier, M.P., Hon. A. B. Routhier, Lt.-Col. A. Evanturel, Mr. O. W. Bedard, Dr. Cote, M.P.P. Alderman A. Galipeault, Dr. M. Fiset, Hon. J. C. Kaine, Col. Turner, Mr. W. H. Wiggs, Mr. F. Carrel, Mr. T. J. Murphy, Rev. F. G. Scott, Mr. H. M. Price, Dr. N. E. Dionne, Mr. Chas. Grenier, Mr. P. B. de la Bruere, Dr. Art. Simard, Mr. J. E. Prince, Mr. J. A. Charlebois, Mr. Cyr. Tessier, Dr. A. G. Doughty, Mr. Phileas Gagnon, Mr. Byron Nicholson, Senator Landry, Mr. Ferd. Laroche.

MEMBERS OF SUB-COMMITTEES

Finance Committee—President, Mr. P. B. Dumoulin; secretary, Mr. E. E. B. Rattray; Hon. E. B. Garneau, Mr. G. E. Amyot, Mr. L. P. Sirois, Mr. Chas. Grenier, Mr. Cyr. Duquet, Mr. E. G. Meredith, Mr. J. H. Holt, Mr. J. B. Laliberte, Mr. W. A. Marsh, Mr. Wm. Price.

Committee on History and Archeology—President, Hon. Thos. Chapais, M.L.C.; vice-presidents, Mgr. C. O. Gagnon, Mr. G. M. Fairchild; secretary, Mr. Ernest Myrand; Mgr. Hamel, Rev. Amedee Gosselin, Mr. Phileas Gagnon, Colonel Hubert Neilson, Mr. H. M. Price, Mr. Cyr. Tessier, Mr. Ernest Gagnon, Rev. F. G. Scott, Rev. Camille Roy, Sir James LeMoine, Mr. P. B. Casgrain, Rev. L. St. G. Lindsay, Mr. Eug. Tache, Dr. N. E. Dionne, Mr. E. Joly de Lotbiniere, Dr. Harper, Dr. Bacon.

Committee on Works and Embellishments—President, Alderman Lemay; secretary, Dr. P. H. Bedard; Hon. Rod. Roy, Mr. A. Lachance, M.P., Mr. C. F. Delage, M.P.P., Alderman Fiset, Mr. O. W. Bedard, Mr. John Hamilton, Mr. W. D. Baillarge, Mr. Elz. Charest, Hon. J. C. Kaine, Mr. L. A. Carrier, M.P., Dr. Cote, M.P.P., Alderman Messervey, Alderman Drouin, Mr. P. B. Dumoulin, Mr. C. E. Gauvin.

Members of the Consulting Commission—Hon. Sir Frs. Langelier, Mr. E. E. Tache and Lt.-Col Wm. Wood.

Committee on Publicity—President, Mr. G. A. Vandry; secretaries, Messrs. Fenwick and Nazaire LeVasseur; Mr. J. Hone, Mr. D. Watson, Mr. Frank Carrel, Mr. J. Mercier, Mr. T. LoVasseur, Mr. G. Belanger, Mr. Mont. Joseph, Dr. Ed. Morin, Mr. O. W. Bedard, Mr. H. Dumont.

Committee on Sports—President, Lt.-Col. Ray; secretaries, Mr. August Malouin and Mr. Frank McNaughton; Lt.-Col. Turnbull, Major Hethrington, Lt.-Col. Ashmead, Mr. T. J. Murphy, Mr. E. E. B. Rattray, Mr. Jos. Ahern, Lt.-Col. Turner, Dr. Dussault, Ald. Art. Picard, Mr. F. S. Stocking, Mr. D. Watson, Mr. F. Carrel, Mr. C. de Rouville, Mr. M. Foley, Mr. Jas. McCarthy, Dr. A. Simard, Mr. S. H. Hill, Mr. J. S. Thom, Mr. J. G. Scott, Mr. W. Learmonth, Mr. N. Lavoie, Mr. A. Labrecque, Mr. Jos. Savard, Lt.-Col. Evanturel, Mr. Geo. Tanguay, Mr. J. A. Carrier, Mr. Fr. Glass, Mr. G. C. Scott, Capt. LeDuc, Mr. R. Davidson, Mr. W. Hinds.

Committee on Programme—President, Mr. O. W. Bedard; secretary, Mr. K. S. Fenwick; Mgr. Marois, Mgr. Gagnon, Mr. J. E. Martineau, Hon. Mr. Choquette, Rev. F. G. Scott, Mr. Cyr. Duquet, Hon. Thos. Chapais, Dr. Jobin.

Committee on Hotels and Lodgings—President, Mr. Jules Hone; secretary, Mr. G. A. Allen; Mr. P. B. Dumoulin, Mr. E. E. B. Rattray, Mr. R. H. Gale, Hon. E. B. Garneau, Mr. E. Lemay, Mr. C. de Rouville.

Committee on Music—President, Mr. Jos. Vezina; secretary, Mr. J. A. Bernier; Mr. Ernest Gagnon, Mr. Leon Dessane, Mr. E. A. Bishop, Mr. A. Lavigne, Mr. J. A. Gilbert, Mr. Wm.

LIEUT.-COL. B. A. SCOTT
Deputy Commissioner of the Official Guests Committee of the National Battlefields Commission.

Reed, Mgr. J. H. Harvey, Mr. Gustave Gagnon, Mr. Georges Hebert, Mr. Jos. Cropeault, Mrs. Kennedy.

Committee on Legislation—President, Hon. Sir F. Langelier; secretary, Hon. Mr. Landry, Mr. Wm. Power, M.P., Hon. Mr. Choquette, Mr. A. Lachance, M.P.

Committee on Costumes—Mr. A. J. Painchaud, Mr. W. H. Wiggs, Mr. O. W. Bedard.

Committee on Enrollment—Hon. Chas. Langelier, Mr. L. E. O. Payment, Mr. W. Price, Lieut.-Col. Turner, Mr. G. Scott, Mr. G. Van Felson, Mr. Ed. Laliberte, Mr. Blouin, Mr. Fectean.

Committee on Procuring Horses—Lieut.-Col Turner, Lieut.-Col. Ashmead, Mr. G. A. Vandry.

Committee on Sale of Tickets and Privileges—Mr. W. H. Dunsford, Mr. E. J. Cockburn, Mr. Neuville Belleau.

Committee on the Pageant Lawn—Mr. Kenneth Molson and Mr. Bertram Foy.

Committee on Receiving Guests—President, Sir Francois Langelier; secretary, Mr. W. A. Weir; Deputy Commissioner, Lieut.-Col. B. A. Scott, assisted by Mr. F. Hawkins, Lt.-Col. J. P. Landry, Lt.-Col. Bacon, Major H. O. Roy, Major K. F. Gilmour, Major A. C. Dobell and Capt. J. S. O'Meara, Mr. H. F. Gray.